# Endorsements

I was inspired when I read **Ushering In Your Spouse.** This book moved me with its thought-provoking insights that prepare you for one of life's most important decisions. Choosing the God assigned mate for your purpose is critical to every journey, and Jasmine has written a powerful book that provides encouraging and practical biblical instruction. I highly recommend obtaining a copy of this book to add to your list of gifts for every single, divorced, or widowed person in your life who is hoping and praying to be married or remarried. This book is filled with essential information for every Kingdom-follower choosing to obey God's instruction in their quest to be married with both purpose and daily Joy.

SANDRA STEEN
Founder and CEO
Sandra Steen Consulting,
LLC, and The Joy Institute
Author of *Who Stole My Joy*

This story moved me to tears and gave me hope in the redemptive power of God. This book will inspire you to be better prepared in seeking a spouse and having a healthy marriage. Like the woman who was caught in adultery must have felt when her condemners were ready to hurl rocks, Jesus saved and forgave her. Her story gives hope.

So does the story of Jasmine give hope that no matter what trial you face as a child or in a relationship, the Lord wants to save and redeem you for His Kingdom purpose. This book will encourage you to overcome obstacles to live a life of hope in Jesus and healthy relationships with others.

JOHN VAN PAY
Senior Pastor
Gateway Fellowship Church
Northwest San Antonio, Texas
Author of *Marathon Faith*

Jasmine Hartswick gives us invaluable insights, penned from the richness of her own life experiences. Her authentic wisdom and wit are rooted in having walked in the shoes of one who brings compassion and comfort to others. You'll find help and understanding that will help you prepare and usher in your spouse. This book will help you realize you too can make a difference!

KATHRYN VAN PAY
Pastoral Care and Counseling
Gateway Fellowship Church
Northwest San Antonio, Texas

# Ushering In Your Spouse

### The one God has chosen for you

# Ushering In Your Spouse

The one God has chosen for you

*Jasmine Hartswick*

Disclaimer: Certain names in this book have been changed to protect the identities and privacy of those involved.

Their identities and events in one chapter have been modified for their protection.

Please note: The author uses capital letters when referring to God and any of His names. She also chooses not to capitalize the name of satan or related names, as she gives no acknowledgment to this looser or any of his demons.

Queens of Valor Ministry
San Antonio, Texas
jasminehartswick@queensofvalorministry.org
www.queensofvalorministry.org


Cover and interior design by Jasmine Hartswick
Cover photo was taken on Tom and Jasmine's wedding day




ISBN 13 PB: 978-1-7353123-0-9
ISBN 13 HC: 978-1-7353123-1-6
ISBN 13 eBook 978-1-7353123-2-3

Printed in the United States of America

# Dedication

## It is with great honor and a humble heart that I dedicate this book to our loving Lord

There are no words that could describe the gratitude I have for all the things You have done, for all that You are doing, and all the things You're going to do in my life. The greatest gift of all was sacrificing Your life for mine!

*For God so loved the world that He gave His only begotten Son, (Jesus) that whoever believes in Him should not perish but have everlasting life.* (John 3:16)

You have spared my life from death, three times! You accepted me as I was. Full of sin, covered in shame, living a life filled with hurt, pain, regret, anger, unforgiveness, bitterness, fear, and doubt. You looked down from heaven and called out my name by Your saving grace. When I called upon Your name, (Jesus) You saved me! You shined Your light on the darkest parts of my life and gave me hope for a new beginning. The second I surrendered my life to You, on February 28, 1993, a miraculous journey began.

*Therefore, if anyone is in Christ, he is a new creation; old things passed away; behold, all things have become new.* (2 Corinthians 5:17)

Time after precious time, You have shown me great mercy. Every single time I fell and failed, You were there to pick me up and embrace me with Your loving arms. You have been with me through every storm, every trial, every heartache, every loss, every emergency, and especially the times I should be dead.

*You comprehend my path and my lying down and are acquainted with all my ways, for there is not a word of my tongue, but behold, O Lord, You know it altogether. You have hedged me behind and before and laid Your hand upon me. Such knowledge is too wonderful for me, it is high, I cannot attain it. Where can I go from Your spirit? Or where can I flee from Your presence? If I ascended to heaven, You are there; if I make my bed in hell, behold, You are there. If I take the wings of the morning and dwell in uttermost parts of the sea, even there Your hand shall lead me, And Your right hand shall hold me. If I say, "Surely the darkness shall fall on me," even the night shall be light about me; indeed, the darkness shall not hide from You, but the night shines as the day; The darkness and the light are both alike to you. For you formed my inward parts; You covered me in my mother's womb. I will praise for I am fearfully and wonderfully made, marvelous are Your works, and that my soul knows very well. My frame was not hidden from You when I was made in secret and skillfully wrought in the lowest parts of the earth. Your eyes saw my substance, being yet unformed. And in your book, they all were written, the days fashioned You, for me when as yet there were none of them.* (Psalm 139: 3-16)

It wasn't until the day the eyes of my heart were opened that I comprehended You had a plan for my life all along. It was as though, all the questions I ever had, were turned on like a lightbulb. You quickened my understanding, and able to see all the answers from all the years of asking, wondering, and doubting. I know in all truth and in the deepest part of my heart and soul, You have never, or ever will leave me nor forsake me. You carried me when I could no longer walk. You've shown Your light before me when all I could see was darkness. You have loved and accepted me unconditionally, and You breathed Your breath of life into me. My life truly belongs to You and I am eternally grateful!

*"Yet Who knows whether you have come to the kingdom for such a time as this?"* (Esther 4:14)

It has been 29 years since I gave my life to You and asked You to come into my heart. You have taken me out of the darkness into Your glorious light. You have led me, walked beside me, taught me, reproved me, transformed me, made me strong in my weakness, and courageous in my fears. Now, You have taken my long journey and commissioned me to write this book so that I may leave a legacy of Your pure and unconditional love. Lord, may Your voice guide me and Your words be written to glorify You.

Thank You for this honor.

# Acknowledgments

I would first like to give a special thanks of gratitude to my husband, Thomas, for always believing in me, covering me in constant love and prayers, and living a committed life beside me with our one true God. I would also like to thank all my family, especially my children, who have prayed, supported, and encouraged me during the process of writing this book. To all my friends and to those whom I don't personally know, who prayed for me through prayer requests, I thank you. When I first mentioned to my pastors, John and Stephanie Van Pay that I was commissioned to write a book, they immediately gave me their blessing and words of affirmation to inspire my ability to do it. So, thank you pastors for your love, prayers, and support. An extra special thanks to my endorsers, Pastor John Van Pay, Sandra Steen, and Kathryn Van Pay, who took time out of their very busy schedules to read my book and approve it with sincerity of heart. To my spiritual mom, Agnes, who has lifted me and my family up in prayers for so many years, I can't express the gratitude I have in my heart for you. You have loved and treated me like your own daughter, and you will always hold a special place in my heart. I would also like to show my deep gratitude to Dasia Leatimua. Had it not been for your obedience to the Lord in speaking His word to me about writing this book, I wouldn't have ever begun this journey. Most of all, thank You Holy Spirit for leading, guiding, and speaking to me through the whole process of creating this book for Your glory.

.

# How This Book Came to Fruition

It all started on a vacation trip to Hawaii. My husband and I went to visit our best friends, Roger and Fiona Ledoux, who were also our worship leaders when we were stationed at Spangdahlem AFB, in Germany. Over the past 17 years, we have come to know and call them family. They have two daughters. The oldest is Elianna, and their second, they named after me, Analei Jasmine.

They have a home in Kapolei, Hawaii where they graciously hosted us for our entire stay. I must say, that was the best vacation ever! It was another gorgeous day on July 21, 2017. When evening fell, Roger and Fiona were having a bible study at their house for members of their church family. They had prepared a delicious meal and snacks for everyone to enjoy. As the bible study came to a close, we all gathered together for thanks and prayer. After that, we all just hung out. After all, there was still plenty of food, music, and good friends. I met one of the wives and we just kind of had this spiritual connection as we sat and talked about the Holy Spirit. Her name was Dasia Leatimua. She was very pretty. During our conversation, she just looked at me and said, "You are going to write a book. But it's not going to be a regular book.

It's going to be like a "how to manual" and it's going to be a success. And I'm going to buy one." Dasia had just prophesied to me. I just thought to myself, "I don't know anything about writing a book." I left it at that.

On the way back home, while in flight, I prayed to the Lord and said, "Lord, if that was a word from You, then I need confirmation because I know absolutely nothing about writing a book." Eighteen days later, during the week of August 9th through the 16th of 2017, I was awakened by the Lord every morning at exactly 3:00 a.m. The second I woke up, I immediately spent two hours in prayer and then I would fall back asleep. I was having many prophetic dreams during this time about myself and my husband. It was right in between the point of me falling asleep or waking up that I would clearly hear His voice speaking to me. I was also having visions. I knew something was going to happen, because God was waking me up every day at 3:00 a.m.

It was on the seventh day of my very early awakenings, exactly at 3:00 a.m. that I woke up. When I opened my eyes to the darkness of our bedroom, I began to get flooded with all these ideas of a book that was to be written. God was just pouring the names of chapters into my mind, what the chapters were going to be about, personal experiences, and a lot of information for this book that lasted for two hours. I almost got to the point of asking God to slow down because I wanted to retain all the information He was downloading into my brain, but I didn't dare. I laid there for a few minutes after the Lord was done, thinking about everything He just revealed to me. I then said to Him in prayer, "Lord, You are going to have to give me the title to this book." He immediately answered my prayer and showed me a vision. I saw in this vision all the ideas, words, and chapters

twirling around like a whirlwind. All the words were
dissipating

into the tail end of this twister. The end of the twister then inverted, turned inside out and into a book. I then saw what the book looked like in detail. The title read: Ushering in Your Spouse- The one God has chosen for you. God also showed me that the letters would be written in gold, like the gold refined in fire. This was indeed confirmation from the Lord! I fell asleep and when I woke up later in the morning, I wrote down everything I could remember. I wrote down the date, August 16th, 2017. It was our 14th wedding anniversary! What a special gift to receive from God, to bless me with a book that was already written as part of my calling. Now, I just have to bring it into existence hear on earth, as it is in heaven!

The next day I had a very vivid dream about seeing the word CALLIGRAPHY. It was written in the font of calligraphy, and it was at the top of a book page. My daughter Angela was standing right next to me. Her name means Angel, messenger of God.

From Wikipedia, the free encyclopedia
Further information: Handwriting and Script typeface
1798 Georgian calligraphy
Calligraphy of the German word "Urkunde" (deed)
Calligraphy (from Greek: καλλιγραφία) is a visual art related to writing. It is the design and execution of lettering with a broad tip instrument, brush, or other writing instruments. A contemporary calligraphic practice can be defined as "the art of giving form to signs in an expressive, harmonious, and skillful manner"

The deed God was showing me in this dream was to write this book. The page in my dream represented the beginning of the book. The visual art was the vision He gave about what the book looked like and how I was to write it. The writing instrument was my hand under the influence of His Holy Spirit. The completion of the book is the art of giving form to signs (confirmations) in writing this book that includes my testimony, writing in harmony with the leading of the Holy Spirit, and using my personal experiences and God's Word to put the chapters of this book in skillful order.

I now had the commission of bringing this book into the world, as God had given me all the ingredients, I needed from His throne room. What an honor to be chosen to write one of His books!

## Another Confirmation

This Word was given to me by Senior Pastor Christina Sosso, Executive Vice President and Co-Founder of Sons of God Ministries International, on the evening of March 30th, 2018, at 9 p.m. A conference was held at Freedom Fellowship Church International in San Antonio, TX. (Home base church of SOGMI)

I was invited by a friend, or I like to refer to her as one of my adopted daughters, Yvonne Garcia, because she grew up with my eldest daughter. She told me about this conference at her church because she knew I loved the prophetic. I didn't know who this pastor was, and I had never been to this church. It was a free conference, but I still had to register due to the limited seating. Before I went to the conference, I asked God for a specific word. I said to Him, "Lord, I don't know who this lady pastor is, I never heard of her, nor have I ever been to this church. She doesn't know me but use her to give me a word specifically about this book I am writing. After her teaching about the prophetic, she began to prophesy over about half the people that were there.

She said she would continue tomorrow until everyone got a word. Pastor Christina, who is from the Philippine's, then asked, "Is there anyone here tonight who won't be able to come back tomorrow?" I raised my hand and she called me up. I stood in front of her with my eyes looking down, when she told me to look at her eyes. As I raised my eyes to meet hers, she began to prophesy to me. These were her words: (From the Holy Spirit)

"Jasmine, you have always been prophetic. You've always been that. You see things and sometimes you don't want to see things happening because you're afraid that they will manifest. And some have manifested in your life. But the Lord has been redirecting your focus. That you focus on the great things and mighty things that are coming up. Don't even think that it's too late for you, that you have lost so much opportunities, and you have lost so much. Don't even say that."

"Because greater things are ahead. Better days are ahead. That's why you felt led to come here. So that the Lord can touch you. And He'll reinstate some of the things that were lost. Restoration has come, don't beat yourself up. Release the past. And step into the newness of life in Christ Jesus. There's a lot of things that you miss before and that you used to do and used to have that somehow, they got stolen from you. But now things will be more exciting and greater things than those that were lost. So, don't ever look back because God is going to speak to you person-to-person, and He will clarify, and He will tell you the things that you will expect, and they will happen before your very eyes."

"You will address, you will be speaking in front of people. You will be laying hands on the sick, you will be prophesying. You will be operating in all the gifts of the

Holy Spirit. That's what you wanted. You wanted to see the manifestations of the supernatural. Well, the Lord says, and this is His promise to you, the supernatural things will manifest first in your life then you can give it away. There's a lot of tidbits of revelation that will come. I see that you're going to write a book one day, an inspiration book. Books, actually." This is where I gasped, put my hands to my heart and bellowed out "Yes! I started one already!" She continues, "Oh, you started one already, praise the Lord! You might review the chapters again because He would want you to add some things, and if you believe this and if you focus and spend time with Him, you will be revising some of those books because things of the supernatural and revelations are coming down the pikes for you." Father let none my words fall to the ground that they shall accomplish what they set out to do in the name of Jesus. Thank You Father for Your love towards Your people, that righteousness is now springing up and I thank You Father for unleashing the power that the Holy Spirit, Your Holy Spirit can only provide as He is our power source, in Jesus's name I pray. Amen! And Amen!"

She then asked, "Can I get an autographed copy? Not can I get, I have to change that. Can I buy one?" Of course, I told her "Yes!"

How amazing is our God to answer our prayers! He really did give me a specific word that I asked for about this book through Pastor Christina Sosso. And Everything else she spoke to me was accurate.

God gave a sister named Dasia Leatimua, in Kapolei, Hawaii a word for me, telling me I was going to write a book. As she spoke those words to me, the book was given life. (God's spoken Word brings life) I heard the words, then took them to the Lord and asked for confirmation. The Lord Himself, then spoke all the details of the book to me at three a.m. and then showed me a vision of what the book looked like, including the title. He chose a very special day because it was my 14$^{th}$ wedding anniversary. Then, seven months later, He uses a prophet to confirm the writing of this book. And that is how this book came to fruition.

# Prayer

"Lord, I pray for everyone reading this book. Open their hearts to receive Your Word, as I know You will personally be speaking to them. Use my testimonies to shed light into their lives and to bring real life encouragement for those who need it. Prepare their hearts and minds to acknowledge anything they could relate to in my writing, so that You may bring change and truth into different areas of their life. I pray that they will be filled with Your gift of hope for their spouse, as they wait upon You, in Jesus's name, amen.

*Wait on the Lord; be of good courage, And He shall strengthen your heart. Wait, I say on the Lord* (Psalm 27:14)

# Contents

# (Contents Continued)

# Introduction

## A Summary of My Hell

I was raped in my early twenties, witnessed the death of a shooting victim, had a close encounter to being abducted, lost two sisters to murder, and lost two babies due to miscarriage. I had three marriages that ended in divorce because of the addiction to alcoholism, abuse, adultery, abandonment, and threatened life. The people I thought were my friends, stole everything I owned and caused me unimaginable pain. I was filled with a deep hatred towards men and bought a gun with intention of killing someone. I was overtaken with a spirit of murder. There were times when I had no place to go and had to spend the night at the park with my babies. I suffered a very traumatic back injury. I lost my mom when she was still young. My life was filled with betrayal and deep darkness. Heavy anguish and depression filled my heart. I would just push through all the agony, trauma, and destruction going on in my mind and emotions. And after everything that I had suffered through, I was desperately hanging on by a thread of hope; I knew God was out there.

With all that said, I want to encourage everyone that no matter how bad the circumstance in your life or anything you may be going through, there is hope, healing, and restoration that can only come from the redemptive power of the blood of Jesus and His Holy Spirit. As you read the chapters of my life, I know there will be many of you who can relate because you went through the same ordeal or something similar. I encourage you not to skip any of the chapters in this book. You might miss something God is trying to reveal to you, whether to teach you or to help you in your own healing process. That's what this book is all about. Taking you through a journey of hope, healing, restoration, and being made whole. After this proven process, you will be more than prepared to usher in the spouse God has for you. Even if you're already married and struggling, or feel a lack in your marriage, you too can still obtain that Godly marriage you've been praying for.

When God commissioned me to write this book, I had no idea what I was in for. It has been a long journey with many obstacles, trials, errors, and attacks. Despite of what the enemy tried to do for evil, God has turned it into something good. As He always does.

Before I met and married my husband Tom, I married someone I should not have. It almost cost me my life. But because of the enemy's evil and murderous plans towards me, I was divinely taken to a place where I would meet my true husband. God wanted me to share my testimony on what happened, so that I can help others not make that same mistake. But there is so much more that you will learn. There is a whole lot of gold in this book. I'm not talking about these little golden nuggets. I'm giving you solid chunks of gold! So, I want to invite you into my personal life journey to find out how God saved me through it all. You know when you have a calling on your life, the enemy is going to try to take you out. Well, I should literally be dead three times. God has preserved my life for such a time as this. You will find out how God transformed me, set me free, and changed my life

2

forever. He can and will do the same for you if you allow Him to. Just surrender. I included personal prayers that I pray over you and instructions on helping you prepare yourself for your spouse. So, find a quiet place, grab a pen, and get ready to be launched into a whirlwind of lifechanging revelations!

This is the first book of the "Ushering In" series, which God has commissioned me to write.

JASMINE HARTSWICK

*ouse*

Jasmine Hartswick

# Chapter 1

# Growing Up

This is where it all begins. A journey into the unknown. The story of a child growing up into what seems to look like an ordinary life. But as the years gradually progress, the innocence of that life turns into something of a darkened, upheaved world filled with sorrow, torment, danger, depression, trauma, and agonizing pain. As you read this story, you too will be taken into the world of someone who was lost, broken, scarred, desperate and confused. She was not alone. There was someone watching, following, recording

the events, leading her, and most of all, protecting her.
Though she knew nothing about what was going on or why.
Until one day...the eyes of her heart were opened to a whole
new world. And then everything changed!

I want to give you a little background about myself so
you will know where I come from and so that you can
personally get to know who I was before all hell breaks
loose.

I was born and raised on the Southside of San Antonio,
Texas. I come from a very large family. My mother gave
birth to thirteen children. Six girls first, then seven boys.
These are the names of my siblings and where I fall into
place from oldest to youngest. Lilly Ann, Yvonne Alma,
Consuelo Marie, Stella Marie, Jasmine Marie, Theresa
Marie, John James Henry, David Bohumil, Daniel Claude,
Christopher Lee, Brian Anthony, Patrick Zachary, and
Adam Timothy Cortez. There would have been another, but
my mom lost one.

My youngest memory was inside my crib. It was
against a wall in the living room. This was a very small
house. I was two years old and had very blonde curls. More
than Shirley Temple, if you know who she is. Of course,
later in life, my blonde hair would turn into an auburn
color.

One night when everyone was in bed, I saw numerous
black figures running back and forth from the front of the
living room to the back of the house. There appeared what I
could see, some sort of white door that was placed in front
of my crib. I remember reaching out my small arm touching
the door to see if it was real. I felt it and somehow knew I
was safe behind it. I wasn't afraid of the black figures that
seemed to be having fun in the dark. But they didn't come

near me. I didn't know they were demonic spirits, until many
years later. There are a lot of things we don't understand as

little innocent ones, but God places a calling on our life before we are even born. He gives and anoints us with special gifts to fulfill our callings and destinies. When He knows we are
ready to understand, He will reveal those gifts to us. I was able to see those demonic spirits at the age of two because one of the gifts He gave me was the spirit of discernment.

*For to one is given the word of wisdom through the Spirit, to another the word of knowledge through the same Spirit, to another faith by the same Spirit, to another gifts of healings by [a]the same Spirit, to another the working of miracles, to another prophecy, to another discerning of spirits, to another different kinds of tongues, to another the interpretation of tongues. (1 Corinthians 12:8-10)*

God used a white door as a symbol of purity and entrance into the spiritual and prophetic realm. The door also represented His protection covering me.

We were living off Mission Road, right next door to San Jose Mission. It is considered to be *Queen of the Missions*, because it is the oldest one in Texas. The house was my grandmother (my dad's mom) Anita's and step-grandfather Henry Antonin's house. He was in the Air force, so we lived in that house for about five or six years until they came back home. I have memories of my grandmother reading us tarot cards. She would tell our fortune, read our palms and had a crystal ball. I would learn later in life that was all witchcraft and why I saw those demonic spirits running around. She had an open door into the dark realm. She used to tell us some pretty scary stories about how she could feel someone sit beside her on her bed at night, when no one else was there. Or she could see the imprint of a body lying down next to her. She would see dark shadows and hear voices speaking to her. But she would repent and get delivered from all this later in her life.

We always had these beautiful peacocks in our back yard
that came over from the church grounds. We used to chase them to try to pull the feathers off. But when they would spread their feathered trains and expose their beauty, I would just be in awe of their splendor. My grandmother ended up with vases full of these colorful beauties. When they would let out their cry at night, it sounded like they were screaming, "Heeelp!" It was a little scary for me. But then my other sisters would mock them and soon I was listening to a quartette that echoed back to the peacocks. When grandfather Henry came home from the Air Force, he got a job at the Century South Theatres as a security guard. He would bring home huge bags of popcorn and feed the peacocks. They just loved it.

One day, I was standing in our back yard playing around, when I looked up and saw my dad with his rifle. He was aiming towards the very back. My sister Yvonne was standing under a tree and a snake was in mid-air attempting to wrap itself around her neck. I heard a shot and saw the snake drop to the ground. I and my sister ran inside. Nice shot dad!

My grandfather, Frank George Cortez (My dad's dad) had served in the Army. He became a physician and later owned a mortuary. He used to give us rides in his ambulance when he would pick us up from school. Later, he got a job working for the government as an embalmer. He was sent to Viet Nam to take care of the bodies and then send them home. I remember his last postcard to us. He wrote that he was planning a visit before Christmas to come and see his grandchildren. He told us how much he loved us and God willing, he would see us soon. The day for his visit never came. He died of a heart attack at his desk, in Viet Nam. I cried for my grandpa. He was so nice and loving towards us. A great man to be missed.

My dad too, served in the Army. My grandparents signed some papers so that he could join right before he turned fourteen and be able to use the GI Bill for schooling to become a doctor. He was a Medical Administrative Specialist and served in Japan for almost two and a half years. He re-enlisted into the Air Force and served for a short while. He is a World War Two Veteran and has been honored in various ceremonies and parades as the Grand Marshall.

## It's a Boy!

For years, it was just us girls. Six of us running around in pretty, little dresses, pig tails, bows, and barbies. Then, one day we got a huge surprise from our parents. My mom was pregnant again. My dad wanted a boy so bad! When the time came, I remember a lot of excitement going on, but I didn't know why. I was only three. A lady came over to our house and was tending to my mom. I didn't know she was a midwife. Hours later, I hear a baby crying, then a loud shout, "It's a boy!" My dad was ecstatic! They named him John, after my dad, and James Henry as his middle name, after my step-grandfather. My dad went out to celebrate the birth of his son. He used to tell my mom that he drank and got drunk because it was her fault for not giving him a son. (Really?) Then, when she did give him a son, he had to go out and celebrate. Like... go out and get drunk celebrate. The only thing I can remember that related to my dad being an alcoholic was that night when he came home. I heard a loud noise in their bedroom. My sisters had said that he fell behind the heater. He did fall, but it was because he was drunk. He was a Police Officer for two years but got thrown out of the force because he got in a fight at a bar when he was

off duty. After the birth of my second brother David, was the day my dad quit drinking. That was 59 years ago. He founded   the ARC, which stood for Alcoholics Recovery Center in San Antonio, Texas. I remember going to the meetings with my whole family. We were all young.  And when someone stood up to speak, they would say, "Hi, my name is ------and I'm an alcoholic." That was many years ago, but the AA community knows my dad very well. He has been honored in many states and around the world for holding one of the oldest sobriety dates. He was invited to be a guest speaker at a convention with over 65,000 members attending.

My mom went on to have six more boys later in the years, the last one at the age of forty-two.

My four older sisters went to the school across the street. I must have been around five years old at that time. My little

sister and I used to watch all the kids come out and be guided by the nuns, while they were taken to church. We used to yell out at my sisters passing by and wave at them. Every year they would have a huge Easter egg hunt and a procession of some sort, where they would make crowns of flowers and wear them in their hair. They all looked like little princesses in their Easter dresses.

On easter morning, we would wake up to a row of Easter baskets, starting from oldest to youngest. My dad would tell us stories about the "Easter bunny" running around in the back yard. Then we would have an Easter egg hunt in our backyard.

I remember we would have parties with our family. My dad would fill up this empty fish tank with doughnuts. There were pinata's, lots of food, and drinks set out on the picnic tables, deserts, music, and a lot of fun. My Aunt Janet would show up in her mariachi costumes and sing her heart out. She was a living miracle. But you will find out about her miracle in another book.

When I was old enough to start school, my dad enrolled me and my sisters in a parochial school. We had to wear red and white plaided uniforms and black and white school shoes. We had nuns for teachers and priests to spank and discipline the children. They carried rulers that they used to spank the palm of our hands. St. Phillips Catholic School is where I attended for my first three years of school. My sisters
and I used to be pulled out of our classrooms so that we could sing in front of the students. They would take us down the halls to show off our talent in singing. We would be placed in
plays and concerts as The Cortez Sisters. My dad would also have us sing for his clients. I remember we all received a silver dollar and thinking what a treasure that was. I held on to it for many years, until one day it got stolen. I was actually, sad about that. It felt like one of my memories with my sisters was taken away. Decades later, I was sharing that memory with my brother Brian, in his kitchen. I told him the silver dollar was from 1890. He got up from his seat and went to his bedroom. When he came back, he handed me an 1890 silver dollar preserved in a case. He gave it to me as a gift. I was astonished and hugged him with gratitude. It was as if he handed that memory back to me. What a big, little brother he is!

# The Duplex

17

My dad bought a duplex that was located at 126 Verne Street. It was on the next street over across S.W. Military

Drive. He had the wall separating the duplex knocked down and made into one house. There were two bedrooms in the back. One for the girls and one for the boys. Two sets of bunk beds were in each room with a couple of twins. We had three couches in the living room. My parent's room was on the opposite side in the front with a crib in it. Thank God there were two full bathrooms.

All the girls were given different chores to help out. We rotated daily. Two would sweep, one would wash dishes, one of the older girls would wash dirty cloth diapers, one would dust, and another help set the table. My mom had a silver pitcher that she would make sweet tea in. I remember lining
up all the cups and filling them with that sweet delight. We had a huge table that sat in the middle of the house with benches on the sides and chairs on the end. There was also, a highchair for the baby.

When Christmas came around, we always had these very huge glass-colored lights hanging on the top our house. The Christmas tree would be perfectly decorated, and gifts were underneath. On Christmas Eve, my dad would make a trail of flour or sugar, maybe both, to make it look like snow. He would tell my little brothers that Santa had come down from the attic. We had lots of aunts and uncles, so there were plenty of gifts for each of us. I always got extra gifts from my Aunt Rosie because she was my godmother, as well.

## Mr. President

My dad was working as a car salesman. He used to drive different vehicles home. I remember being in the sixth grade and attending Terrell Wells Middle School. My dad drove me and my little sister, Theresa, to school in a limousine one day. He pulled up and got out of the Limo dressed in his black suit and tie. When he opened the back door to let us out, a young man jumped on the top of the school fence. He proceeded to yell out, while waving his arms, "Hi Mr. President!" Then all the other kids ran to the fence to watch. He honestly thought my dad was the president. Everyone else started waving, jumping on the fence, and saying hi. So, my dad just waved back at them. I thought it was hilarious.

## Home Feast

Every weekend someone would come and deliver a massive amount of barbacoa, tamales, tortillas, and drinks. There was also, a small buffet of Pan Dolce. (Sweetbread from the bakery) That was our routine feast every Saturday. Sometimes my dad would come home late at night and yell out, "Wake up babies! We're going to have a feast!" He would have several buckets of ice cream and cookies spread out on the table. We would fly out of our beds and run to the dining table. We sounded like a small army getting ready for battle. There were clanking of bowls, silverware being thrust across the table, and bodies scrambling to find a seat. My dad meant well, but this didn't make my mom too happy, as we would not want to go back to bed or sleep.

## Drop Box

I don't remember ever going shopping. My dad would come home with huge boxes filled with clothes of different sizes for the girls. He would dump it in the middle of the living

21

room and whatever we found that fit us, is what we got to keep. My four older sisters, more or less, wore the same size, as I and my little sister did. We used to share all our clothes with each other anyway, even what we used to call the everybody drawer. It was a huge drawer filled with clean underwear and socks. It would have taken my mom hours to

sort them out, so she just made one drawer. If you could have seen the enormous pile of dirty clothes in our washroom, you would have thought up ways to cut back on time as well. I guess my dad figured out it was just too much on my mom, so he hired a maid to help my mother out. I remember over the years, having maybe two or three. This was when I was

in elementary school and attending Carroll Bell. Theresa, my little sister, and I would walk to school which was a couple of blocks from our house. It was a lot safer back then. You could sleep with your windows and doors open. I made some true, lifelong friends at that school

## Incoming Plate

My parents used to fight a lot. I don't know why, I just wished they wouldn't as any child would hope. Well, it was mostly my dad. My mom was the quiet type. She barely ever got angry unless it was something super bad. There were maybe a couple of times that I could count on one hand where she got really upset and raised her voice. My dad had a bad temper, so if something wasn't right in his eyes, everyone heard about it. We would scatter like roaches when he came home from work because no one wanted to be around in case he got angry and started yelling. I remember how we used to get all lined up in a row to get spanked with the belt because no one would confess to doing something my dad didn't like. By the time he got to me, he was calmed, and I didn't get it as bad. I found out later in life, my eldest sister Lilly would sometimes fess up to the crimes so that the rest of us wouldn't get spanked. My dad always said, "Big ones first," so she was always first in line. I love her for doing that and being a great protective sister.

My mother just usually let my dad scream it out.

Sometimes I wished she would have yelled back at him and told him to leave. His favorite saying was, "I'm leaving, and I'm not coming back!" I used to think to myself, "Good! Don't come back! I hate you yelling at my mom!" I have a vivid memory of my dad throwing a plate of spaghetti at my mom and her just moving her head out of the way, so the plate

slammed into the wall behind her.

My parents were divorced after the birth of their thirteenth child, even though they were separated before then. My dad filed for the divorce. My mother never got married again. She was a Catholic and totally stayed true to her faith.

We saw my dad come and go for visits but, they became scarce. So, we all became a broken and very dysfunctional family. My mother did the best she could, but we lived a very poor life after my dad left. All I knew was that he was some sort of financial consultant. He used to travel all over the

world and bring all kinds of gifts for us when he would visit. My mom had this small China cabinet in the living room that was filled with artifacts from all parts of the world. My brothers would pull down on the drawer if it was slightly open, trying to climb it somehow. There were many topples and falls. Most of the items in the cabinet ended up broken. We too, in our own ways, were broken inside over the years. Some, more than the rest. I think it was harder on my brothers than on me and my sisters. They needed that father figure in the house. This caused a lot of animosity and anger in my family. Including myself.

# Stranger

One sunny afternoon, I looked out the window and shouted, "Mom, there's a man coming up our sidewalk!" She asked who it was, but I didn't know. When he came closer, I realized it was my dad. I hadn't seen him in a very long time. He had a briefcase in his hand and was very anxious to come inside. As we all went to give him our greetings, he asked that all the windows be closed and for us to shut the door. We never had air condition. Our ceilings were high, so the fans we used were usually enough to keep us cool. When he

opened his briefcase, it was full of money! I understood that he had put together a huge deal between two companies and they paid him compensation for it. That day, he paid off the mortgage on our home. That is one thing I am so glad he did

for my mom because it lifted a huge burden off my mother's shoulders. He stayed a few days but left again.

# The Rat Patrol

Our home was occupied by rats and roaches, but they usually came out at night. The rats were taken out by my brothers in the evening, who would lie on the floor, wait for the intruders to emerge, and use their BB guns as a weapon of annihilation. You could hear the sound of victory, for each one that got a fatal hit. Different traps were conjured up by my brothers, to see which ones would capture the most rodents. I was quite entertained by my little brother's creative imaginations.

# No Food in The House

We witnessed my mother struggle hard, trying to feed us and barely making ends meet. Mom didn't get any child support. She really couldn't work because there were two toddlers and a baby in diapers. The rest of us were in school.

We did get free breakfast and lunch, which helped out a lot. The summertime seemed to be more challenging. One summer, all we ate was bread and butter. Sometimes no bread, sometimes no butter. I think that is why I hate white bread. Other times, there was just absolutely nothing to eat. I opened up a kitchen cabinet one time to find an open box of raw grits. There were pieces of roach parts in it. I was so

hungry; I ate what I could out of the box. I now understand why the homeless people have no problem digging for food out of the trash. My heart goes out to them.

# Finding Free Food

I remember a couple of my siblings and myself made a discovery, while exploring dumpsters in our neighborhood. We used to walk across the all-famous Southwest Military Drive. We would dig in the HEB (grocery store) trash can to

see what we could find. We discovered all these different packages of food that were thrown away. They were all still in containers or wrapped packages. When we looked at the dates, they were all only a day or two old. We can take all this food home! We discovered a way to get food! We loaded what we could carry in our arms and take it home. We made this a regular visit, taking bags with us so that our family might have something to eat when there was nothing.

My Aunt Manuela and Aunt Theresa would frequently visit my mom. They were her older sisters and they used to call my mom Baby. I know they helped her as much as they could. I used to love to hear them speak to each other in Spanish, even though I didn't understand what they were saying. Our church helped by sometimes paying our bills and bringing us food. My little brothers would run outside and

yell out, "FOOODDD!!!" I can laugh at that now, but it wasn't funny then.

## Answered Prayer

I saw my mom on her knees every single night. She had an altar above her bed and prayed her rosary and personal prayers faithfully. She would walk us to church every single Sunday for about a mile. We looked like a bunch of little chicks following the mamma duck. She sang in the choir, and

I used to love watching her sing out with all her heart. She had a beautiful voice. My favorite song that she used to sing was Ave Maria. I never knew what the translation meant, but I really didn't care. I just adored listening to her voice, as she sang it out. I found out many years later, it was the Hail Mary prayer.

I believe God had to have answered her prayers for help. She started getting help from the government by waiting in

a line for these huge boxes of cheese, corned beef, bread, and milk. They told her about food stamps and welfare, which she totally qualified for. They sent an agent to our house to physically confirm that she had thirteen children. The look on the woman's face was priceless when she saw our squadron run into the living room. We never had to worry about food again. She also got a check that was enough to pay all our bills and buy essentials. My favorite gourmet meal was from Griff's Hamburgers, right off Pleasanton Road. We got thirteen hamburgers for a dollar. Thank You, Lord, for sending us help and for my mom's faithful and relentless prayers. I asked her one day, why she didn't report my dad for not paying child support. Her heart was so full of God's mercy and love, she said he would have ended up in jail and she just could not do it. She truly was a saint!

## Highschool Mischief

I was now in high school, attending Dillard McCollum High. I was in the ninth grade, what they called a fresh fish. (freshman) I had three of my sisters in the same grade, as juniors. One had been held back and one had started early.

The eldest was a senior. So, there we were. All five of us. One of my teachers asked my name during roll call. When I said, "Jasmine Cortez." She blurted out, "Oh my God! Not another Cortez!" Little did she know there were many more to come.

When it was my turn to be the senior, I kind of got into some mischievous behavior. I used to light up bottle rockets and send them soaring down the halls, whaling a high pitch tone, until I would hear them explode. Then you could see me high tailing it to another building, so I wouldn't get caught. There were also firecrackers that would visit all the trashcans, leaving behind a trail of smoke and the sounds of a small machine gun. I can also recall the rolling of colored smoke bombs into the crowds of students when switching classes. I just thought it was so much fun. You couldn't do that nowadays. I would have been arrested and labeled a terrorist.

I basically skipped the first two weeks of my first class, in my senior year. I used to hang out with five male friends. We would go to the corner convenience store and get drinks. Then we would walk back to school, go across the street, and go into the Monte. (An area with lots of shrubs and trees) We stayed there until the next bell rang. One day the vice-principal saw me coming up the steps and asked me where I was coming from. I ran as fast as I could across the grass when he decided to chase me down. I ran and opened the door to the back end of the cafeteria, which was being used as a

study hall during school. It was full and all the students watched me fly across the room at full speed. The teacher just glanced at me and then looked to see who I was running away from. When I pushed the door open to freedom, I continued down the outside courtyard and then into the next building, where I hid inside the girl's bathroom. I waited to

see if I was going to have to make a grand escape out the bathroom window, which I totally would have been able to slide out of. I waited. I sighed with relief, as I slowly opened the door and saw the coast was clear.

The next day, I was walking to one of my classes when the vice-principal tugged at me and asked, "Wasn't I chasing you yesterday?" I just gave an innocent look and said, "No sir, it wasn't me." I smiled and he let me continue on my way. Of course, I was dying of laughter on the inside.

I had a really sweet girlfriend who was very shy and quiet. For some reason, she wanted to hang out with me during the times I would skip school. So, I let her tag along. I told her that the school security would keep an eye out for students who looked like they were trying to leave campus.

One day we were at the back gate, when all of a sudden, a police car pulled up and asked what we were doing. I remember yelling out, "Run!" We ran as fast as we could, cutting across the field and taking a shortcut into the Monte. I grabbed her hand and shouted, "Slide!" We both slid right under a bush that was just big and low enough to hide us. I had previously marked that bush as my hideaway. The police officer's footsteps ran right past us, as we covered our mouths to hide our laughter. When we knew he was gone, we crawled out and did a dance of victory, while cracking up in laughter so hard that we almost peed in our pants. After we had several more times of running, jumping fences, and avoided being caught, my friend thanked me for bringing her out of

her shell. I don't know if that was a good thing or a bad thing. Needless to say, I decided if I was to graduate, I should start going to my first-period class. I walked in and sat down at an empty desk. The teacher never asked who I was or where I had been. It was as if I had been going to class all along.

My favorite class of all time was Art. Me and two of my buddies used to sneak food and have a picnic in the back of the art room. We brought in snacks, drinks, fried chicken

from the food court, and anything else we could muster up. Our Art teacher was pretty laid back, so it was easy to hide what we were doing. He always stayed in the front of the class. After he did roll call and I had my meal, I would crawl out of the window and walk the ledge that went around the whole second-story building. I used a pole that was attached to the brick wall to let myself down. I did this for a while until my teacher caught me. He said he wouldn't have me suspended if I promised not to do it again. I agreed. I started to really get into my artwork. I had taken four years of art while at McCollum. One of my oil paintings was displayed in our school's Evening of Art Gallery. I remember someone wanted to buy my painting for his mother. I had painted the head of Jesus, with the crown of thorns on His head, and blood dripping onto His face. They were very insistent on buying the painting, but I said, "No."

All my family is blessed with very artistic abilities. Remember, my grandfather, Bohumil Oravecz was an artist. My mom could draw very well. I know she got her talent from him. Even my dad used to paint. All our talents would be used later in life.

## Getting Caught

Proms came and went. I never went to a dance or any other high school event they had. Never a cheerleader, in band or any other activity. That just wasn't me. I liked creating my own fun. The only thing I did go to was several retreats through our church. My little sister and I would have to work for our way. So, we would clean out the sister's gardens and do whatever work needed to be done around the convent. It belonged to The Schoenstatt (a beautiful place) Sisters of Mary. Since some of my friends from school also attended these retreats, I was happy to go. They were held in Lamar, Tx. The huge convent with dormitories was right on the water. There was a long peer we could hang out at. We were assigned our dorm rooms and were fed three meals a day until the retreat was over. We would have meetings, prayer time in the tiny shrine, and sing songs together. When nighttime came along, the sisters would walk us to our dorm rooms to make sure we got in bed. When we knew it was safe, we would visit each other rooms, to see who was awake and to share what snacks we had. I would always instigate sneaking out at night and walking to the peer. One evening, a group of us decided to go downstairs to the kitchen for a midnight raid. One of the sisters heard us and we all split up, scrambling upstairs, or hiding downstairs. My friend Mary Ann and I ducked inside a closet. We tried hiding our chuckles, but the closet door slowly opened to find us both covering our mouths and peering up at the sister standing in front of us. She calmly said, "Come with me girls." I honestly thought she was going to spank us! Instead, she led us to our dorms and asked us to go to bed. We just replied, "Yes, sister." She stood there and watched us get into bed. We must have laughed for about fifteen minutes, until our stomach's hurt so bad, we had to stop and wipe the tears from our eyes.

We still snuck out at night and raided the kitchen but were more discreet at our misbehavior. Those were some of the best times spent with my friends. My eldest sister, Lilly, joined the sisters in Lamar and served there for fifteen years of her life. After getting seriously sick, she made the decision to leave the convent. She had every right to do this, as sisters
do not make a vow to stay in, as nuns do. I myself was very happy that she came back home.

## Eighteen-wheeler Versus Bug

Several of us got jobs. We bought our own clothes, as the hand-me-downs got pretty worn out. I got a job when I was sixteen. I worked for a nonprofit that helped low-income families. I was a receptionist. We had a facility that allowed
parents to drop off their children during the day, so they could work and not have to pay for childcare. The children were given snacks every day. Whatever was leftover, instead of throwing it away, I was allowed to take it home. This included small cartons of regular and chocolate milk,

41

which was a treat for us. We were used to drinking the powdered milk.

My supervisor used to give me a ride home. She couldn't see past some bushes at the stop sign one day, so when she drove on, I heard her yell out. We were suddenly hit by an eighteen-wheeler. The Beetle Bug we were in spun around several times and landed in a yard that was three feet above ground level. After the shock, we realized we were miraculously alive. Had you seen the damage to the beetle, you would have been bewildered as to how we walked away. She was very badly bruised and hurt her arm. I was sitting
right behind her, but I walked away without a scratch. I walked home from then on. I was afraid to get into a vehicle.
It took a long time before I was able to take the bus or get a ride from anyone.

## Changes in The House

My mom got a job working at Solo Serve. She got off food stamps and welfare. She worked hard and never missed a day. She took the bus because she never learned to drive. I never saw my mom sick. She was such a loving woman, who never complained about anything. And she was fearless! Her door stayed open to every one of us, even when we got older and got ourselves into trouble. She loved us unconditionally, no matter what.

As the years went on, my other older sisters moved out of the house. Consuelo (Connie) went off to college, Stella married her high school sweetheart, who joined the marines and had a beautiful daughter. Yvonne got married and moved to Champagne, Ill. And that left me and my little sister, Theresa and all my little brothers left in the house.

43

I was still working at SNAC (Southside Neighborhood Assistance Corporation) and helped my mom with what I could. This was a summer job, so I was able to buy my own school clothes and shoes. I also tried to learn to cook to help out. I remember my mom teaching me how to make flour tortillas. My first attempt was a disaster. The shape of the tortilla came out looking like a splattered mess. And when you bit into them, they cracked and crunched into pieces. I was so disappointed, but my mom lovingly said, "You just need to practice." And she was right. I mastered the technique and eventually made the best tortillas ever.

It was my turn to graduate high school. I couldn't believe I made it. I think it was by the grace of God and my prayers that I graduated high school. I hated school and never did my homework. I even flunked math, my worst subject, but my teacher passed me anyway, because he said he believed I had potential. I was very grateful he did that for me. Praise God, we all graduated and got our diplomas. All thirteen of us!

I got a ride from a friend and my aunt would take my mother and a few siblings to the Joe Freeman Coliseum to watch me cross the stage and receive my diploma. It was such an exciting day for me and my friends, as we dressed ourselves in our green cap and gowns. Our school colors were green and gold, so we had a gold tassel hanging from our caps. As we lined up in order of our names, the orchestra began to play Pomp and Circumstance. The all-famous graduating march. When they called my name, I was so happy to hear a huge and loud cheering from all my family and friends. I was so grateful to God for answering my prayer. Afterwards, we went home to celebrate.

**store for my life after ning of a future filled with darkness, danger, death, and destruction.**

# Ushering In Your Spouse

# Chapter 2

# First Failed Marriage

It started many years ago when I would encounter my first failed relationship. I had just graduated high school. I met Joseph at the community swimming pool. I kind of ran away from home to live with him and his sister's family. My little sister had made my life difficult for the last couple of years I was at home. Many years later, I would find out why. After

I moved out; we were fine. We became close. I guess I left because I didn't want to deal with the drama anymore. This was very shocking to my precious mama because I had never done anything like this before. I always obeyed her and rarely ever talked back.

I was still an eighteen-year virgin when I graduated. I had it in my heart that I was going to save myself for marriage, but it didn't quite work out the way I planned. A short time into the relationship with this guy and I find out that I am pregnant. When I told my mom, she was very happy to hear that I was going to give her a grandchild. This would be her second, as my older sister Stella had already given her a granddaughter, named Deborah.

Since I was raised a Catholic, I was sort of forced into marrying someone I didn't love. It was very much frowned upon in the church for what I did. I didn't want to marry him, but I figured I would give my baby a name, then divorce him. I knew nothing about life, and I was very naïve. I didn't even know I was with child. I was still in my tight jeans, but they told me I was four months pregnant. I was five feet one and a half inches tall and weighed 105 lbs. Well, I thought, "At least I graduated high school." Then my thoughts went into the joy that I was going to have my own baby! I was excited, happy, and scared, at the same time. I prayed, "God, just help me do this." I thought of my mamma who did this thirteen times. If she can do it all those times, then I can do it once.

Now, getting back to other reasons why I didn't want to marry this guy. One of his brothers told me that when we first met, he lied about his age. He told me he was 18, when in fact he was only 16. My mouth dropped when I heard this. I was now married to a sixteen- year- old and having his child. When I first moved in with him and his sister's family, it didn't take long before I met the other five of his brothers and other sister. All of his brothers drank and smoked pot. I was introduced to this, and I remember getting drunk on half

a beer. I then shared in their indulgence of getting high on pot. (This was before I knew I was pregnant) His brothers were always fighting with other people including the neighbors.

Joseph wasn't working at the time. I was still working for SNAC, which helped low-income families. He would steal money out of my purse to go out drinking with his brothers. One time I was arguing with him because I didn't want him to leave again, when out of no-where, his hand came across my face so hard, it stunned me for a second, then I cried in shock and hurt. He had the nerve to tell me, "See what you made me do!" The neighbor called the cops because they heard all the yelling. He ran off before the cops got there. It was nighttime, so they gave me a ride to my mother's house. She comforted me with love and compassion. I did NOT want to marry him, but like I said, I had to. I stopped drinking beer and smoking pot the second I found out I was pregnant. His drinking got worse, and I decided I would stay married to him because I felt sorry for him and thought I could help him quit drinking. Oh, what little I knew about alcoholism and its destructive behavior. There was definitely the absence of the magnitude this stronghold had on Joseph's life. Much less, what a stronghold was.

## An Angel Is Born

I remember one day giving him an ultimatum, when I was now about eight months pregnant. We were at a park, and I said, "Make a choice, me and your unborn child, or your beer." He thought for a moment then said, "My beer." Then he walked away. If at the time, I would have known how sick he was in his mind; I wouldn't have let his answer make me feel like I was dirt. My heart wouldn't have sunk deep into my chest, and I wouldn't have allowed a spirit of rejection to overwhelm me. I got a ride back home with his sister, but things only got worse from there.

I was playing basketball one day with my sister-in-law and her kids at another park one day. I was in my ninth month of pregnancy. I remember throwing the ball into the basket and getting really excited that I made it in. As soon as I made the basket, I went into labor. My sister-in-law drove me to the hospital. I was in labor for six and a half hours. It honestly wasn't as bad, or long as everyone said it would it be, being my first child. I thought it felt like really bad cramps. Maybe it was all the walking I used to do. When I got my biggest contraction, I pushed, and out came my beautiful baby girl. When they brought her to me, I fell in love with her. She was so tiny. Her dark hair matched her big brown eyes. She had the cutest little button nose, and her smile melted my heart. God gave me such a precious gift. She looked like a little angel. (Messenger of God) So, I named her Angela Marie. I continued the middle name going on in our family.

Joseph was not at the birth of his daughter. I was so happy and pre-occupied with this tiny miracle that, I honestly didn't care. No one seemed to be able to find him. I don't remember much of my hospital stay or when Joseph finally showed up. My world changed when I had my angel. She brought so much joy into my life.

Our time living with Joseph's sister came to an end. We are now living with his parents, along with one of his brothers, his other sister, her six kids and husband. There were fourteen of us crammed in a very small house with only

Ushering In Your Spouse

two bedrooms. We slept on the living room floor and his brother slept on the couch. The house was infested with rats and roaches. The family was infested with lice, so of course,
my long hair that was down to my waist, got invaded too. I hated everything about living there. I didn't want to burden my mother by going back home with a baby, so I suffered it out.

Joseph would disappear for days at a time and would just leave me, and our baby abandoned. There was no food in the house at times, or diapers for Angela. His sister would usually buy food with her food stamps, but when she wasn't there, what could I do with no car or money. I would carry my baby and walk eleven blocks to my mother's house just to feed myself and my daughter. My mother and I were very close. Most of my brothers still lived at home. After I got something to eat and borrowed some money for diapers, I walked back to the nightmare house. I did this quite often. One of those times when I was walking home, I was passing one of the neighbors. He hated Joseph and his brothers. I was aware that he had a shotgun and was pointing it at me because he knew I was one of the wives. I was so scared. I thought he might shoot me. I held my daughter close to me, as to protect her somehow. When I got inside the house, I closed the door and just broke down and cried.

When Joseph came home four days later, it was late at night, and he was drunk. I had put my baby on the couch, since his brother wasn't there. He stumbled in the dark and just fell right on top of my angel! I screamed and his sister had to help me get him off. I was so scared, but she seemed to be ok. The curve of the couch stopped the impact of his drunken weight.

55

The next morning, I explained to him that I was leaving him. His parents were nice, and both worked, but they too drank. They would make a big circle in the back yard with
chairs and a bonfire, and all the family and friends would sit there and get drunk and high. This usually led to fights of all
kinds. Fist fights were the usual. Knife and gun fights were usually away from home, thank God!

# Leaving San Antonio

Joseph pleaded and swore like thousands of other times, to give him another chance to make things better for us. I always gave him so many chances, just to be let down. He said he had an uncle in Houston who might be able to help because he owned several houses. He called his uncle who gave him a job. I had to wait for him to come and get me after a few months so that he could get settled in with his job and a house. I visited my mom as much as I could and stay as long as I could, while he was gone.

When he came back with a car, I was really surprised that he kept his word. We packed what little belongings we had and left San Antonio. I was never so relieved in all my life. The house was very nice and had three bedrooms. It had a nice yard and his uncle just lived across the street. I put the baby's crib in the center room where there was plenty of light and space for her. We took the huge bedroom as our own. I was trying to figure out what I could do with the third front room. Within two weeks of my happy time, one of his brothers shows up with his girlfriend and all their stuff to move in. I was so angry! He didn't even tell me! He explained that they would pay half the rent and help out with bills and groceries. This was one of the nicer brothers, so I had to calm myself down. There was nothing I could do about it. After they settled in, it wasn't long before his other brothers showed up. Are you kidding me? They all came to party and get drunk. And of course, Joseph was all too happy to join them. This became a regular habit on weekends. I hated it and we fought all the time because of it.

Joseph didn't keep his job and would disappear for days with his brothers. The one brother and his girlfriend would also, go away at times. I ended up turning to stealing to get food for myself and Angela. I did it several times, until I got caught. I was so scared because I had my daughter in the stroller and my backpack hanging from it. When I got to the register to pay for a twinkie, the owner looked at me and said, "What else do you want to pay for?" I knew I was busted. I pulled out a large can of ham, some pastries, baby food, chips, and milk. I was so embarrassed! I started crying and told him that I was sorry and that I only did it to feed my baby. He made me promise never to go back to his store and he would not call the police. I promised, thanked him, and never went back. I was so angry and hurt. Another promise broken, along with my heart.

Joseph's aunt agreed to watch Angela, so that I could find a job. I told his uncle what was going on, so he gave me some money to tie me over. When Joseph came home, his uncle was waiting for him in our kitchen and tore him a new one!

I got hired as a waitress at a dance hall. They were very popular in Houston. My neighbor was really nice and gave me rides to work. I made really good tips, but I didn't like working there. One night on a weekend, I came home from work and was wondering where Joseph and my baby girl were. I walked to the corner bar, and sure enough, there he was with my Angela sitting on the barstool where she could have fallen off. I was so furious! How could he take her to a bar with a bunch of drunks and so much smoke? I was fuming inside! I grabbed her and quickly walked back home with her. Tears were running down my face as I thought of how

we moved away, just to end up in the same, if not worse, predicament. I quit my job and told him he had to work, or I would leave. He went back to work for his uncle but had to walk across the street to get a ride. He totaled the car we had, while driving intoxicated.

I became very close friends with our backdoor neighbor. Lisa was very much aware of what was going on in our lives. Her and her husband did not like Joseph or his family at all. They began to help me out with food and money whenever I needed it. I was so grateful for their generosity and friendship. Now, I didn't feel like I was all alone.

Lisa told me they were hiring at the company she worked for. She graciously took me to her job, where I filled out an application and got hired that same day. I would be able to go to work with her. My plan now, was to save some money so that I could go away and start a new life.

*Ushering In Your Spouse*

# Chapter 3

# The House of Witchcraft

You know the old saying, you jump out of the frying pan into the fire? Well, that is exactly what happened to me. I met a married man, Carlos, who swore he was divorcing his wife. We started messing around at work and I was just enjoying

all the attention that I was getting from him. It seemed like a good thing to me at the time because he was a manager in my department, so if I did not like the job I was doing, he would move me to another one. It was only a few weeks into

the job, that I decided I no longer wanted to deal with Joseph and his family. I was done!

Carlos asked if I wanted his help in moving out of the house and away from those people, to be with him. I accepted his offer. I was just so relieved to be getting away from the turmoil I was in, I didn't even think about what I was really doing. I pretended I was sick and stayed home with Angela. He waited around the corner with his truck at the corner bar. When I called to let him know the coast was clear, he came over and we loaded the truck with everything that belonged to me. I put all my daughter's little dresses, shoes, and outfits that I bought her in a bag. The first thing I would do when I got paid, was to go shopping for clothes at K-Mart for my baby girl. Doing this this made me happy. I bought her crib, stroller, and walker at the thrift store. She was one-and-a-half-years-old when we left.

Carlos took me to his parents' house. They lived in the Heights area. We were introduced and my situation was explained to them. They agreed to take me in. I was confused because I thought I was going to live with Carlos. NO. It turned out that he was still living with his wife and two daughters across town. He swore that he was still working on getting a divorce and that his wife agreed to it. He said that we would get our own place. In the meantime, I would stay there.

These people were sick in their minds. The mom was into witchcraft, and they were both very perverted. They lied, stole, cursed, were unsanitary, and were abusive. Carlos would come to visit me, ask for money, use me, and fill my

head with lies. He was very manipulative and controlling. Yet, I continued to believe all the lies I was being told. I had to put up with his disgusting parents and all their voodoo and witchcraft spells and curses. They kept an eye on me and made sure to call their son to give their report on my behavior and my where abouts.

I got another job at a huge tool company and was doing very well financially. I gave the grandmother money for rent and food. After I saved enough money, I left the witchcraft house and got my own apartment. I did not tell them where I was moving to. A girl who worked with me and lived in the same apartment complex helped me move. We became friends. She had a son and a daughter. Her babysitter began to watch Angela for me. This was so convenient for me. I lived in the apartment for about a year and a half. I really liked it there. It was peaceful for me. Everything was close by. There was a small grocery store right by us. I could just walk over there whenever I needed something. I loved sitting outside on the balcony in the back and listen to music.

As time would have it, Carlos found out where I lived. He said he followed me home one day from my job. I don't know why I kept falling for and believing his blatant lies and deception. I allowed him to use me and take money from me that I worked hard for. He never stayed with me for more than a couple of hours. Just enough time to get what he wanted from me.

He started to go to my job and cause trouble, break into my apartment with his wife and steal whatever they could from me, including money. Then, he would beat up his wife and make her call me to tell me they were getting divorced and that he loved me and not her. He literally gave her a black eye that I saw for myself. They were both twelve years older than I was. How naïve and gullible, I must have seemed to them. Nevertheless, I kept this inappropriate relationship with this man. I cannot explain why I allowed myself to be tangled up in another web of deception.

# A Dead Man

One day, I heard some sirens right outside of my apartment. I went outside on the balcony and saw some firefighters and paramedics. I went down to talk to one of them to ask what happened. Before he could answer, I saw a man lying on his stomach. He was dead. He was shot in the back by the owner of the store, over a pack of hamburger meat that was tucked in his jeans. I was so sad for this man. Perhaps he was just trying to feed his family, as I had stolen to feed myself and my baby. I was very perplexed by this situation. I left the scene, taking one last look at the dead man on the ground.

A few days later, I went for a walk to go to a different grocery store down the street. I left my daughter with my friend, so she could play with her kids. I noticed an older man driving very slowly behind me and watching me. I went to the other side of the street. When I turned around to see if he was still there, he held out a hundred-dollar bill. Are you kidding me? Do I look like a prostitute to you? I looked at him with a disgusted face and told him to get the hell away from me. He drove off in a hurry. I looked like a young teenager. I always got carded for everything. So, this made me even more upset because he must have thought I was a teen. He could have been a sex-trafficker for all I knew. I would still ask God to help and protect me. I had a bare minimal relationship with Him. I didn't know what a prayer life was.

I just talked to Him when I thought I needed Him. I had such a void in my life, I had no idea what it was.

# Chapter 4

# The Rape

I was taking the bus to work very early in the morning. We were able to work as much overtime as we wanted, so I took advantage of this. A friend of mine was watching my daughter. The buses were running two hours late so, I was at the bus stop at four a.m. in order to be at work on time. A dark grey van pulled up and the guy driving asked me if I needed a ride. He said that I could trust him. I was already waiting for an hour, so I hopped in and told him where I had

to go. I was twenty-three years old at the time. The guy went off on a tangent about how his girlfriend had broken up with
him. He told me his name and where he worked. He was terribly upset and hurt. I listened to everything he was saying. He passed my street destination and drove into an abandoned warehouse parking lot. My instincts told me I was in trouble. I had not noticed the empty beer bottles lying on the floor of the van. I also, didn't realize this guy was drunk. When he was preoccupied with something in the back, I slowly unlocked the door, reached for my backpack, and then flung the door open and jumped. He was able to grab a hold of my long hair and I felt myself being dragged back into the van. He met my throat with a very large, sharp knife. He got terribly angry and yelled at me, "You -----! If you try anything like that again, I will kill you!" I was forced to the back of the van where I was terrorized and raped. When he was finished with me, I lay there on my back, trembling, crying, and horrified. He took the knife and held it above me. I just knew this was going to be the end for me. I prayed the only prayer I could remember, which was the Our Father. I had grown up as a Catholic, so that was what came to mind. I was praying it as fast as I could before I felt the deadly piercing of his knife. He looked down at my chest, where I was wearing a crucifix. He grabbed it, stared at it, and slammed it back unto my chest. In an angry voice he said, "Yeah, He's protecting you!" He sat there in a frozen position and let me go.

We were so close to my job, so I walked the rest of the way to get to work. In those days, the woman was always made out to be the blame for such things. So, I never reported

71

what happened to me. I did not worry about pregnancy because I was on my cycle. When I got to my workplace, my supervisor saw me and immediately knew something was wrong. She allowed me to leave with a friend of mine. I was shaking and crying but, I was grateful to be alive. I thanked God for protecting me.

I tried to move on the best I could, but something happened inside me. I was filled with such a hatred towards men! It consumed every fiber of my being. This man sexually assaulted me with force. He threatened my life with a deadly weapon and fear. He then violated, invaded, dishonored, damaged and deeply hurt me physically, emotionally, mentally, and spiritually.

Two weeks after I got raped, I was walking back home after work. A car pulled up beside me and the man was insistent that I get in. I kept saying no, but he parked his car in front of me and jumped out. He was angry, saying he was only trying to be nice. All the flashbacks of my rape flooded my being. I felt paralyzed. I heard some yelling across the street. It was a couple of young men yelling at me from the second floor of some apartments. They told me to run across to them. They yelled out that they were Christians, and they would help me. That was the first time I ever heard the phrase, Christians. This man came at me, but right before he could grab me, I felt an invisible push and I ran across the street. By the time I got across, the young men were standing there to help me. One of them took me home. He was genuinely nice and said he would pray for me. After that, and another incident, my hatred toward men intensified. I bought a gun. I wanted to kill someone!

I took some much-needed time off from work and used my sick leave to go home and spend it with my mom and family. I never told my mom because she had enough to worry about. As a matter of fact, I never told anyone until many years later. My supervisor was very understanding and allowed me to take as much time as needed. She had already guessed what happened to me and reassured me that it would stay between us.

I went to my old church, St. Lawrence Catholic Church. I walked in and looked for an old priest that I always thought looked like a walking angel. When he saw me, he could see the desperation and pain in my face. He took me to his office and closed the door behind us for privacy. I broke down and let everything out in my tears, my anger, my brokenness, and my hatred. I even told him I bought a gun. He was so gentle in his prayers over me. I could really feel the love of God penetrating my heart, through him. I never felt that before! After I calmed down, he reached inside a drawer and told me he was giving me his own personal wooden crucifix. As I held it in my hands, I looked at the body of Jesus hanging on the cross with His nail pierced hands and feet. Something rose up from deep within and I felt a miraculous healing taking place inside my heart and soul. Hatred left me! I no longer had the desire to kill someone. I got rid of the gun. I will never forget Father Paul Fritchell. He was indeed an angel to me. When I heard that he passed away years later, I cried for him.

# Chapter 5

# My Second Child Is Born

Five months have passed when I found out I was pregnant. I was already in my third month. My cycles were inconsistent, so I couldn't tell. I told Carlos but he denied my baby was his. That was fine, because I knew this child had a Father in heaven who loved them more than any man could!

I made plans to move on. I continued to work and save some money in case of an emergency. I would see Carlos here and there, but when I refused to give him any more money, he stayed away more. I was in my eighth month now. Of course, my car would break down! Or did it? I had to walk to work in the heat, wearing steel toed boots for three miles.

When I get to work, I am informed that I am getting laid off. What? Within a few weeks, I lost my job and apartment. Then, my so-called friend stole everything I had except the clothes on my back. She even took all my baby shower gifts I had gotten from work. She stole all the clothes I got from a co-worker for my little girl, so I was left with nothing! She left with her kids and didn't let anyone know where she was going.

## Back To The Witchcraft House

I had to crawl back to Carlos's parent's house. I had to get on food stamps and welfare and buy clothes for myself, my daughter, and baby at the thrift store. I had to sleep on the floor with roaches, since they got rid of the mattress I had left there. I still don't know why I wasn't allowed to sleep on the couch. My daughter was around three years old. I kept her close to me because I didn't trust those people.

I was now in my ninth month and due any day. Two weeks go by, and no baby yet. The doctor tried to induce labor, but the baby just didn't want to come out. So, they sent me home to wait it out. The next day, I was made to clean the whole house by myself. They were very dirty people. I found all kinds of objects that I knew were being used for evil. There was a jar with a raw egg filled with liquid and what looked to be my long hair. I found a huge dirty rubber penis in their bedroom. When I went to change my sheets, there was something that looked like dried skin

in the shape of a snake that was hidden under my sheets.
They                          had                          all

kinds of books on witchcraft, spells, and incantations. I always felt something very eerie and haunting in the house.

I woke up in the night to find the old lady rubbing an egg all over me and saying stuff in Spanish. I was very scared and trembling when I saw her crack the egg into a jar and the egg was full of blood. She hurried back to her room and left me there terrified in the dark. I was in pain all night. I went into labor the next morning and the old man dropped me off at the hospital at eight a.m.

The nurses put a wrist band on me and had me dress into a gown. As I was getting ready, I told the nurse I had to go to the bathroom. She led the way and said, "Pull on this emergency cord if you need to." I sat on the toilet to pee, when all of a sudden it felt like I had to poo out a watermelon. I pushed once, but I could feel the baby's head coming out. I yanked on the cord and the nurse came running. She said, "What is it?" I said, "The baby is coming out!" She replied with, "No, you're just having contractions." She helped me up off the toilet and as I was walking back to the hospital bed, I could feel the baby, so I was walking like a duck with a trail of blood spots behind me on the floor. The nurse saw it and said, "Is that you bleeding? Come up here and let me have a look." When she saw that I had crowned, she yells out, "DELIVERY!" Three other nurses came to rush me down the hall, while banging the bed on the corners of the walls, trying to get me into the delivery room. One said, "Don't push!" I thought, "I won't have to, you're going to bang the baby out!"

The doctor said, "No time for anything." No time for an IV, pain medicine, or nothing. I had my baby all natural. The doctor says, "OK. You can push!" When I did, it was like a moment. The doctor declares, "It's a boy!" I cried, as I looked up and saw this perfect little round head with black curly hair and a tiny body squirming and crying. Then I passed out of pure exhaustion. Apparently, I had been in labor during the night, but I thought they were just cramps from over working myself, cleaning the nasty house. My son was born at eight twenty-four a.m. That means it only took twenty-four minutes to give birth after I arrived. The nurses brought my son to me after I woke up. I held him in my arms and just admired him and stared at him, for what seemed to be hours. Oh, how I loved this little guy! I thanked God he was perfect. I named my son Manuel, which means, "God is with us." It is the Spanish translation of the Hebrew Emmanuel. This is a very popular boys name in Spain, where a lot of my dad's ancestors came from.

After three days in the hospital, my son's aunt and uncle, who took care of Angela for me, picked me up. They were very nice people and were nothing like their brother or parents. I introduced Manuel to his big sister. She gave him a hug and kiss. She was only three, but understood she had to be gentle with him. We were taken back to the house of witchcraft. To my astonishment, there was a twin bed waiting for me, on the other side of the living room. I was small, so Angela and the baby still fit on the bed with me. I know it was Manuel's aunt and uncle who put that bed in there for us, so we all didn't have to sleep on the floor.

## The Black Owl

About a week after I gave birth, my son's umbilical cord fell off. His grandmother put it inside my pillowcase and told me to leave it there, to protect him from the Lechuza. She told me it was a huge owl that came at night to steal the souls of newborn babies. I swear, a few days later, I heard a loud scream in the front yard. I looked out the door and sitting on one of the lower branches of their tree, was a huge dark black owl that was at least four feet tall. When I saw it, shivers ran up and down my spine. I slammed the door shut and asked for God's protection. I didn't tell the grandmother, for fear she was the one who conjured it up and this information would heighten her practice of witchcraft. Too many frightening and freakish things happened around that house.

Carlos actually brought his wife and children to live with his parents because he got kicked out of his in-law's house. So, there we all were, living in the same house with him bothering me and his wife cursing at me. I slept across from them. They brought in their mattress and put it on the floor at night, then picked it up in the morning and leaned it against the wall. One late evening, while I was asleep with my babies, I felt someone take my son out of my arms. It was his grandmother. I saw her hand him over to Carlos. He was looking at him and they were whispering, so I couldn't hear what they were saying. I was afraid because I didn't want them putting a curse on him, or his wife getting angry, for carrying my baby. When they saw I was watching them, the grandmother handed him back to me and said that she was just showing him to Carlos. I got my son and put him on the opposite side of me, where she couldn't get to him again.

Carlos's parents would tell lies about me, which made things worse. I would find a bunch of witchcraft crap that was geared towards me. When the others would be outside, the disgusting old man, who was fat, bald and had a missing arm, would try to talk me into having sex with him to keep it in the family. How utterly repulsive and grotesque! He told me if I said anything, I would be sorry.

# Sleeping In The Park

Several times, out of nowhere during the night, I would get kicked out of the house and forced to spend the night at the park with my two babies. I would have slept in my broken car, but it was parked at Carlos's sister's house. I had to walk with them in the dark. There was a small, netted hammock climber for kids, so I laid a small blanket on top and put Angela to sleep in it. I kept Manuel in the stroller bundled in his baby comforter. I stayed up watching them all night to make sure nobody came around. I was terrified but prayed for God to protect us. I knew I absolutely had to get away from this tormenting ordeal.

# Chapter 6

# New Year's Eve Shooting

I went back to work and after a few weeks of constant overtime, I was able to buy my very first car. It was a white Impala. No more buses, no more asking for rides, no more walking.

I was still in this toxic relationship with Carlos, but not so much anymore. Sometimes it was three weeks or

even a month before I saw him again. He would go to my job and
disassemble parts to my car, so that I couldn't leave. When

I tried to start my car, he would be waiting for me, and I was
forced to listen to him. I didn't dare intentionally get him angry, as I knew he had a very bad temper. Just a few days prior, he got passed security at my job. My boss informed me that he was at the gate where I worked. I turned and saw him, but I got scared and told my boss to call security on him because I did not want to talk to him. He was holding a possum in his hands. Why? I have no idea, but when my boss told him to leave, he stormed off cursing, and slammed the poor possum into the brick wall and killed it. Security made sure he left the premises.

I was invited to go to a New Year's Eve party with Carlos's sister. Veronica and I got along pretty good. She was considered the black sheep of her family. I didn't want to leave my kids on New Year's Eve. She was so persistent that I gave in to my better judgment. I got my neighbor to watch my kids. She was very nice. Angela was four and Manuel was one. I didn't want to drive, so Veronica came to pick me up. There was a total of four of us. We were going to a huge dance hall, where a very well-known band was playing. For the most part, we all had fun dancing. I only danced with them, not with any man. I was not into drinking, so I passed on the alcohol. The band played a lot of the songs we liked, so we stayed on the dance floor most of the evening. I couldn't help but feel that I should have stayed home. It was like I was having fun, but I really wasn't. Something just kept bothering me on the inside.

The leader of the band saw me and wanted to talk to me. He asked if I wanted to go on tour with them. I was thinking, this guy is a complete stranger to me. I declined the offer and went back to my company.

The countdown came around to bring in the New Year. Everyone counted down, "Ten, nine, eight, seven, six, five, four three, two, one, ........HAPPY NEW YEAR!" Glasses were clinking, people were hugging and kissing, confetti was being blown unto the dance floor, and the band began to sing Auld Lang Syne, "Should old acquaintance be forgot,"......... tears started filling my eyes. A deep sadness came over me. Something inside me was crying out for someone or something. After the song, we were all ready to go home. People began heading to the exit door.

We wanted to beat the crowd, so we were already next to exit the door. But for no apparent reason, I let four other people leave ahead of us. When they exited and walked towards the parking lot, a car drove by shooting many bullets into the crowd. The four people that we let in front of us all got shot. There were screams, panic, running, falling, and cars leaving as fast as they could. We got split up during the chaos.

I ended up standing above a husband and wife that got shot. They were two of the four we let in front of us. The man had a bullet right in the middle of his forehead. His body was shaking like a fish trying to grasp for air. The wife was on her knees, crying in torment for her husband. A bullet shaved across her forehead and her skin was hanging with blood pouring out. I stood there watching the man die. I was in shock and couldn't move. A few moments went by when I felt a huge tug on my wrist. It was Veronica, pulling on me to take me away from the scene of death and danger.

I don't remember the drive back home. I got my babies from my neighbor and crawled in bed with them. I cuddled them close to me. I was so terrified that I could not go to sleep
for several days. I called in sick. I just wanted to stay safe at home with my children.

None of us talked about what happened. I remember hearing on the radio that the husband died on the scene and the wife died the next day. Now I know why I didn't have any peace about going out that night. I wish to God I would have listened to my gut feeling. It was a horrific experience that haunted my mind for a very long time.

# Chapter 7

# Attempted Murder

Since I had a good relationship with Veronica, she came and got me and my little ones to go live with her. I was so relieved to get away from those evil people. We had our own room and beds to sleep in. There were no roaches to crawl on us. I bought another crib for Manuel. I helped Veronica out with groceries off my food stamps. She had an older son who was about ten. We did good together in that house. We helped each other out. If one or the other had to go somewhere. we were each other's babysitters whenever we needed be. We didn't lack anything. All the neighbors were friendly and helpful.

During the year I stayed with Veronica, Carlos would make his rounds. Not too often, but just enough to keep his curiosity at ease. When Manuel was four months old, I had him baptized and his aunt and uncle became his godparents. We had a small party to celebrate, without Carlos. When he turned one, we had a huge neighborhood party for him. All the kids had a lot of fun. I hadn't felt that relaxed and enjoying the time with everyone in a long time. The neighbors brought different foods and Veronica made enchiladas and menudo. I had a big cake for him, a pinata, and games. Angela had fun with all the other little girls. I was so happy to be safe with my children.

Within a few weeks, Veronica said to me, "Carlos is outside and wants to talk to you." He opened the door and tried to get in, but She stood in the doorway to block him. While he stood there mouthing off his lies to me again, I told him, "I am done with you and all your lies. I don't want to see you or have anything to do with you ever again! Go back to your wife and kids and leave me and my children alone!" He became enraged and started cursing and calling me all kind of names. He said he could pick up any -----off the street. His sister pointed outside and told him to go on into the streets. He left.

Later in the night, I was called to the kitchen and informed that he was outside and demanded to talk to me. Veronica did not get along with her brother and often had fights with him. I wasn't going to go outside, but she said he wasn't going to leave until he spoke with me. She told me that he had his two girls with him, so she didn't think he was going to do anything to me. She asked me to make him leave. I figured I owed her this favor.

When I went outside, there he was, sitting in his car with his two daughters in the back seat. They were maybe five and six years old. His car was sitting in the dark where you really couldn't see him. I went around to the driver side and looked at his face. I was frightened and could sense danger in the air. His eyes were filled with hatred and rage. Before I could say a word, he pulled out a .357 magnum and pointed it at me. He said with a vicious voice, "If I can't have you, nobody can!" I knew in my heart I was about to die. The next few seconds went into a slow motion of episodes. He pulled back on the trigger with intention and intense force! I remember closing my eyes and sort of ducking, as if my body could shield me from the fatal impact of the bullet. The sound of the gun rang deep into my ears......... then silence.

I stood there in complete shock and stunned at what just happened. I got my bearing, stood up straight, and saw the look on my killer's face. He was devastated! The gun jammed! He could not finish what he intended to do. I watched as he slammed his foot to the gas pedal. You could hear the wailing of his tires screeching all the way to the end of the street and then making a violent turn. I ran inside and told his sister what happened. I went to my room where my babies were and embraced them with relief and gratitude. I was crying hysterically because I came so close to losing my life and never seeing them again. I thanked God for protecting me, yet again. His sister called the police and after our report, they put out an APB on him. I called his wife and told her what he did and that the police were out looking for him. Before I hung up, I told her with sincerity that I was sorry for everything and for her not to worry about ever seeing or hearing from me again. I really don't know what happened to him after that because I used all the money I had, to fix my car and go back home. My mom welcomed me and her grandchildren with loving and open arms.

Living in Houston for those three years were the absolute worst years of my life!

# Chapter 8

# Second Failed Marriage

The second marriage was with whom I call my high school sweetheart. Even though he had already graduated from my high school, I was still in school. He should have been my first. I met him through his sister who was my best friend at the time. I was a senior at McCollum High School. His sister had a photo of me in a bridesmaid dress standing next to her,

because we had to do a mock wedding for our homemaking

class. When he saw the photo, he asked her who I was. Apparently, he wanted to meet me. So, she invited me to go to her house to meet her brother.

When we got to her house, she took me to her living room and asked me to wait there. I stood there wondering what he was going to look like and if I might like him. She came back with Brandon, introduced us, and then we just started chatting. I thought he was very attractive and had a nice body. He thought the same of me. That day was the beginning of our encounters and secret meetings that lasted for about a month. I had to hide him from my mom because I wasn't allowed to date until after I graduated. Although, I did have previous secret boyfriends. I would break up with them because I got bored.

I would go see Brandon after school at his mother's house that was just down the block. I thought he was the most handsome guy and I fell in love with him. He had to return back to his duty station, so during the rest of my senior year, he would call, send letters and gifts. All done through his sister. I was supposed to wait for him to come and get me after I graduated because he was in the service on leave, when we first met. After I did graduate, as I mentioned earlier, I was having trouble at home, I moved out and didn't wait for him.

Over the years that had passed, I kept all his letters and everything else he sent me while I was still in high school. I still loved him. I used to pull out his pictures and look at them, regretting that I didn't wait for him.

I remember when I was at one of the lowest times of my life in Houston, I was standing on the front porch of the witchcraft house and I said, "God, I don't know if You really exist anymore or not, but if You do, I want to see Brandon one more time. Even if it's just to say hi and bye."

When I moved back home, I went to visit his sister. She told me that her brother had gotten out of the service and moved back to San Antonio. She said that he came over for dinner every night, if I wanted to wait around to see him. I couldn't believe it. When evening came and she saw him pull up, she had me wait in her bedroom. When he came in, he asked, "Who's car is in the driveway?" She said," "Someone you know." He replied, "Who?" Then she announces, "Jasmine." With a surprised voice he asks, "Jasmine? The Jasmine Cortez?" She says, "Yes. The very one." I heard footsteps coming down the hall. My heart was racing. He opens the door and we just looked at each other with huge smiles, then greetings, and then we embraced. God answered my prayer. He heard me.

It felt as though we just picked up where we left off. He graciously took me in with my kids as if they were his own. Brandon moved us in with him in the house he was renting. I was forbidden to work, wear shorts outside, no shirts that revealed the shape of my chest, and no lipstick. And of course, I complied. We had lived together for two years and were happy. After the two years, we decided to put the money he was paying for rent, into buying our own house. He bought us a house where the kids could go to school, right across the street. There was also a grocery store right on the corner. I was very happy where we moved. This was the first place I lived where I could call it my OWN home.

I had the need to be legally married to him. He agreed to get married through the justice of the peace at our home. I was still a Catholic, so I was reminded that we were living in sin because we were not married through the church. Then, four years later, I was advised that we should get married through the Catholic church because we were still living in sin. So, we got married through the church.

His, occasional drinking went from bad to worse, until he was a full-blown alcoholic. I didn't know it at the time, but
I was an enabler to him. I made sure the fridge was stocked with beer, I made him gift baskets with beer, and I would serve him his beer. I was very ignorant about the disease, addiction, and destruction of alcohol.

# First Miscarriage

Right after I told him that I was pregnant, he tells me that he was going to bring his ex-wife and daughter back to live with him. So, that meant me, and my kids were getting thrown out. I spent the whole weekend being traumatized with the thoughts of being abandoned and trying to figure out what I was going to do. I never cried so hard in my life. My heart was being crushed into a million pieces.

When we went to his parents to tell them, his dad hit the roof! He told him that he needed to stay with me and start with raising his unborn child, instead of trying to start over with his first, who was already four. Brandon adored his dad. It was a major shock for him to see his dad so angry with him. His dad always did like me, not his mom. His mom was yelling and pointing at me saying, "I told you I didn't want her! I wanted the other one. I didn't want this one!" She made sure I knew this by hanging his ex-wife's pictures where I couldn't miss seeing them. I run to the bathroom crying my eyes out and feeling like my heart was being ripped out. I was devastated, angry and hurt. His mom comes pounding on the door and tells me that Brandon was leaving, and **I needed to go**. Not long after we got home, I started bleeding and pain intensified. Brandon took me to the emergency room, where I lost our baby. I was three and one-half months. Cause of death......... trauma.

The marital issues continued to grow worse. Mental, verbal, and emotional abuse were taking a toll on me. It became a habit for him to always be gone on weekends to get drunk at whatever bar his co-workers were hanging out at. If he took me to a party, he would turn his seat away from me as if he weren't with me and didn't know me. That was worse than always leaving me at home. I overheard some of his co-workers calling him names in Spanish. They were very bad. They implied that he was a man whore. I was wondering why they would call him those horrible names. I just totally forgot about it.

One time he said he was going to a family-oriented BBQ at a bar, but he said I couldn't go. I was friends with a couple of the wives of his co-workers. One of them called me and asked if I wanted her to come pick me up so that we could hang out. I had told her yes. I had never gone anywhere to look for Brandon or to show up where he was. This was the first time and I figured it was o.k., since he said it was family oriented.

Everyone was sitting outside on picnic tables. When we got to where Brandon was, a female who was sitting right behind him and very close, put her hand on his thigh and said, "Here they come to check up on you." I sat down next to him and noticed his dad sitting with him. Across from him was a woman he was buying drinks for. He began to curse me out in front of everyone. He was extremely drunk. It was in Spanish, so it was very vulgar, degrading, and humiliating. I started to cry, and the woman got up and left. His dad kept telling him to be quiet, but he only got louder and uglier. I don't know where my friend went, so I got up and went to sit inside our car. After a little while, I saw

Brandon looking around to see where I went. When he saw me inside the car, he came charging at me, like a ravenous pit bull. He flung the door open making a scene in front of everyone. He was raging in anger, screaming, and cursing right in my face. A couple was banging on the door saying, "Come with us! Come with us!" His dad was yanking on him, telling him to leave me alone. We ended up leaving and on the way home, we got rear ended by another vehicle. This jolted the drunk right out of Brandon. He took me back home and then drove off with his dad. He spent more hours drinking the night off. I never went anywhere he was at, trying to hang out with him, ever again.

There were times he wouldn't come home. All the signs were there that he was cheating on me, but I chose to ignore them. I lived in my own world of denial. We got to a point of sleeping on opposite sides of the bed. It was like we were living in the same house but living separate lives. I forced myself to stay with Brandon. After all, what would I do or where would I go? He had already made me believe that I was worthless, useless, and lost without him. Inside I was miserable, but I played the part of being a happy wife on the outside.

## My Sister Stella is Murdered

I will never forget that day. I was at home alone, when I received a phone call from my niece, Debra. When I said, "Hello," she told me with a voice that was distraught and in shock, "Aunt Jasmine, my mom is dead. "What?" I replied in disbelief. Debra replied with these words, "She was stabbed, and they found her body behind a dumpster.".........I could barely gasp out, "Oh my God!" My mind went racing like a whirlwind and my heart filled with ache I never knew before.

My thoughts went immediately to my mom. What a deep sorrow she'll have to face with the death of one of her own daughters! It already felt like a huge chunk was taken away from our family.

I called the city morgue and asked questions about a possible identity of my sister. I described what she looked like and that she had a scar on the right side of her cheek, where her abusive boyfriend had kicked her in her face. They hesitated but wouldn't give me any information. They said a family member had to go in person to identify the body.

I drove to my mother's house and met my sister Connie there. The eldest of my brothers, my sister, and my husband went to the morgue. I just couldn't bear to see if it was my sister, nor was I prepared to witness what they would unveil. My insides were in a huge, twisted knot, waiting for them to get back home. When they finally got back, after what seemed to be an eternity, I looked at my husband and he nodded his head yes, letting me know it was my sister. I felt my heart drop into the pit of my stomach, as I began to sob tears of anguish and anger. I will never see my sister again, talk, or hang out with her. Someone took her life away. She was murdered! Not only did they stab her many times, but they also slit her throat and did unimaginable and unspeakable things to her body. They marked her with signs of the occult.

An investigation took place, but everyone who knew her and hung out with her, claimed they knew nothing. None of their stories matched up to what took place that evening. We know she was at the wrong place, at the wrong time. She left the bar she was at with a male who was giving her a ride. They don't know if she was going home or to another bar.

Someone there knew who he was, but nobody was talking. The identity of the man was never found. My

family was left missing one of the girls. We were referred to as the
Cortez girls, since there were six of us. My sister Stella was

a year older than I was. She was beautiful, had the kindest heart, and would give you the shirt off her back, even though she didn't have much. She was a very talented graphic artist, who was published in a local magazine in Tucson, Arizona when she lived there, and you could see her local works around San Antonio. She had one daughter, Debra Denise, whom she loved very much.

I remember how beautiful her funeral was. She looked so peaceful, and her beauty stayed with her, even in death. The funeral home was filled to the max with family and friends. I was sitting with my family, as people made their way to the front where Stella's casket was, to say their farewells to her. As the line of mourners finally slowed down, someone caught my eye as they slowly approached my sister with a steady and rhythmic step. I looked closer through my drenched eyes to behold the sight of my little brother, Brian, who was in his Marine Blue Dress Uniform. He made his way to the front side of his big sister, facing us all. He stood there for just a minute, standing at full attention. He then raised his hand to his forehead and made a valiant salute to honor our sister, Stella Marie Flores. Oh, how I just became undone!

My little brother had flown in from where he was stationed. He came and sat next to our mother. She stood strong and courageous that day. During the funeral procession to the cemetery, I looked back out of the limo window, where I witnessed an unending row of lights following behind on the highway. I told my mom how beautiful I thought that was. My mamma cried and said, "And she thought she didn't have any friends."

My sister always had boyfriends who used and abused her. They would beat her and pull the phone from the wall, so that she couldn't call for help. One of them left her with

cracked ribs. This went on for years. It broke my heart to see
and know this. Two weeks before her death, I witnessed her face get kicked in by her last boyfriend, causing her cheek to split open with blood pouring out. She never pressed charges against anyone. The next day I prayed a prayer that haunted me for a while. I said this to God. "God, if this is the life that my sister is going to live for the rest of her life, then please just take her home, so she won't suffer anymore." Two weeks later, is when I got the call from my niece that she was murdered. I felt so guilty for that prayer. I didn't want her life to be taken away in such a brutal way. I carried that guilt and torment in my heart. I was then filled with a fear that I couldn't comprehend. When my husband was gone at work and my kids at school during the day, I had the need to turn on all the lights, even in broad daylight. I put the TV and the radio on. I would get images of my sister's dead body in the morgue and all the horrible things done to her body. At night, if my husband went to the bathroom, I would go sit by the door because I didn't want to be left alone. If I had to go to the store, I would check inside the car and look underneath to make sure no one was there. Fear had gripped my life.

One day after many months following my sister's death, I was visiting my mom and she told me something that stunned me. She said, with such a calm voice, "We all have to forgive whoever it was that killed Stella." I wasn't expecting those words. I didn't say anything, but I thought to myself, "I will never forgive the person who murdered her!" After a long time passed, fear and guilt finally left me alone. Not completely, but enough to give me strength to deal with my failing marriage.

This man took my heart and over the years just chipped away at it in pieces. I wasn't going to let this happen to the
point of no return. I started praying and asking God to give

me the strength to end it with Brandon.

Soon after that, I found out I was pregnant with my fourth child. When I told Brandon, he was happy. This triggered a very short season of him being nice to me. Everything was going fine until about the fourth month. I started spotting blood and got scared. I went to see the doctor and he explained to me that my placenta was falling. He said I needed to stay in bed and do absolutely no lifting at all. In time the placenta would move back up on its own and the baby would be fine. So, off to bed I went. Brandon and the kids helped me with the housework. He even tried not to be gone all night when he went out drinking. Within three months, I was informed that my placenta was back to normal, and I could resume normal activity, with the exception of heavy lifting. I was seven months now. Brandon continued to drink. Any birthday party we had for the kids turned into a drinking bash for him and his family. Any party we were invited to by his family was just another event for drinking. I was so sick of it. I didn't even want to attend any celebrations they had anymore, but I thought about the kids and wanted them to have fun. I always made sure Easter, Christmas, and birthdays were something they could remember.

## My Third Child Is Born

I'm now in my ninth month of pregnancy; this baby is supposed to be born on my birthday. I never wanted to know the gender of the baby until they were born. So, it's time! I started having contractions early in the morning. This child is coming a week early. We get to the hospital and the nurse is trying to get hold of my doctor. I am at three centimeters,

so they said we still have plenty of time. They hook me up
to

an IV and all the monitors. My contractions are getting stronger. Still no word from my doctor. I asked for some pain medicine. They checked me again and couldn't believe I jumped from a three to a ten in such little time. Brandon waited in the waiting room because he said he didn't want to see everything. That he was old fashioned. His sister was in the room with me. As soon as they gave me an epidural, baby was ready to be birthed. The doctor still wasn't there. The nurse had to perform the delivery. She said, "Push." I literally just pushed slightly, as if I had to pee, making only a small grunt. Out came the baby and over the crying, I hear, "It's a girl!" Total delivery was two and a half hours. The doctor showed up in time to finish up with me. I named her Christina Marie because the name Christ was in it. She was just a bundle of cute, adorable, sweetness. She surely captured my heart! Brandon came in to hold his baby girl. He was very happy.

When I got home three days later, I called Angela and Manuel to come meet their baby sister. They were too cute in how they hugged and held her for the first time. I had her crib set up in our bedroom. I guess now that I was good to go, and Christina was born, Brandon went back to his usual habits. Four months went by, and he was in full force again. One night while I was watching TV and the kids were in bed, Brandon asked me something about a female friend of mine, which really upset me. How could he ask me that? I used a curse word in my response to him and his hand came swinging across to backhand my face. That's it. I knew the physical abuse was inevitable. When I tried to talk to his

mom about what was going on, she had the audacity to tell me, "If I had to put up with it, so do you!" I was completely shocked and stunned with her answer. I never confided in her again!

Whenever I threatened to leave, Brandon would standin front of me like a bully and laugh. He would say things like, "Look at you! You think your all bad with your threats. Why are you crying then? You haven't left me yet; you're never going to leave me! Your fat, ugly, and nobody is going to take you in with kids the way I did." I was skinny and attractive. Men were always looking at me, but Brandon made me feel ugly on the inside and out. He also told me that if I ever got fat, he would throw me out of the house.

I tried to live a normal life with him, for my kid's sake. The years just kept going by. I stayed in the marriage for all the wrong reasons. Divorce was against the Catholic church. I stayed for my kids. I stayed out of fear. I stayed because I had no confidence and very low self-esteem of myself. I hid the bad stuff between us, so my children wouldn't find out. They never saw him passed out on the floor from being drunk. They never saw him stagger into the house so intoxicated that he would just plaster himself into the wall and lose consciousness where he fell. They never heard him cursing at me or belittling me. They never saw him swimming in his own vomit on the floor or sprawled outside on the ground. I tried to shield them as much as I could from his inebriated world. I didn't want them to lose respect for him.

## Second Miscarriage

I had gotten a job working at Sam's Club. At this point, I didn't care if Brandon approved or not. He was working a different shift on his job, so he was able to watch Christina who was about three years old. I found out I was pregnant again. This was my fifth baby. Brandon didn't seem too thrilled about it. I was a cashier and had to move a lot of heavy items from one cart to the other. One day I started spotting blood. I told my supervisor but was informed that if I couldn't perform my regular duties, they were going to let me go. They themselves didn't know what to do with me, because I was the first pregnancy they had to deal with. So, I continued to work and lift all the heavy items off the carts and the next day I lost the baby. I was close to four months. I was sad, but not overwhelmed with grief because we were still having a lot of issues in our marriage. My boss gave me time off work to recuperate.

Months turned into another year. Christina is four years old now. Our *normal* life consisted of going on vacations, celebrating holidays, and birthdays. I really tried hard to be a good wife and mother. This marriage was poisoned with the toxic addiction of alcohol, abuse, and adultery. I too had my own issues that needed to be dealt with. I was pretty messed up. I wouldn't find out how messed up I was until later. I used to yell when I would get angry. I tried really hard to stop because it reminded me of my dad yelling at my mom and getting angry all the time. No matter how hard I tried, I couldn't control it. I began cursing as well. Most of the people I worked with swore, so I just picked it up from them. I cursed worse than a sailor.

I was at the end of my rope, but stuck it out another year, only to add the worst year of misery. The only thing that kept me from letting go, was the thought that he would never cheat on me. Even though the signs were there, I deceived myself by blocking it out of my mind. I don't know how much time passed between the time I started asking God to help me leave this relationship and the night Brandon came home from being gone all day. He was drunk. I looked at him and noticed several purple marks on his neck. I

121

couldn't deny what I was seeing. Reality just punched me in the face. I yelled and said, "What the hell is on your neck?"

He ran to the bathroom to look in the mirror. I yelled again saying, "Are those hickeys?" He never let me do that to him. So, since he got caught and couldn't deny it, he just sat there in his drunken stupor. I asked him with tears running down my face and my heart being filled with a deep dark betrayal, "Why? I have always been here for you!" He says in a very angry and arrogant shout, "Because it was there! I'm glad you found out; cause now I don't have to hide it anymore!" He starts to sway and then blacks out. I stood there looking at him in disgust and just wanted to punch him as hard as I could with everything that was in me. I just couldn't do it. Instead, through the pain that was piercing my heart and the tears that blinded my eyes, I emptied out his drawers and packed his suitcases. "You're out of here!" I yelled. I missed work the next day. The truth came out about all his affairs. Would you believe they were all with heavy women? I'm not saying this to be mean in any way, shape or form. But he threatened me that if I ever got fat, he would throw me out! He did other things that I couldn't comprehend. He also disclosed that he cheated on his first wife as well. I made him take his suitcases and told him. "Get out!" He looks at me and says with a haughty tone, "I have plenty of friends who will take me in." I replied, "Well then, go live with your friends!"

A few days later, his mother comes knocking on the door while the kids were at school. I wondered, "What the hell does she want?" She actually wanted to know what my plans were. Not that it was any of her business, but I told her I was

going to file for divorce. You would think it was her I was divorcing for the way she reacted. She exploded! You would think she would be celebrating, since she hated me so much.

I know her deep anger and envy was because I was setting myself free from the hell I endured, and she never did. You see, Brandon was an exact carbon copy of his dad. And his dad's dad. I asked her not to tell Brandon, but that was like telling her to sound the alarms. A few hours later, I got a call from a distraught Brandon. He thought I would NEVER leave him or NEVER file for divorce. After our conversation, my anger was triggered deeper than I could have imagined.

His mom had bought him a jacket that advertised beer. I hated everything that had to do with drinking. I took a pair of scissors and shredded that jacket, like Freddy Kruger had gotten to it. I had been saving Brandon's ex-wife's wedding album for his daughter. That thing got destroyed! I also, cut up a shirt I had embroidered for him that had the emblem of the service he was in. I took our wedding picture and slammed it until the glass broke. I just felt the need to destroy something. All this anger surfaced, and I didn't know what to do with it. I cried all day while the kids were at school. When they got home, I tried to be strong and not show my inner pain.

Two weeks later, Brandon comes drunk to the door late at night and says he wanted to see his daughter. I told him no and never show up drunk again. As he was driving off, I noticed his suitcases were still in the back of his truck. He shows up again, in the morning and asks if he can come back. He says, "Can't I move back in, and we just live the way we did before?" I asked him, "Are you insane? What happened to all your friends you said would take you in?" He said nothing. I still had compassion for him, so I let him come back for a month and sleep in the middle room, until he found an

apartment. He moved less than a mile away from us. His mother used to call me to find out who was parked in my driveway. Really? What are you doing, spying on me?

Brandon allowed me to keep the house we bought. It wasn't paid off and there was still a large mortgage debt. I gave him the recliner I bought him for Father's Day from the kids. I gave him our bedroom set, one of our TV's, a table, some dishes, kitchen utensils, and other various household items. I helped with the necessities for his apartment. After his year lease was over, he called and said, "My lease is over." And I replied, "Yeah, so?" "Well, I thought since it's been a year that we would get back together," He proclaimed. My response to that was, "NO! I have moved on. I will never go back to that life! You need to just move on as well because WE are never going to happen again."

Our divorce was finalized, but that began another hellish season with joint custody. In short; having to put up with his girlfriends who were all very much over weight, driving drunk with our daughter in the car, having to call the cops on him because he refused to bring her home, filling her little head with lies about me, letting her down by not coming for her when he was supposed to, and just breaking all the rules that were set in our divorce.

I also found out his mother and sister were lying about me to the people I worked with, while they were shopping. My neighbor, who was related to them, told me they were telling everyone that Brandon divorced me because I wouldn't let him go anywhere without me. What a joke. I just told them that they needed to lie about me to hide the embarrassment he brought to their family.

I continued to work to support myself and my children. I always had to work weekends. Brandon usually took care of Christina for me. The times he couldn't watch her, I had to ask my son to help because Angela was now working, herself. I remember being at the register one day, crying because I felt my children were growing up without me and I was missing out on so much time with them. I know the divorce was hard on my children. It pained my heart to know

that they were going through their own hurts because of this. Divorce effects our children more than we know. I wish I could have just taken all their hurt and anger and put it on myself. Children don't deserve the heartache of divorce. But I had to do it. Not just for myself, but for them as well.

# Chapter 9

# The Miraculous Day I Got Saved

## This Is My Testimony

I was introduced to a younger man I met through a close friend and co-worker. She was dating his brother. She told

me he was in town for a little while and asked if I wanted to meet him. So, I agreed to go on a double date with her. We hit it off and spent time on the phone before we dated. We had only been seeing each other for a short while when his mom invited us to a crusade. I had never been to one in my life, so I was curious and wanted to go. We accepted the invitation and all three of us went together. It was at the Joe Freeman Coliseum in San Antonio, Texas. It was a Benny Hinn crusade, and I had no idea who he was. I had never heard of him before. The place was jam packed already, so we had to make our way to get seats on the upper level, way on top. I could see the platform that looked to be in a shrunken size because of how high up we were. There were huge TV monitors on either side of the platform. So, either way, we could see what was going on.

When the worship team began to play, the pastor stepped out on stage and began to sing, "Hallelujah," repeatedly, as the whole auditorium joined in. Something was happening all around us. You could feel it in the air. I was in awe at the thousands of thousands of people singing in one accord. It didn't matter what denomination, the color of skin, young or old, or their background. They were all there for one reason. Every single one of those people were there to worship God! This is what I had been looking for, this is what I wanted, this is what I needed! To be in unity with the body of Christ. It was as though I was being drawn into something way bigger than I could ever imagine. And I knew that God was the center of it all. I joined in the singing with all my heart. For every Hallelujah I sang, I felt myself go deeper into a place that was being prepared for me. I didn't understand what that was, but I pressed in for more of God and what He had in store for me. As the worship continued, the atmosphere was filled with an intense holy presence. Pastor Hinn lifted his finger to his lips to quiet the worship team as he said, "Just a whisper." Our voices faded

out, as only the music was playing now, in a very quiet and peaceful sound. All our hands were lifted in reverence and honor to our God. He prayed a prayer of blessing over the whole auditorium, invited the Holy Spirit to have His way, then after a few minutes, everyone was asked to sit down.

He introduced himself. He was all in white and so were the hundred pastors who were sitting on stage with him. He said, "I don't know a lot of these pastors up here with me, I do know a few of them." He mentioned two of their names, they stood up and then sat down. Then he said, "Oh, and this is Pastor John Cortez." To my disbelief, I looked closely, and I said loudly, "That's my dad!" I said out loud again, "That's my dad!" Again, in disbelief, "That's my dad????"

The last I heard of him, was that he was in prison for fraud. I didn't know if that was true or not at the time, but there he stood on stage with Benny Hinn! Whaaatt??? I was very much perplexed! I hadn't seen or heard from my dad in years. I didn't care where he was or if I ever saw him again.

While I sat there and listened to the pastor preach, his words really hit me where it hurt, deep in my heart. I knew I was harboring unforgiveness towards my dad, so right there and then, I chose to forgive my dad for everything. Subtly, all the hard feelings, all the anger, and the hurt melted away that had been rooted in my soul. When Benny Hinn's preaching was over, the beautiful worship songs began. He gave an open invitation for anyone who desired to give their life to Jesus, to come down to the alter. I couldn't get there fast enough! I stood there with open arms and humbled myself before my God. I repented of all my sins, prayed with pastor Hinn and asked Jesus into my heart.

With tears running down my face, I felt the pure and un-conditional love of my Savior penetrate to the hidden chambers of my heart and flood it with a blissful flow of intimacy with Him. It was almost too much to bear.

While standing there surrounded by hundreds of others who just got saved, Pastor Hinn said he was going to blow on us and we would fall under the anointing of the Holy Spirit. I didn't believe in getting slain. I used to mock people about that because it looked like they were being forcefully pushed down to the ground. And speaking in tongues, I thought they just made up some ridiculous sounds and forced them out of their mouths. So, I stood there talking to God, "OK, God. You know me. You know I don't believe in this stuff. So, if it is true, You are going to have to show me Yourself."

Benny Hinn blew on all the people to my right. I thought that the majority might just give a *courtesy fall*, but they all fell down. I was in the center group. I stood there telling God, "Well, it's our turn. I'm going to look like an idiot because I will be the only one standing. OK God, show me!" When Benny Hinn blew on us, in a split second, a huge bolt of lightning struck right in front of me! All I could see was this tremendous, bright, pure, and glorious light that burst out of this bolt when it crashed against the floor. The second that it did, I experienced an explosion of un-believable peace and warmth that I never felt before in my life. It seemed to saturate my being. I felt like I was melting and gently fell to the floor. I stayed down for a few moments just lying in the power and presence of God. I couldn't move, open my eyes, nor talk. That was the moment of truth, from God Himself! I got slain in the Holy Spirit! When I did get up off the floor, it felt like I was drunk. I really didn't know what was going on, but it sure felt good!

After the alter call, I made my way to the stage where I was greeted with security. Literally, men in black. I climbed a few steps and told the security that I needed to talk to my dad. They asked me who my dad was, and I said, "Pastor John Cortez!" To which they responded in an un-believing tone, "Pastor John Cortez is YOUR dad?" I said, "Yes! I need to talk to him!" So, one stayed on guard and the other went to call him. I will never forget the look on his face when he saw me! His mouth dropped open wide, his eyes filled with surprise and tears, and as I climbed past the security guard to the platform, we embraced. He told me that he had been praying for thirteen years for one of his thirteen children to get saved. That was me!!!

God restored our relationship as father and daughter. He also restored all the years that were lost between us. I also found out that my dad was wrongfully accused and imprisoned. However, only God can turn something bad and make it good. While my dad was in prison, he gave his life to the Lord and studied to become an ordained pastor. God used him to minister to the other prisoners. I didn't know it at the time, but he was the one who organized and put together the whole crusade with Benny Hinn. Little did he know, God was using him to bring his daughter into the kingdom and set me up for my own salvation and destiny. Wow! All that for me! Thank You Father God! Thank you, dad for your faithful and continued prayers for your children. I love and appreciate you.

## Transformation

God began a life changing process in me. He began to heal all my hurts, brokenness, sorrows, regrets, and failures. Also, to deliver me from all the powers of darkness.

This was not an overnight process. This took some time and surrender on my part. He removed different layers of darkness that plagued my life, in different seasons of my life. He filled my heart with love and compassion. He was filling me with Him. I could feel a deep change taking place within my soul. He restored all my sorrow for joy. He renewed my strength. He lifted me out of the darkness of hell and raised me up into His glorious light. He saved me from death and gave me a place of eternal life with Him in heaven. I was no longer just going through life but living it abundantly with the help of my Savior Jesus, and His Holy Spirit.

*For He made Him who knew no sin to be sin for us, that we might become the righteousness of God in Him* (2 Corinthians 5:2)

*Jesus answered and said to him truly, truly I say to you, unless one is born again, he cannot see the kingdom of God.* (John 3:3)

I was indeed born again. God has molded, conformed, and transformed my life into His beautiful image. I truly am a new creature in and through Christ. You see, it isn't enough just to love God, do good, and go to church. You must have a personal relationship with His Son, Jesus Christ. You need to be filled with his Holy Spirit.

*If you confess with your mouth Jesus as Lord and believe in your heart that God raised Him from the dead, you will be saved; for with the heart a person believes, resulting in righteousness, and with the mouth he confesses resulting in salvation.* (Romans 10:9-10)

*Jesus answered, truly, truly I say to you, unless one is born of water and the Spirit he cannot enter into the kingdom of heaven.* (John 3:5)

*For the wages of sin is death, but the free gift of God is eternal life in Christ Jesus our Lord.* (Roman's 6:23)

Being a Christian does not mean that you will not face difficulties or hardships. It does not mean that everybody will love you and be your friend. Now that you belong to the Lord, the enemy will do everything in his power to keep you down and in the same place from which you were in bondage. However, you now have the weapons of spiritual warfare and God on your side! The Bible is His living Word and contains everything you need to be victorious in life.

*My brethren, count it all joy when you fall into various trials, knowing that the testing of your faith produces patience. But let patience have its perfect work, that you may be perfect and complete, lacking nothing. If any of you lacks wisdom, let him ask of God, who gives to all liberally and without reproach, and it will be given to him. But let him ask in faith, with no doubting, for he who doubts is like a wave of the sea driven and tossed by the wind. For let not that man suppose that he will receive anything from the Lord; he is a double-minded man, unstable in all his ways.*
(James 1:2-8)

After I got saved, I began to get attacked, ridiculed, and falsely accused by a few family members, my ex, and my neighbor. A brother I used to be close to, outright dis-owned

143

me because I left the Catholic church. Over the years, he called me names, judged me to other family members as to why I was going to hell, told me to my face how evil I was, and belittled me in front of my own children. Oh, how my kids wanted to tell him off! I told them that we just needed to forgive him, he was their uncle, and they still needed to show respect. You see, the enemy wants you to doubt your salvation. he wants to keep you down and out. And now that I was saved, he was mad as hell, because he lost my soul to Jesus!

My mother was so loving to me. We went to lunch one day and I explained to her my experience in being saved and that I considered myself to be a Christian without being tied to any religion. She listened with her heart full of love and with her beautiful smile said, "I don't care what you call yourself, so long as I still have you." My mother was a Catholic, who believed in Jesus, as Savior. That is the love of the Father to us. He doesn't care what we call ourselves: Catholics, Pentecost's, Baptists, Protestants, Lutherans, or Presbyterians. So long as we believe in His Son, Jesus Christ, as our Lord and Savior and in His Holy Spirit who comes to dwell in those who believe. God is not a God of religion. He is a God who cares about the substance of our heart!

Eventually, the few members of my family who didn't really understand me leaving Catholicism, came to peace with my decision and salvation. The eyes of their heart were opened to the truth. Except the one brother.

Even as a Christian, we have to endure heartaches, trials, and battles. It wasn't until I gave my life to the Lord that He began to reveal His purpose for me and why I had gone through such tragedies. This was the time where He answered my prayer when I asked him years ago, why I was going through all that heartache and turmoil. He was going to use me to minister to other women. I had to go through everything I went through, so that I could relate to them on

a personal level and in different situations going on in their lives. God was going to use me to bring healing and deliverance to their lives. It's one thing to say, "I understand

what you're going through." But if you've never experienced what they went through, then you really don't understand. I would know how to pray for them, what to pray, and teach them how to pray, as well. I knew how to minister to these women because I lived and went through the experiences myself. And I was victorious. I became a Queen of Valor! (Great courage in the face of danger, especially in battle.) This only happened with the weapons of warfare that our King Warrior gave us, the full armor of God. He also, surrounded me with warring angels as I used His Word to bring destruction to the enemy. When I spoke His Word, He rose up inside me and placed His sword and shield in my hands. When the enemy faced me, he faced the Lion of Judah roaring back at him.

*"Fear not, for I have redeemed you; I have called you by your name; You are Mine. When you pass through the waters, I will be with you; And through the rivers, they shall not overflow you. When you walk through the fire, you shall not be burned, Nor shall the flame scorch you. For I am the Lord your God, The Holy One of Israel, your Savior. (Isaiah 43:1-4)*

Our life does not belong to us. We were created to serve Him. He gives and plans our life. He uses our life and our testimonies to help and encourage others. We must give

Him all the honor, praise, and thanksgiving for the wonderful things He has done in our lives.

*And they overcame him by the blood of the Lamb and by the word of their testimony, and they did not love their lives to the death. (Revelation 12:11)*

*I will declare Your name to My brethren; In the midst of the assembly, I will praise You.* (Psalm 22:22)

*However, Jesus did not permit him, but said to him, "Go home to your friends, and tell them what great things the Lord has done for you, and how He has had compassion on you."* (Mark 5:1919)

**Your testimony is the key to set someone free from their own prison, the solution to someone's dilemma, or the answer to someone's life changing event. It may be the encouragement someone needs for something difficult they are going through or the hope for that someone who is desperate. We should always be ready to testify of the goodness of our Lord!**

*For God so loved the world, that He gave His only begotten Son that whoever believes in Him shall not perish but have everlasting life.* (John3:16)

*There is therefore now, no condemnation to those who are in Christ Jesus, who do not walk according to the flesh, but according to the Spirit. ² For the law of the Spirit of life in Christ Jesus has made me free from the law of sin and death.* (Romans 8:1-4)

*That if you confess with your mouth the Lord Jesus and believe in your heart that God has raised Him from the dead, you will be saved. For with the heart, one believes unto righteousness, and with the mouth confession is made unto salvation.* (Romans 10: 9-10)

This is what I ask people, "If you were to walk outside and get hit by a car that takes your life, would you know without a shadow of a doubt where you would spend eternity?" If you don't know the answer to that question, or you know God has been tugging at your heart for some time now, I urge you to ask Jesus into your heart, to be Lord and Savior. You may never have another chance. Maybe you are reading this right now, and this is your time. We are not promised today or tomorrow. You have nothing to lose but everything to gain. Please, don't pass up this opportunity to allow yourself this lifechanging, lifesaving miracle.

# Prayer for Salvation

(Just say this simple prayer, but really mean it in your heart.)

Dear Jesus,

I come to You right now, where I'm at and just the way I am. I ask You to please forgive me for my sins, for I am a sinner. I believe that You died on the cross for all my sins and that I may be healed and set free. I believe that You resurrected on the third day and sit at the right hand of the Father. Jesus, I ask You now to come into my heart and take over my life, as I surrender it over to You. Thank You for reconciling me back to our Father. I confess and accept You as my Lord and Savior, Jesus Christ. I surrender my life to You now, so that You can transform me into Your image. Holy Spirit fill me now and dwell in me all the days of my life. In Jesus's name, amen.

*Therefore, if anyone is in Christ, he is a new creation; old things have passed away; behold, all things have become new.* (2 Corinthians 5:17)

This means that you have been given a clean slate. Your past has been washed away. You are no longer a slave to sin but set free by the washing of the blood of Jesus. You are not the same person that you were before you got saved. The Holy Spirit will now begin in you a transformation from the inside out. You will begin a journey of being conformed to the image of Christ. You will begin to hate the things you used to love (sin) and love the things you used to hate (righteousness). My journey began many years ago and continues to this very day. I have so many testimonies on what God has done in my life and that of my children.

*As far as the east is from the west, so far has He removed our transgressions from us.* (Psalm 103:12)

After that great and faithful day, on February 28th, 1993, my life began to change at dramatic paces. I learned that in order to begin the healing process, I had to forgive everyone who had ever hurt me or my family.

*"For if you forgive men their trespasses, your heavenly Father will also forgive you. But if you do not forgive men their trespasses, neither will your Father, forgive your trespasses.* (Matthew 6:14-15)

I was very new to this, so I asked God to help me do what I needed to do. He prompted me to get a piece of paper and write down the names of people I needed to forgive, and why.

If I came to someone I didn't know, I just prayed, "Lord, You know who they are."

# This Is What My Name And Reason List Looked Like:

**1.** Lord, I forgive <u>Joseph</u> for his lies, neglect, abuse, adultery, and for not providing for me and our daughter, as a husband and father should have.

**2.** Lord, I forgive <u>Carlos</u> for all of his lies and manipulation, abuse, stealing, denying his child, using me, and attempted murder on my life; which You saved.

**3.** Lord, I forgive <u>the man that raped me</u> (You know who he is) and took so much from me that was not his. I forgive him for causing me to go through such a nightmare of emotional turmoil. I forgive him for putting a hatred in my heart towards men and for wanting to take my life, which You saved.

**4.** Lord, I forgive <u>Brandon</u> for his abuse, adultery, belittlement, manipulation, lies, and trauma he caused in my life and in our marriage. I forgive him for causing heartache in my children.

**5.** Lord I forgive <u>the person who murdered my sister, Stella,</u> in such a brutal way, (You know who they are) and took her from us. I forgive them for making a hole in my family's hearts and causing us all much grief, pain, and sorrow. I forgive them for leaving her only daughter without a mother.

**6.** Lord, I forgive <u>my dad</u> for leaving my mother to raise thirteen children by herself, after he left. I forgive him for not supporting us and making it so hard on my mom and us. I forgive him for the times he was a millionaire and didn't put money aside for us or for our mother, so that she didn't have to struggle the way she did. I forgive him for being an absent parent and leaving my brothers without a father figure. I forgive him for everything he did and did not do.

**7.** Lord, I choose to forgive <u>anyone and everyone</u> who has ever hurt me or any of my family. (You know who they are and what they did.)

**8.** Lord, I choose to forgive <u>**MYSELF**</u> for all my mistakes, bad choices, and failures. For the prayer I prayed for You to take my sister home. For not being the mother, I wanted to be and should have been for that season in my life. For all hurt I caused especially to my children, or my family.

**9** Please forgive me Lord for all the times I hurt You, my Abba Father.

# Make Your Own List

1. _____

2. _____

3. _____

4. _____

5. _____

6. _____

7. _____

8. _____

9. _____

10. _____

11. _____

12. _____

13. _____

14. _____

15. _____

16. _____

17. _____

18. _____

19. _____

20. _____

After I made this list, I read it out loud so that satan and his demons and author of unforgiveness could hear my words, as I declared them unto the Lord. I envisioned myself, placing this list at the foot of the cross and watching the blood of Jesus cover it. I found myself being released from a blanket made of oppression and depression, guilt, anguish, torment, brutality, manipulation, control, and hostility. I experienced layer after layer of this heavy blanket being ripped away as I continued to call upon the name of Jesus, again, and again. That was the day the Lord covered me with His tapestry of peace and tranquility. I was free from the torments of my past.

*Now the Lord is the Spirit; and where the Spirit of the Lord is, there is liberty.* (2 Corinthians 3:17)

Forgiveness is a way of life. The enemy will continue to bring all of these past offenses to your mind. The moment this happens, you need to take your thoughts captive to the obedience of Christ. Just say, "NO, I forgave that offense or that person. I refuse to pick it back up. I rebuke this thought in Jesus's name."

If you continue to entertain that thought, you are going to find yourself being tormented with what the person did and playing it over and over again in your mind, until you have no peace of mind. Your thoughts will be flooded with thoughts of revenge, anger, what you should have said, what you should have done, and then you are back to square one, having to forgive again. I know it's hard, but you must take your thoughts captive immediately. The thought itself is not a sin. It's what you do with the thought afterwards.

Allow the Holy Spirit to quickly erase that thought so that you can go on with your day in the love, peace, and joy of our Lord!

*For the weapons of our warfare are not carnal, but mighty in*
*God for pulling down strongholds, casting down arguments and every high thing that exalts itself against the knowledge of God, bringing every thought into captivity to the obedience of Christ.* (2 Corinthians 10:4-5)

Jasmine Hartswick

In time, after my own salvation, all my children got saved and water baptized. My son-in-law Armando, my daughter Angela Marie, (they were still newly- weds) and my
little one, Christina Marie, were baptized on the same day at my dad's church. What a triple blessing that was! They were slain in the Holy Spirit. Christina was speaking in tongues at the age of seven. Myself and my son Manuel had been water baptized at a church we had been attending before the others followed. Thank You for saving us Lord!

*And if it seems evil to you to serve the Lord, choose for yourselves this day whom you will serve, whether the gods which your fathers served that were on the other side of the river, or the gods of the Amorites, in whose land you dwell.*
***But as for me and my house, we will serve the Lord.***
(Joshua 24:15)

# Chapter 10

# My Sister Theresa Is Shot And Killed

I honestly don't remember who it was that called me to let me know that my little sister had been shot at her house. I know that Brandon was there, to pick up Christina for his weekend with her. When I dropped the phone after hearing those words, I jumped into my car and raced to her house. She only lived a couple of blocks away from me. I remember slamming my brakes in front of a police car. There was the yellow crime scene tape all around her property so that no one could pass. I tried, but an officer stopped me. I explained that it was my sister in there, but he held me back. Another officer came by my side and offered me a cold soda to help calm me down. I knew him. He was one of the officer's that had responded to my calls when Brandon refused to bring my daughter home, or when he left our four-year old sleeping in the car outside in the cold of winter, so that he could drink with the neighbors, or when he would be driving while intoxicated with her in the back seat.

I stood there right in front of my sister's house, knowing she had been shot, but not knowing if she was still alive. An ambulance was flashing its lights, right at the end of her driveway, but inside the crime scene tape. There must have been a half dozen police vehicles with officers coming in and out of her house. I knew my two nephews and my sister's boyfriend were inside. As I watched the door open, two paramedics rolled out a stretcher with a body wrapped in a black bag. I knew it was Theresa. "NNOOOO!!!" I cried out! As the crushing sight began to overtake me, I felt two arms embrace me. It was my brother Brian. We held on to each other, as we watched my sister be loaded up into the ambulance and drive away to the morgue.

It had been three years since the death of my sister Stella. Now my family has to face more pain and suffering because of another one of my sister's being murdered. My only little sister is gone. She too was beautiful, loving, giving, and an artist. But she too suffered from an abusive boyfriend. She had young two sons. I can't reveal their names.

164

We found out, the reason for the drive-by shooting at my sister's house was because her stepson and my nephew were
in rival gangs. We had absolutely no idea of this. No clue whatsoever.

My sister was going to college to finish her degree. She had an exam that day and was excited that she scored a high grade on it. She came home early to celebrate with a special dinner with her boys. When they were done eating, my sister stepped out to the back porch to give her dog the bones. A barrage of bullets began hitting her house, while her boyfriend and boys were inside ducking on the floor to escape the shooting. She was shot in the head and died instantly.

It was so hard losing another daughter, sister, mother, aunt, and friend. Not just because she died, but because someone murdered her. They cut her life short. All the feelings of my other sister came back. But something was different. It didn't grip me like before. The pain didn't overwhelm me, nor did fear. I knew it was because I had been saved and not the same person, I was the first time. My Savior had me in this. I got my strength and courage from Him. Now I know where my mom had gotten hers from. I could lean on Him and rely on Him to get me through this ordeal. My mother's words came back to me when Stella was murdered. "We need to forgive the person who killed Stella." I needed to forgive the people who were involved with the drive-by that killed Theresa. I asked God to help me do this. So, I prayed like I did before.

"Dear Lord, I choose right now to forgive all the people involved with the death of my sister, Theresa. The driver, the shooters, the company in the car, and the leader. I forgive the gang involved in this murder. I pray for justice for Theresa, in Jesus's name. Amen.

*Repay no one evil for evil. Have regard for good things in the sight of all men. If it is possible, as much as depends on you, live peaceably with all men.   Beloved, do not avenge your-selves, but rather give place to wrath; for it is written,*

*"Vengeance is Mine, I will repay," says the Lord. Therefore; "If your enemy is hungry, feed him; If he is thirsty, give him a drink; For in so doing, you will heap coals of fire on his head." Do not be overcome by evil but overcome evil with good.* (Romans 12:17-21)

We used the same funeral home that we used for my sister Stella. It was as though we were reliving the same memories, emotional trauma, and loss from our other sister being murdered, as well. I couldn't comprehend the level of evil someone could possess inside of them, to be able to take an innocent person's life. This tore my heart. I couldn't even imagine what my mom was going through, losing two daughters to murder, but like my mother, I hung on to the strength that could only come from the Lord. Theresa's funeral was beautiful.

Years later, I would find out by my dad that both my sisters had given their lives to Jesus. Each one just two weeks before their death. Three years apart, they went to visit my dad at his church and surrendered themselves over to their Savior. That gave me such peace, knowing they were both in heaven with our precious Jesus.

## More Shots Fired

About four months after my sister Theresa was shot and killed, I got a phone call from my sister Connie that my mother's house had been targeted with a drive-by shooting. My mother was okay, but I couldn't help thinking, "What if."

I jumped in my car and drove to my mother's house that was about half a mile away. As I pulled up, I saw my mother standing there on the porch with some of her friends from church. I ran to hug her and cried as I held her. She reassured me that she was okay. I said, "I know mom. God was protecting you. My tears are tears of gratitude." Everyone that was gathered there to support my mother, joined hands as we prayed for her protection and her home. Some of my brothers still lived with her.

Apparently, the same gang that shot up my sister's house, found out that my nephew would visit my mom's house. They decided to do another drive-by, to a house they believed my nephew was in. The miraculous thing about this is, my mother's bedroom faced the street, and the police found a bullet in the wall about one foot right above her head. My mother didn't hear any of the shots. She woke up to some wall fragments on her face. The police concluded that they must have gone by around four or five in the morning. They found numerous gunshots in the wall of her bedroom and the living room. None of the bullets got past the front rooms. We praised and thanked God those bullets did not take another life from our family. And again, during our prayers together, we chose to forgive everyone involved in this shooting. There was never another incident of shootings after that.

# Chapter 11

# Being A Christian In An Immoral Relationship

First, let me explain what a relationship is, pertaining to males and females. (According to Collins Dictionary)

**Relationship**: between two people, is the way in which they
feel and behave towards each other. If you feel a particular emotion or physical sensation, you experience it.

**Experience** is used to refer to the past events, knowledge, and feelings that make up someone's life or character.

So, there I was. A brand-new Christian. I was involved in a relationship with a man that led to much sin and on an endless merry-go-round. I'm only even mentioning this because I don't want anyone wasting their time on someone who will never commit to you. I'm not saying that Ryan didn't have genuine feelings for me in the beginning of our relationship. He told me that he loved me many times but loving someone and committing to someone are two totally different things. You see, someone can show you in many ways that they love you, but they won't take that one step that will join you together in marriage. They will be forever happy just being with you and getting all the fringe benefits of that relationship, so long as they don't have that forever bond! And there are many reasons why people have the fear of marriage.

## I can't even begin to cover them all, but here are a few:

**1.** They went through a horrible marriage, to include a devastating divorce.

**2.** They have a trust issue. (Male or female)

**3.** They are afraid it won't work out.

**4.** They see it as an end, instead of a beginning.

**5.** They're parents had a really bad marriage.

**6.** They think the other person will change, once they get married.

**7.** They don't believe they deserve a spouse

**These are all legitimate reasons in people's heart and mind, but God can heal ALL things!**

*In the multitude of my anxieties within me, Your comforts delight my soul.* (Psalm 94:19)

*Trust in the Lord with all your heart and lean not on your own understanding; In all your ways acknowledge Him, And He shall direct your paths.* (Proverbs 3:5-6)

**You need to allow God to direct your paths that lead to your future, in every area of your life. Especially, if you seek to be married. There is hope for everyone who desires a spouse.**

*For whatever things were written before; were written for our learning, that we through the patience and comfort of the Scriptures might have hope.* (Romans 15:4)

*For I know the plans I have for you," declares the Lord, "plans to prosper you and not to harm you, plans to give you hope and a future.'* (Jeremiah 29:11 NIV)

**God has a future for you and your spouse, but you need to be willing to totally surrender your own plans for His.**

In the early stages of this relationship, we had a very good *friendship*. I would encourage him and pray for him during a difficult time in his life. My mistake was being alone with him. We eventually gave into sin and that started the
decline between us, our kids, and of course, our Lord. I already knew that fornication was a sin. I knew it displeased God and I was convicted in my heart every time I failed. I'm going to describe the type of relationship I had with this man.

For the years I spent with him, I could never say no to him. After all, I loved him, and I wanted to please him. The problem was, he didn't care that we were sinning. Since he was a Christian himself, I couldn't understand why it didn't bother him. When we would go out, he would stare at other women and make a grunting noise when they would pass by, or he would see them bend over to pick something up. This really bothered me. I thought it was rude and disrespectful.

One time we met with another friend of mine and her boyfriend for dinner. I noticed he was staring at her and checking her out. He didn't even try to hide it. When we parted ways, he asked, "So, what did your friend think of me?" I told him that she said, "Jasmine, he is not only ugly, but dog ugly!" His response was, "Too bad, because I wanted to bone her." I got angry with him and then he tells me, "Look what you're doing. You're ruining our night out."

Ryan would at times make my children do things I wouldn't have let them do. He would keep my son outside with him till three a.m. on a school night, while he drank. And I was made to stay inside so that he could talk to my son. Lord forbi, what he was discussing with him. I know it wasn't anything good. He would make him come inside to bring him another beer. When I got totally fed up, I made my son come in and go to bed. Why did I put up with that?

I was in the shower one day and without any warning, I

felt a bucket of ice and water being poured over my head and body. I screamed as the freezing cold shocked my body. He told my child to do it. Who does that? He wasn't being funny; he was just being mean.

This man would also have sexual discussions with my children, which he had no business doing. I didn't find out until after the fact. His mouth was full of vulgar cursing. This made me to believe that he had a lot of anger and un-forgivingness in his heart.

At other times, Ryan would tell me to get ready so that we could go out and he would come pick me up. I would be waiting for him all night, with no show from him. He never called me back and I would find out he went out by himself and picked up another woman. I honestly don't know why I stayed with someone who treated me the way he did. These are just a few examples of his character.

Towards the end of our years together, he ended up moving away to a nearby city, making our relationship long distance. I was kind of glad for this because it meant during this time, I could go to church, enrich my prayer time, and ask God to make me strong whenever I was with my boyfriend. We saw each other whenever he could get off work and drive up to see me or I would drive to go see him. Without fail, I would fall into sin and feel so bad after-wards. I also put him first before my children. I dropped everything for this man and left my kids behind, not caring about their feelings or needs. I was very selfish with my time. My children should have been my priority. Not him! I was a very bad example of being a Christian to my children. When you give into sin, you give the enemy a right to come into your life and cause heartache, strife, division, and all other matters of demonic activity.

Eventually, our relationship started to die because we

kept giving into sin.

*For the wages of sin is death. but the free gift of God is eternal life in Christ Jesus our Lord.* (Romans 6:23)

*Then, when desire has conceived, it gives birth to sin; and sin, when it is full-grown, brings forth death.* (James 1:15)

**These verses don't only pertain to physical death, but also to the soul (mind, will, emotions) and spirit (wisdom, communion, consciousness).**

Ryan began to make me feel like I was no longer good enough for him. He began criticizing everything about me; my hair, the way I danced, dressed, and even began to ridicule me. He took me to the doctor one day because I had pain in my ear. The doctor told me it could be jaw related, so I should go see a dentist. Ryan actually laughed at me and made fun of me for it. He made me feel really bad, insinuating I was stupid.

When we first met, he had low self-esteem. I helped him build confidence in himself. I would always compliment him, encouraged him, and make him feel like he was important. There was a time that I went to visit him, and he told me that his neighbor thought I was a hooker. His neighbor told him I was way too pretty for him to get anyone like me. I just encouraged him not to listen to those types of comments because they were said out of jealousy. His friends and co-workers on the other hand, were always telling him to go out with other women and that he had so many to choose from. (Not in such nice words) So, he started to flirt with other

women in front of me and ask me to go away. He did this all the time, now. He also had other women calling him. Is it any surprise that I would develop a suspicious and jealous spirit? Especially when his little one would blurt out, "Oh! Guess
who came over last night?" And he would shush her up and say, "Nobody!"

I remember someone mentioned to me that Ryan had told them, I had hung his pictures on my wall like a *shrine* to him. He made it seem as though I were obsessed with him. Are you kidding me? I had a few photos of us together and one of him standing alone. These were in my hallway, which you couldn't see unless you went to the bathroom. This man sure thought a lot about himself.

*God has given me grace to speak a warning about pride. I would ask each of you to be emptied of self-promotion and not create a false image of your importance. Instead, honestly assess your worth by using your God-given faith as the standard of measurement, and then you will see your true value with an appropriate self-esteem.* (Romans 12:3 TPT)

Since he thought that I was *idolizing* him, which I was not, I decided to take down the photos of us together and the *one* of him. I threw them in my closet. That way, he had nothing to complain about. I was already contemplating the possibility of a breakup.

Ryan called and asked me one day, if I would get with one of his friend's wives so, that he and her husband could watch. (Where did he come up with these disgusting ideas?) Of course, I did not do it! These are the type of things he would ask me to do. I would have never looked at porn, but

181

he introduced me to it and because of my disobedience, my morals and integrity declined the longer I was with this man.

Once, he asked if he could do my sixteen-year-old daughter. My daughter was and still is very beautiful. When I got angry with him, he said he was just kidding. I know in my heart, he was not. Who would joke about something like that? I don't know why I didn't just break up with him right then and there. Maybe the fear of being alone? I don't know. He had a spirit of perversion that I had slowly given in to, but the Holy Spirit's conviction was strong upon my heart. I cried and told God I was sorry, every single time I gave in to him. And this man never felt bad about anything. I hated myself for doing everything I knew God didn't want me to do, and for not doing what my Lord, heart, and conscious wanted me to do.

*For what I am doing, I do not understand. For what I will to do, that I do not practice; but what I hate, that I do.* (Romans 7:15)

*But now, I have written to you not to keep company with anyone named a brother, who is sexually immoral, or covetous, or an idolater, or a reviler, or a drunkard, or an extortioner-not even eat with such a person.* (1Corinthians 5:11)

*Don't be fooled by those who say such things, for bad company corrupts good character.* (1 Corinthians 15:33)

*Do not be wise in your own eyes; Fear the Lord and depart from evil. It will be health to your flesh, And strength to your bones.* (Proverbs 3:7-8)

One day, as I was looking out of my bathroom window, I saw Ryan's car pull up my driveway. I got irritated and literally got a knot in my stomach. I really didn't want him there. I closed the curtain and waited for him to ring the doorbell. When I answered the door and let him in, I asked him, "If I don't have sex with you, would you get it from someone else?" And without hesitation he said, "Yes." I don't know exactly what you would call this, but it certainly wasn't love. When he came in, we were standing in my living room next to the bathroom. He looked at the bare wall that used to display our photos. I will never forget the staggered look on his face! It took everything inside of me not to react. He said, "I have to leave!" I told him, "You just got here." He left in a hurry, leaving a trail of mortification behind, as he was no longer hanging on *HIS* wall of fame. After some hours went by, he came back. I shouldn't have let him back in my house or in my life, but there I was again, entangled in that web of sin.

I had been having nightmares about me dying in these very horrible ways. My dream world for the past year was flushed with God, showing me prophetic warning dreams of what was going to happen to me if I continued to disobey Him. The death of this relationship happened because I feared and loved God more than I loved this man. And since he did not want to marry me, God told me the man who does will get all the blessings he said no to. You see, early on, when we were at church one day, God told this man, "Marry her and I will bless you." He flat said, "No" to God. Remember that God is a gentleman. He will not force anything on us. He gave this man the choice to say yes and be blessed. Instead, he passed up the blessings God would have given him. Why did I stay with him? I would have saved myself and my kids a lot of strife and heartache. This is what happens when you have false hope. (Confident feelings about something that may not be true.

The very last night spent with this man, I had another nightmare. He had to wake me up because he could tell I was having a bad dream. I woke up and my heart was pounding
so hard, it felt like someone was using drumsticks on my chest. Tears were running down my face in the dark. He turned over and just fell back asleep. The dream was fierce and more real than any other time. With this particular dream, I believe this one was a night vision. I was on top of a pile of people. We were all stacked up on what looked to be an army tank without the tank canon. I was on the top center. As this tank moved forward, the other people were being rolled under and crushed by the tank treads. They were all screaming in torturous pain. I could hear the crushing sounds of their heads and bones as they were being pulled to their death. Blood was gushing out from all around them. The movement of the tank seemed to come to a slow motion, as I too moved slowly backward to avoid being pulled down and brought under the tank treads, to my own crushing death. As I was yelling out in fear and trembling at the terror that I was in, I felt something pulling on me. That's when I woke up to the hands of my boyfriend, waking me up. I knew without a shadow of a doubt, I had to end this relationship before he walked out the door the next morning. We had a cup of coffee and really didn't say much. I was praying really hard and asked God to intervene for me. My boyfriend turned to me and asked, "What were you dreaming about?" I didn't tell him the details of my dream, just that I had been having nightmares and that I knew it was God warning me what would happen if I kept disobeying and remaining in sin. God answered my prayer and gave me the boldness to break up with him and I said to him, "We need to get right with

185

God and our kids. If God wants us back together, He will make it happen." Ryan gathered his belongings and walked out the door. I took a very deep breath of *relief* as he drove away. We never got back together, and I am so happy that I did not

pursue him. He was with someone else that very weekend. He used her for a while, like he did me.

Within the next few days, I began to have pain in my lower abdomen. I went to the doctor, and he confirmed I had a STI (sexually transmitted infection). I called Ryan and told him wat the doctor said. I also told him as God as my witness, he was the only one I had slept with. Sin was certainly manifesting in me physically. He said he was going to call a woman he picked up at the airport a few days before, whom he slept with. After he slept with her, he slept with two other women that same day, before he came to stay with me. I was so hurt and angry that he would take a risk in exposing me to his deceitful and cheating exploits. I was treated, but I don't know if he was.

I also found out through my friend that he was telling everyone it was I who gave him the STI. God knows that was not true. The enemy will use the very people you trusted to falsely accuse you. I know I disobeyed God. And the consequence of my sin manifested in my body. Repentance of sin means you turn away from your sins. That is why I broke up with this man who was full of it. I know the blood of Jesus made me clean again. I knew that I was still His daughter.

*You shall not bear false witness against your neighbor.* (Deuteronomy 5:20)

*"Do not fear, for you will not be ashamed; Neither be disgraced, for you will not be put to shame;* (Isaiah 54:4)

This man used to always tell me, "You deserve better." He was perfectly correct in saying this. God knew that he would say no about marrying me. I believe in His grace and mercy, He was trying to save me from the sin of death, had I chosen to stay in this relationship. I just wish, I hadn't figured it out years later. I was what you call a *baby Christian* when I first got together with him. I had so much I needed to learn in my walk with God! And during those years, I did learn very important life lessons. Lessons that would change my life according to God's will for me. I learned how I was supposed to be treated and what kind of Godly relationship I should have. I learned how sin can cause death in every area of your life. God never gives up on us, but loves us so much, as to convict us and warn us of the dangers we invite into our lives. First and foremost, I learned that my children are more important and should always come first before anything or anyone else, besides God. I also learned that my life is not my own. Jesus paid the ultimate price for me. I knew through this ungodly relationship, that I needed to start living my life according to the will and purpose God called me to. I had a long journey ahead of me. It would not be easy. But I knew every step I took towards my calling was worth it. My priority was God first, then I needed to make amends to my children and with the help of my Savior, I would become the mother they deserved.

Sin causes death in relationships. Not just with each other, but with our Savior. It also causes death in our emotions, in our standard of morality, and even in our bodies. It causes damage with family members who are being affected by it. Sin is an immoral act and is a transgression against our loving God.    Sex outside of marriage defiles the temple of the Lord, which is us, and the sacred union that God created to make a husband and wife *one flesh*. As we are *One* with the Holy Spirit.

*Flee sexual immorality. Every sin that a man does is outside the body, but he who commits sexual immorality sins against his own body. Or do you not know that your body is the temple of the Holy Spirit who is in you, whom you have from God, and you are not your own? For you were bought at a price; therefore, glorify God in your body and in your spirit, which are God's.* (1 Corinthians 6:18-20)

Thank You Jesus for dying on the cross and taking away all our iniquities, transgressions, and *all* sin, if we truly repent. I forgave this man for the way he treated me, and I asked my children to forgive me as well. God transformed me into the loving mother He created me to be. My children came first, God restored the time I lost with them, and I made sure I was there for them throughout the years, no matter what they needed. We have such a loving Father who has such a compassionate heart!

If you are in a relationship that is similar to the one, I just described, this is not what God wants for you. Do not settle for someone who just uses you for their own benefits or whatever they can get off of you. Do not settle for someone who is never going to commit themselves to you in marriage. Do not allow someone to put you down, make you feel worthless, is abusive to you in any way, shape, or form, (physically, emotionally, sexually, financially, verbally, or spiritually) and do not believe the lie that you don't deserve better.

After looking back and learning what a true Christian is, I can say that this man was not a Christian. Just because
you are standing inside a bank, that doesn't make you rich. Just because you live in Hollywood, doesn't make you a movie star. Just because you call yourself a Christian, doesn't mean you are one.

*Beloved, do not believe every spirit, but test the spirits, whether they are from God, because many false (Christians) prophets have gone out into the world.* (1 John 4:1) (Emphasis mine)

This scripture is telling us to put the person to the test. Is he or she living according to what the Word *of God says how we are to live? Is he or she living a* lifestyle that would be pleasing to the Lord? In other words, are they a living example of Christ? What does the fruit of their life look like?

*But the fruit of the spirit is love, joy, peace, long suffering, kindness, goodness, faithfulness, gentleness, and self-control. Against such, there is no law.* (Galatians 5:22-23)

The Bible, which is our *Life Manual*, speaks about the manifested fruits of the Holy Spirit in a Christians life. These should be the characteristics, behavior, beliefs, and qualities in a person who believes in Jesus Christ. Yes, we are human, we make mistakes, and bad choices. **"We will never be sinless, but we can sin less."** (My own quote) The good thing is, that we can take it to the cross and repent, get up where we fell, and continue our walk with the Lord. We learn and grow from our mistakes. God enjoys His children who have a teachable heart. We continue to pursue a life that is pleasing to the One who gave His life for ours. This is the life of a true Christian.

God only wants the very best for us. He doesn't want us to settle for second best. This is so true when it comes to choosing our spouse. He is going to give us someone who is perfect for us. He knows us through and through. He knows every detail about us. If we lack something about ourselves, He will match us with someone who will balance us. We will be a perfect match for each other. We won't be perfect in ourselves, but perfect for each other. Don't try to make it happen on your own. Wait on God!

*Now the Lord had said unto Abram: "Get out of your country, from your family and from your father's house to a land that I will show you. I will make you a great nation; I will bless you and make your name great; And you shall be a blessing. I will bless those who bless you, And I will curse him who curses you; And in you all families of the earth shall be blessed." (Genesis 12:1-3)*

Let us look at what happened to Sarai. She tried to help God keep His promise to her husband Abram. As if, He needed her help. It had been many years since the Lord had promised Abram that he would be a great nation. His descendants were supposed to make his name great, but he and Sarai had not even born one child yet!

## Hagar and Ishmael

*Now Sarai, Abram's wife, had borne him no children. And she had an Egyptian maidservant whose name was*

194

*Hagar. So Sarai said to Abram, "See now, the Lord has restrained me from bearing children. Please, go in to my maid; perhaps I shall obtain children by her." And Abram heeded the voice of Sarai. Then Sarai, Abram's wife, took Hagar her maid, the Egyptian, and gave her to her husband Abram to be his wife, after Abram had dwelt ten years in the land of Canaan. So, he went in to Hagar, and she conceived. And when she saw that she had conceived, her mistress became despised in her eyes. Then Sarai said to Abram, "My wrong be upon you! I gave my maid into your embrace; and when she saw that she had conceived, I became despised in her eyes. The Lord judge between you and me." So Abram said to Sarai, "Indeed your maid is in your hand; do to her as you please." And when Sarai dealt harshly with her, she fled from her presence. Now the Angel of the Lord found her by a spring of water in the wilderness, by the spring on the way to Shur. And He said, "Hagar, Sarai's maid, where have you come from, and where are you going?" She said, "I am fleeing from the presence of my mistress Sarai." The Angel of the Lord said to her, "Return to your mistress, and submit yourself under her hand." Then the Angel of the Lord said to her, "I will multiply your descendants exceedingly, so that they shall not be counted for multitude." And the Angel of the Lord said to her: "Behold, you are with child, and you shall bear a son. You shall call his name Ishmael, Because the Lord has heard your affliction. He shall be a wild man; His hand shall be against every man, And every man's hand against him. And he shall dwell in the presence of all his brethren." Then she called the name of the Lord who spoke to her, You-Are-the-God-Who-Sees; for she said, "Have I also here seen Him who sees me?" Therefore, the well was called Beer Lahai Roi observe, it is between Kadesh and Bered. So, Hagar bore Abram a son; and Abram named his son, whom*

*Hagar bore, Ishmael. Abram was eighty-six years old when Hagar bore Ishmael to Abram.* (Genesis 16:16)

It has now been 14 years since Hagar gave birth to Ishmael. All those years, Sarah was tormented because she could not bear any children. Now, let us look at what the Lord does for her, twenty-five years after God promises Abraham, he would become a father of many nations through his own son.

*Then God said to Abraham, "As for Sarai your wife, you shall not call her name Sarai, but Sarah shall be her name. And I will bless her and also give you a son by her; then I will bless her, and she shall be a mother of nations; kings of peoples shall be from her." Then Abraham fell on his face and laughed, and said in his heart, "Shall a child be born to a man who is one hundred years old? And shall Sarah, who is ninety years old, bear a child?" And Abraham said to God, "Oh, that Ishmael might live before You!" Then God said: "No, Sarah your wife shall bear you a son, and you shall call his name Isaac; I will establish My covenant with him for an everlasting covenant, and with his descendants after him. And as for Ishmael, I have heard you. Behold, I have blessed him, and will make him fruitful, and will multiply him exceedingly. He shall beget twelve princes, and I will make him a great nation. But My covenant I will establish with Isaac, whom Sarah shall bear to you at this set time next year." Then He finished talking with him, and God went up from Abraham.* (Genesis 17:15-22)

God had already established His covenant with Isaac, before he was even born. God had a plan all along for Sarah to give birth to him, but because she was impatient, she made her maidservant a wife to her husband, trying to make God's promise come to pass. God does not need our help! Even though Ishmael was still blessed, he was not the chosen one to fulfill God's covenant with Abraham. It was Isaac!

Let me encourage you. If you are desiring to get married and you have been waiting for a while, wait upon the Lord during the process of *ushering in* your spouse. This is a multi-part collaboration.

(According to Wikipedia)

**Collaboration:** the process of two or more people or organizations working together to complete a task or achieve a goal. Collaboration is similar to cooperation.

**Cooperation:** the process of working together to the same end.

Most collaboration requires leadership. Teams that work collaboratively often access greater resources, recognition and rewards when facing competition for finite resources. The great thing about *our* collaboration and cooperation is that it is between us and the Holy Spirit. God's resources, recognition, and rewards far surpass anything this world can bring us. Only God can provide infinite (limitless or endless in space, extent, or size; impossible to measure or calculate) resources that are perfect for what He wants for us.

**Do not settle for Ishmael! Wait for the promised covenant. The spouse that God has chosen for you!**

# Chapter 12

# My Precious Mother Is Called Home

I'm going to estimate the time to be towards the end of February to the beginning of March, when I got a phone call from my nephew Sonny (my sister Theresa's youngest son) that my mother was taken to the hospital. I asked, "What happened?" He said, "I don't know, but we were watching TV and I turned and saw grandma with her head lying back and

she was lifeless. I called 911 and Uncle Brian."

My mother was taken to Southwest General, which was very close to where we both lived. When I arrived at the emergency room, I found a couple of my sisters there and some of my brothers. They told me, mom had congestive heart failure, which caused a stroke. I couldn't believe it.

I'm going to share with you the type of woman my mother, Stella Oravecz Cortez was. She was a loving and devoted wife, mother, grandmother, great-grandmother, sister, aunt, and loyal friend. She was smart, funny, giving, creative, an artist, and seamstress. She used to make her own maternity clothes. She was a very diligent and hard worker, dedicated in all things, and anyone could depend on her. She was a faithful intercessor and prayer warrior. The strength and endurance she carried within herself was supernatural. She had a heart of gold that radiated the love of God. My mother was beautiful inside and out.

She was left to live as a single mom and raise, care for, and support thirteen children on her own, after my dad left her. She never complained about anything. She had the sweetest spirit and even in her correction over us, there was still a gentleness. If we had any activities at school, she would walk as far as it took for her to be there for us; most of the time, a little over one and a half miles. She loved us all and did the best she could possibly do for each of us, under her circumstances. She truly was a saint!

My mother was quick to forgive anyone who hurt her or our family. She forgave my dad for everything he had done to her. I asked her once, "Mom, would you ever take dad back?" She said, "No. I don't have any animosity or grudges against him, I just don't love him anymore. Not in that way." "I don't blame you, mom." Was my response with a huge hug.

When the 911 call was dispatched for my mother, it was the paramedics who worked with my brother at Fire-Station #16, who responded. They tried to get there as fast as they could because they knew it was my brother's address. My brother Brian (firefighter) was off that day, so when he got the call from my nephew, he rushed over from his fiancé's house. He got there before the paramedics. I could not even imagine what was going on in his head, seeing our mother like that. She was sitting on the couch with her head back. She had no pulse. My brother must have been flooded with a hundred thoughts and emotions. Just the night before, my mom asked Brian, "Can I have a hug?" He told her, "Mom, you don't need to ask, I'll always hug you." She said, "Well, it might be my last hug. You never know when it will be my last night." So, of course he hugged my mom.

Two months prior to this, Brian had a conversation with my mom about dying. Since he was a firefighter, he asked her what she wanted him to do in case something happened to her. What if she had a heart attack? Did she want him to resuscitate or do CPR? She told him to do what his heart tells him.

My brother did CPR on her, until the paramedics came. They took over and transferred her to Southwest General. After what seemed an eternity, the results on my mother were devastating. She was brain dead. There was no brain activity. Her brain stem was undamaged, so she could still hear us and breath on her own.

I remember feeling this rush of loss flood my insides. I loved my mother so much! We were very close. I would never hear her lovely voice again, feel her hugs, hear her laugh, have lunch together, or bring her grandchildren to see her. I would never be able to look into her beautiful eyes and tell her I loved her, again. My heart was missing her already.

Tears ran down my face, as I held on to a friend, who had showed up at the hospital to give moral support.

Mother was in the hospital for about a week, then transferred into hospice where all the family would be able to go see her and make their last visits. It was hard enough seeing my mom in such a state, but the enemy used my brother who dis-owned me to make me feel worse. He would take his forefingers to make a cross and aim it at me, as if I were the devil. He would tell me how evil I was and tell others I was going to hell. He would hug everyone else good-bye but would barely shake my hand. After he did, he would look at me with disgust and then rub his hands off on his clothes, as If I had leprosy. I decided to keep my distance away from him. I still loved my brother very much, but I didn't have to subject myself to his words and behavior. One day, if he doesn't repent, he is going to have to give an account to the One and only true judge!

I went to visit my mom every day. There were days when all three of my sisters and I were there at the same time. Those were special days for me because we didn't always get to see each other. One lived in Illinois, one was married and always worked, and the other was constantly busy helping others. The nurses reminded us that my mom could still hear us. We would talk to her and tell her what was going on around us. I used to sit by her bedside, hold her hand, and sing to her all the time. We always made sure she was never left alone. One day her pediatrician came to visit. He actually delivered all of us. His name was Doctor Guajardo. He was married to a famous singer. I just don't remember who it was. When he saw my mom, he just shook his head and said, "Darn, Stella! You have the strongest heart!" And that she did. The miracle is that she

205

was not hooked up to any machines to keep her alive. (That was her wish) She breathed on her own and her heart just kept beating on its own. She only had an IV in her arm.

Almost a month has gone by. All my aunts, uncles, and cousins has had the chance to visit. Including my dad. And just to let everyone know, when my dad got saved in prison and got out, he made a visit to my mom's house many years ago and asked us all to forgive him. Including my mother, which she had already done. I know there is still some animosity towards my dad, between a couple of my brothers. I do not judge them for that. What is in their heart is between them and God. I love all my brothers and sisters. I am praying for full forgiveness towards my dad for any one of my family members who still hold un-forgiveness in their hearts, because God's word says:

*"For if you forgive men their trespasses, your heavenly Father will also forgive you. But if you do not forgive men their trespasses, neither will your Father forgive your trespasses."* (Matthew 6:14-15)

This verse is for anyone reading this book, as well.

After a day of spending time with my sisters and mom at the hospice care center, I needed to go back home and attend to my daughter. I thought about how I would drive by my mom's house at night in our car and we all yelled out to her, "Hi Grandma! We love you!" We could see her through the screen door, sitting on the couch watching tv. We usually went to visit her on Sundays. During one of our visits, she told me, "Your children have a very special place in my heart." That made me feel so loved and accepted, as the one brother was always using the fact that my children had different biological dads, against me. But that wasn't true. They have our one true Father in heaven who created them and loves them unconditionally. They also have one earthly father. Brandon accepted, loved, and raised Angela and Manuel as his own, despite his issues. I will always be grateful to him for that.

My mother was there for everyone. She didn't miss any birthday parties, baptism's, weddings, graduations, or births. Only my son's birth because he was born in Houston. She was there for any hospitalizations. When my son was in the hospital after he got burned, she was there for me. He was only a year old when it happened. That is another miracle testimony on how God helped me out as a single mom with no insurance and how God did not allow my son to scar on his face, just a little scar on his arm. My mom was there for me in the worst times of my life. She always gave advice about forgiving and showing God's love and mercy. My mom was there for all of us. No matter what.

It was a long day. Christina was in bed now and asleep. It took me a long time, but I finally dozed off.

It was four a.m. when I awoke to the sounds of my phone ringing. It was my sister Lilly to inform me that mom passed away. She told me that her and Connie were with her, and they were holding my mom's hands. I remember telling Lilly, "OK. Thank you for calling and letting me know. Goodnight." I didn't cry. I just thought, "Now she's with Jesus in heaven. I know Abba Father welcomed her into His arms and told her, "Well done, good and faithful servant!" I fell back asleep.

The next morning, I had to tell my kids that their *Grandma Stella* went to heaven. That is when I broke down in tears. It was a very sad day. I cried with my children and the reality kicked in that my mom was gone forever, hear on

earth.

Right before my mother had a heart attack, my nephew Sonny was asking her questions about what it is like in heaven. He said my mother had a big smile on her face, and said, "There's no pain or suffering, just pure joy and happiness." He turned to look at the TV for a moment and when he turned back around, that's when he saw my mother with her head back on the couch. I honestly believe my precious mother was already experiencing heaven during her very last spoken words.

Stella Oravecz Cortez
Born: June 21, 1931
Passed away: April 4, 1998

***Eternally lives on in our hearts and in heaven!***

It was probably about four months after my mother went to heaven, when I was missing her so much that particular day. When the evening came and I fell asleep, I had such a vivid dream about her. I saw a whole lot of magnificent white clouds that seemed to be dancing around. They had a beautiful shimmer of light that outlined them. I knew I was in heaven. Out of these beautiful clouds, a door opened up and the most radiant and bright light came shining through. It was so pure and piercing, but it didn't hurt my eyes. I saw my mother appear at the entrance of the door. She looked so young and beautiful. Her hair was full of curls with red highlights. She looked to be in her thirties. The smile and look on her face, was something I will never forget. She was wearing a long, beautiful gown made of silk and layered with a sheer material, which was something like a fuchsia color.

She loved deep shades of pink. As she stood there looking and smiling at me, she didn't have to say a word. I knew that she was emersed in happiness and that nothing in this earth could take its place. She was letting me know, she was in heaven and that is where she belonged. I hold on to that dream dear in my heart, knowing I will see and be with my mamma again, one day.

# Chapter 13

# Moving Out Of The Southside

After the death of my mother, I really started to contemplate moving away. I hesitated because my son was still in high school. Angela had moved out already. She was married and had her own baby boy. I remember the day she moved out. I couldn't believe my baby girl was going to start her own life.

She is such a diligent worker and would even help me out when I was in a financial bind. She is very smart and outgoing. She is beautiful and has a heart to match. She is a great wife and mother. She was excited to move out on her own, but when she left the house, I cried for her. But I knew God would take care of her.

When my mother died, it felt like all my family got scattered. We had always gotten together as a family for Thanksgiving and Christmas. This was no more.

Over the past five years of living in our house on Formosa, I really needed to get out of that house. There were so many horrible memories that still haunted me. There were a lot of demonic spirits in that house that I had to fight over the years. The enemy was on a mission to tear us apart as a family. Too many doors had been opened up to allow satan and his demons to have access. I had learned a lot about them and how to command them to leave, using my authority as a born-again believer. I can tell you many testimonies that happened in that house, while spiritually cleaning it out. All this will be written in another book that is part of this series.

When I found out through a police officer friend of mine, that there were gangs coming into the Southside to try to take over, that is when I decided it was time to leave.

I put the house up for sale. The agent I worked with had something to do with the government and low- income families, but I didn't know this. I was forced to add brand new carpet with money I did not have. I had to borrow it. I added brand new wallpaper in the kitchen to make it look nicer. I also had to paint the entire inside of the house, which I was able to pay in installments.

I remember my ex-husband asked if he could take over the payments, but I just couldn't see that happening. He would just move right in with his girlfriend, and I would lose any financial gain, since I had paid into the mortgage payments for the past five years out of my own hard-earned money. So, I told him no.

There were several clients that wanted to buy my house. Since I was a single mom, there was one lady who begged me to let her buy the house for her and her son. Since she was a single mom too, my heart went out to her, and I told my agent that I wanted her to get it. She went to look inside the house and ended up tearing all the brand new wallpaper out of the kitchen. When I saw it, I got mad because no papers were signed yet. She said the agent told her it was ok, as if it were her house already.

I hadn't paid the mortgage for a few months. I figured they could take it out of the sale of the house. Somehow, the agent claimed we needed to hurry up and finalize the paperwork or it would go into foreclosure. This seemed strange, as it was only two months behind. I didn't want that to happen, so I talked with the agent and said I would sign. They were going to take the closing costs and the few months that I did not pay, out of my equity, "supposedly" according to the government rule. I spoke to the lady who was going to buy the house on the phone and said that I would sign, under the condition that she would pay me $2500, since I was paying her closing costs and all the other fees that she was supposed to. I told her I needed it, so that I could buy my son the car I promised him. She agreed.

When we were in the title company's office, she walked in, and I reminded her of her promise. She was very rude to me and said with a mean voice, "I can't promise you anything!" I regretted trying to help her out. I just wanted to get this over with. There was still some equity left that should have gone to me. Instead of me receiving it, because this was some sort of government transaction; the lady would be making payments to me until my equity was paid in full.

Totally, not what I expected. I was so disappointed because I didn't get to buy my son his car. She made a few payments to me later, but then they completely stopped. I got a lawyer who found out she filed for bankruptcy. I lost all the money I was supposed to get.

They foreclosed on her. She lost the house. At least I didn't have that hanging over my head. I found out she was a police officer. I just thought to myself, "What kind of integrity did this officer have, using the fact that she was a single mom and having a tough time with her son who was in college, just so I could feel sorry for her?" It was like she fed off my kindness towards her, then turned against me when she got her way. I forgave her and knew God saw what she did.

I found an apartment complex that was on the Northeast side of town. My daughter would be going to the best school in that area. It was very convenient because the bus came right in front of our apartment. My son wanted to finish school at McCollum. His high-school sweetheart, Sheila, attended there as well. I would have to drop him off every morning, but I didn't mind.

I loved where we were. I was so much closer to my church. Some very close friends of mine, Jesse and Esther from church lived there too. They were so nice and helped out any way they could. I had introduced Jesse to my girlfriend, and they ended up getting married. I stood in their wedding and had helped with all the decorating. He was like the *Big Brother* I never had. He was active duty and stationed at

Lackland. I didn't have a washing machine or dryer. I would

have to go to the other side of the complex, but they let me wash my clothes in their apartment, which was just across mine. They had helped with our move there. If I couldn't be at home because of a doctor appointment, Esther let Christina wait there with her and made sure she was home safe from school. I don't know what I would have done without their friendship. I loved them like family. And they really loved Christina.

I was so happy to get a fresh start for me and my kids. We didn't have to live in a house anymore, that felt so oppressed and held way too many bad memories.

Jasmine Hartswick

# Chapter 14

# My Miraculous Healing

## A Devastating Fall

It all began, on a day at work. I was a cashier supervisor, still working at Sam's Club. One of the cashiers turned on her light to let me know she needed help. As I walked briskly towards her, I stepped on a piece of fruit peel that a customer dropped on the floor. My foot slipped and I took a devasting
fall. I flew into the air landing on the concrete floor on my

back. I laid there for a few minutes when someone came to help me up. I was so embarrassed; I told my supervisor that

I was okay. She told me to go sit down in the break room and take a few minutes to regroup. A co-worker walked with me and tried to help me sit down but, I couldn't. Pain began to radiate in my lower back and legs. My supervisor came to check on me and said, "Jasmine you look like you're in a lot of pain, do you want to lie down?" I shook my head yes, as I couldn't even talk through the excruciating pain. She helped me lie down on the floor and told me she was going to call 911. Some other coworkers tried to help me get comfortable by placing towels under my head and back. They said when they saw me fall that I bounced, and they heard a crack. The ambulance came and the paramedics went into the break room to place me on the stretcher. I was taken to the hospital where they gave me some strong pain medicine and took me in for x-rays. The X-ray showed I had broken my tailbone, which sits right on the end of the spine.

They said I would need an MRI later on when some of the swelling went down, so they could see what else was going on that the x-ray couldn't pick up. There was nothing they could do for my tailbone, except monitor with pain medication and lots of rest so that it could heal on its own.

From the moment I fell, I claimed the word of God over my life. While I was in the ambulance, I said, "Lord, by Your Stripes, I am healed!"

*But He was wounded for our transgressions, He was bruised for our iniquities; the chastisement for our peace was upon Him, and by His stipes we are healed.* (Isaiah 53:5)

To get through this two-year tribulation, I had to hang on to every word that I read from the bible, pertaining to healing. I called upon the name of Jehovah Rapha. (The God who heals)

*My son, give attention to my words; Incline your ear to my sayings. Do not let them depart from your eyes; Keep them in the midst of your heart; For they are life to those who find them, and health to all their flesh.* (Proverbs 4:20-22)

*Then the Pharisees went out and plotted against Him, how they might destroy Him. But when Jesus knew it, He withdrew from there. And great multitudes followed Him, and* **He healed them all.** (Matthew 12:14-15)

**ALL:** used to refer to the whole quantity or extent of a particular group or thing.

This scripture tells us that no matter what ailments, sickness, disease, broken bones, mental illness, heart conditions, blood issues, leprosy, deformities, allergies, infections, arthritis, tumors, or missing body parts, Jesus healed every single one of them. Miracle after miracle, from hundreds to thousands of people receiving a miraculous healing in their bodies. If Jesus our Healer can do it for them, He can do it for me. I knew in my heart this was the absolute truth.

Jesus Christ is the same yesterday, today, and forever. (Hebrews 13:8)

*So, then faith comes by hearing, and hearing by the word of God.* (Romans 10:17)

I began receiving phone calls from different lawyers. They wanted me to sue Sam's, but I told them I was a Christian and wasn't out to sue anyone. I told them God would take care of me.

I was bedridden for about a month. I was to stay in bed and just let my body rest to begin the healing process. If I had to get up to go to the bathroom, I had to balance myself on the wall, so I wouldn't fall. My sister and mother would come to help me. An insurance agent would frequent my home, to evaluate my condition and record her findings. I guess they had to make sure I wasn't faking it.

When I was finally able to get out of bed, I graduated to a wheelchair, provided by Sam's. I really couldn't sit comfortably, so I had to sit at an angle to keep pressure off my tailbone. I was also provided with a cushion especially made for relief of these types of injuries. A friend of mine would pick me up and take me to my doctor visits or just to get out and get some fresh air. I remember a trip to the hospital for an MRI on my back. I had to lay still, flat on my back because if I moved, I would have to keep doing it until they got a clear picture. I laid there as wave after wave of pain flooded my whole back, down to my legs. Tears ran down the sides of my face as I prayed to God for strength not to move. The MRI showed damage to my L4 and L5 vertebrae, which are the lowest in the lumbar spine. The disks between these vertebrae are made of a gel-like material surrounded by a thick fibrous ring. This disk provides cushioning and shock-absorbing functions to protect the bones from grinding against each other during spinal movement. Both were
ruptured during the great fall. This explained the chronic pain on top of my fractured tailbone. All on the bottom of my spine.

I can't tell you how many doctor visits I had to go to and how many times my pain medicine was changed due to

*Jasmine Hartswick*

inadequate relief. They finally gave me something that helped a little. It was called Lortab. This medication was a combination pain reliever (acetaminophen) that contained a narcotic (Hydrocodone bitartrate). I remember feeling so relaxed, I forgot about the pain. It helped me fall asleep, as well. Praise God, I didn't get addicted to it. I was able to leave the wheelchair and use a walker.

I went to church when possible. Many people prayed over me for healing, but nothing manifested. I never gave up, knowing that I would be healed.

I began a journey of learning about the gift of healing. I watched countless videos, read a huge number of books on the subject, dug deep into the lives of men and women who had been used in this gift over the years, (Kathryn Kuhlman, Smith Wigglesworth, John G. Lake, Maria Woodworth-Etter, William Branham, Charles and Frances Hunter and others) and became quite fascinated with this gift. I wrote down every scripture in the bible that had to do with healing. I kept myself surrounded with them. And then one day, my heart was filled with the desire to pray for the sick.

I underwent many different types of therapy, from injections, electrical nerve stimulation, heating pads, physical to pool therapies, and pain management. All of this and nothing helped. I now suffered immense sciatic nerve pain all the time. Starting from my lower back, into my hips and shooting down both my legs. It was horrible!

I was coming to the end of a two-year mark. When I would walk, my left leg would just give out, causing me to fall if I didn't have my walker. This went on for a couple of weeks. I went to see my doctor and he said we ran out of options. A test showed that my sciatic nerve was so damaged, if I didn't have surgery, I would lose the use of my left leg. I knew I did all that I could to avoid surgery, but I also trusted

God that He would be with me when I did. Some people I told, about having surgery, tried to convince me not to have it. They told me I would come out worse, or even paralyzed. They told me horror stories of surgeries gone wrong. They begged me not to have it. The enemy tried to instill fear in me. I rejected it and stood firm in my trust and faith in the Lord. I was going to do what needed to be done to get better.

Dr. Lenderman, who would perform the surgery, scheduled me in the month of October. I had family and friends praying for me.

While waiting in my hospital room to get wheeled into the OR, I kept my focus on God and His promises. My doctor came in and asked, "Are you ready? I replied with, "As ready as I'll ever be." "Let's do this!" He replied. I'm lying under the lights and being introduced to the different nurses and anesthesiologist. They hooked me up to a blood pressure cuff, a pulse oximeter to measure the oxygen in my blood, an EKG to monitor my heart, a temperature probe, and an IV. I joked and said, "Wow, all this just for me?" Dr. said, count backwards starting with 20. I didn't, I repeated the name of Jesus, until I was out.

I woke up in the recovery room. A friend from church was sitting by my side. Nurses were working on me, asking me questions, but I was too sedated to answer. I fell back asleep.

I heard my name being called while gently being shaken. Dr. L asked how I was feeling. "OK, I think I need to pee. Can I?" I asked. "Of course, you can! Let me have the nurses help you." He said, motioning the nurses to guide me to the bathroom. They had a booster seat with handles already in place for me. The doc had them walk me around the hall, as he said this was the best thing to do immediately after surgery. Afterwards, was a whole different story.

Friends and family came to visit and offer up prayers on my behalf. On about the sixth day, Dr. L came in to give me instructions and advice on what to expect during recovery. He explained to me that my two lower vertebrae were fused together after the removal of the disk in between them. He did mention that my surgery was the most beautiful back surgery he had ever performed because I was so small and didn't have any layers of fat to cut through. However, severe damage to my sciatic nerve was going to make recovery longer and more at risk. I was to be bedridden again for at least a month. He said he had a hospital bed ordered for me along with other medical supplies I would need. I would have a nurse to check on me every day and to make sure my daughter and I had meals to eat. The nurse would follow the ambulance that would transport me back to my apartment and make sure everything was set up correctly. Removable bars were placed in my shower, along with a shower bench. A high toilet booster seat with handles was attached on top of the toilet. They gave me a long cane with fingers, (Reacher/grabber) so I would be able to pick things up without bending down or reaching for it. I was also advised to keep the wheelchair for emergency.

My friends Jesse and Esther would let the people into my apartment before I got released. Sam's paid for
everything I needed. They even paid for the nurses assigned to do my home health care. They would pick up my medications, prepare meals when needed, change my bandages, help me go to the bathroom, and bathe.

After all was explained to me in detail, my doctor then said to me with a serious look, "You will be in pain and on medication for the rest of your life, and you will walk with a limp." Before he could speak another word, I declared, "No! I don't receive that report. That isn't what my bible says.

God's word says, by His stripes I am healed!" I kind of stunned my doctor, so he replied with, "Well, if that's what you believe, who can argue with that? But you need to wear this back-brace for the next six months. Any wrong move could cause more damage to your spine."

I was released from the hospital the next day. I arrived at my apartment via ambulance, where I was helped into my hospital bed that was placed behind my couch in the living room. It was close to the kitchen and bathroom. My daughter, Christina, was dropped off later. She was about nine years old. She became my little nurse when she wasn't with her dad during her joint custody visits. She kept me company and was also my entertainment. There was a pole attached to my bed that had a cable and triangular bar to help me lift myself, although I couldn't use it yet. Christina was small enough to grab the bar and do flips like a gymnast off the bed.

Someone from my worship team organized a meal train for us. The meals began to get dropped off. When the nurse came for my checkups, she would heat up the food and serve us. One week, we got spaghetti for five days in a row. We thought it was funny, but we still appreciated the time and effort people took out of their lives to help us out.

I didn't lack anything during this healing process. I was receiving a disability check from work, child support, and I would get anonymous checks from people at my church. Esther made sure all my bills got paid. I had all the help I needed while I was bedridden. I had visits from my worship team. Other friends, outside of my church and those who lived in my apartment complex, brought food and anything else I or my kids might have needed.

God is so amazing! He knew what was going to happen. I had just bought a brand-new car, right before my fall.

Getting that car was a miracle in itself. While I was in the office, the gentleman asked if I wanted the insurance that would cover my payments in case something happened, and I couldn't make them. I clearly heard a voice say, "Take the insurance." I hesitated with my answer, but then I heard again, "Yes. Get the insurance." So, I said," Okay sure I'll get it." He finished up with my paperwork, to include the insurance. Before I got into the driver's seat, something caught my attention on the window. On the very bottom right of the window where my hand reached for the handle, I saw an etched-out emblem that said MIRACLE. I drove away that day with my miracle car. My brand new, beautiful, blue-green Cavalier. Two weeks later, I had the accident. Now my car was being paid by the insurance company. How great is our God!

The days ahead would prove to be brutal. I was in constant pain. I got very little sleep because I was so uncomfortable. I had to be careful how I tossed and turned in bed. I was always praying, keeping my eyes focused on God. It was an ordeal just to get out of bed to go to the bathroom or to have a bath.

The good thing about this, was that I was able to minister to everyone who came to visit me. Both saved and unsaved. I was praying and ministering to more people in my apartment on my back, than I was at work. I guess satan thought he could stop me from doing God's work. What a loser!

The attack on my body intensified. I knew the enemy was at work making my recovery a living hell. The more I ministered to people, the madder he got. I was given stronger medication to help me sleep. The doctor gave me a pill that was supposed to knock me out for the entire night, just so that my body can rest and heal. Sometimes in the night, I would wake up out of a dead sleep. I could feel an evil presence next to me. Then I would hear demonic laughter. A voice would begin to tell me that God was not going to heal me. That what I believe is all a lie. Before this fall, I was in the gym all the time. I was a gym rat. I was strong and healthy. "Look at you," the voice would say, "you can't even go to the bathroom by yourself." The laughter got louder. Tears would be running down my face in the dark because of the pain. I would just say, "Shut up devil. You are a liar! My God is a faithful God! His word is true and does not return to Him void. By the stripes of Jesus, Christ I am healed! I rebuke you devil and command you to leave in Jesus's name!" Immediately, silence would come, and the wicked presence would leave. Holy Spirit would help me fall back asleep. I had many nights where I was visited by the hater of my soul. Always laughing, always mocking, always lying, and disturbing my sleep. But I always fought back with the word of God and used the name of Jesus. It got to the point where, if I felt it happening again, I would just repeat the name of

Jesus over and over. I didn't even engage a conversation with them anymore. I saved my strength for prayer.

Two months later, after my stitches were removed, the doctor said I could start to use my walker to take short walks around my apartment, but I absolutely had to wear my back-brace for everything I did. I could only take it off to take a shower with help. Christina would go with me when she came home from school.

We had a beautiful lake and walking trail. There were ducks and geese everywhere. We also had black swans that would chase you if you came too close to their nest. I remember Christina went to go look at the swan eggs, so she went ahead of me. I was admiring the lake when I heard screaming. I looked up and saw her arms flying around in the air, while she ran as fast as she could, as the swans were chasing her and making their loud trumpet sounds. I yelled out, "Run Christina!" Then I burst out laughing, but had to control it, so I wouldn't hurt too much. She wasn't happy with me for laughing, but afterwards, we laughed together about it. When I got tired from walking, I would sit on the edge of a bench with my pillow that I had attached to my walker. These walks were spent in prayer, for healing and thanking God for all His goodness. I had a lot to be grateful for.

It's been about two months since I had surgery. I was always in pain and always on meds. I was walking around better on my walker, but still very careful. I didn't want to trip or twist my ankle on anything, especially going up and down the stairs to my apt. I held on to the rails with both hands and took baby steps until I reached the top or bottom.

My friends would check up on me and let me know what was going on at our church. They told me about a three- day conference with a guest speaker who was going to teach on healing. That really triggered my interest. I told Christina
that I wanted to go, but two days of the conference went by. I just didn't have the strength to go.

On the evening before the last day of the conference, my family got together at a restaurant to celebrate my son's birthday, a day early. This was the first time I attempted to drive. I was extremely careful and drove as slow as I could, with the emergency lights on. Of course, my doctor probably would have gotten very upset with me, as I was not supposed to drive. But I didn't want to miss celebrating with my family. I couldn't stand or sit long. I was up and down the whole time. By the end of the evening, I was

244

totally exhausted. I said my good nights. My son would stay and

hang out and then catch a ride home with his girlfriend, Sheila, and her mother.

Again, I drove home with caution. Christina helped me out of the car and up the stairs. I just couldn't wait to get in bed and pass out. And that, I did.

# My Miraculous Healing

The next morning, my alarm went off at 9 a.m. as it did the last two days. I knew it was the last day of the healing conference. When I heard it ringing, I just turned it off like I did before. I just thought to myself I'm too tired to go. Then I heard a voice say, "Get up and go." I thought, "No, I am too tired." It said it again, "Get up and go." I just laid there, trying to get that voice out of my head. And then I heard with a much stronger voice and urgency, "GET UP AND GO!!!" I was more alert now and knew this was the Holy Spirit speaking to me. So, I pulled myself up and sat in bed, and said, "Okay, okay, I'm going!"

I called out to my daughter Christina. I asked her to help me out of bed. And I told her to get dressed because we were
going to church. She helped me get into a two-piece pair of royal blue dress pants and blouse. I put on my back brace. When we were both ready to go, I carefully went downstairs, while Christina helped me carry my walker and pillow. We got into the car, and I drove to our church that wasn't too far away from us, driving like a ninety-year-old lady. I drove around the back of the church, which went up to the second floor, because I knew they had a handicap entrance. We usually had to climb a very long staircase that led to the second floor into the main sanctuary. As I pulled into the handicap parking, I was greeted by an usher that helped me out of the car and then find seats for us in the back of the

church. I didn't want to sit up front where everyone could see me. So, I carefully sat down on my pillow with the use of my walker. I was probably about fifteen minutes late from the time the conference started.

I sat there listening to every word. Pastor Jim Hockaday was speaking. It was about the power of God and how He heals in many ways. How the shed blood of Jesus brings healing. After only about ten minutes, he pointed across the church and stared right into my eyes and said, "You! The lady in the blue. The Lord says, "He's going to heal you today!" As soon as he said that I felt electricity going through my whole body. I knew the Lord was healing me. I sat there as pulse after pulse of electricity consumed my entire body. I told myself, "This is it!"

People were turned around in their seats, staring at me, waiting to see what was going to happen. Pastor Hockaday ran to the back of the church where I was, microphone in hand and said to me, "There is something going on in your body. Take off that back-brace!" I looked at my daughter and saw her big brown eyes staring back at me. My flesh was reluctant, knowing I wasn't supposed to take it off, but Christ

in me raised up a standard against it! I unbuckled the straps, pulled the Velcro, took off my brace and handed it to my daughter. I sat there still fully engulfed in the healing power of God. All eyes on me, still waiting for something to happen. Pastor Hockaday just went right back to the front of the church and continued speaking on the miracle of healing. While the conference came to a close, the praise band began to play. An invitation was called for anyone who needed healing, to go up to the front to get prayed for. Apparently, I got up and walked to the front without my walker, still under the power of God. When I reached the front, there were hundreds of people all around me wanting to get healed. I saw the pastor make his way through the crowd, passing everyone to get to me. He and his wife stood right in front of me. He looked at me with a mission in his eyes and said, "UH UH!! THER'S NO WAY YOU ARE LEAVING THIS CHURCH WITH A MESSED-UP BACK!!! He and his wife boldly laid hands on me, while I heard the words, BE HEALED IN JESUS'S NAME!!!

I felt myself fall back in the arms of an usher, while they gently laid me on the floor. I could hear everything going on around me, but I couldn't open my eyes. It felt like my body was a huge magnet stuck to the floor. I remember trying to lift my arm up and it feeling like a ton of weights was holding it down. So, I just laid there and let God do what He needed to do. I felt someone get my hand and I was able to sit up. It was the pastor, asking me if I could stand up. As I looked up at him, I felt like I was so stinking drunk. My head was swaying, my eyes were barely open, and I really couldn't talk. So, he just looked at me and said, "Oh, God's not done with you yet! Stay down there." I laid back down, feeling a strong pull of gravity between myself and the floor. I laid there in the presence and power of God, while He performed surgery on me.

After what I thought was only a few minutes, I was able to sit up. Christina helped me get to my feet, as I was still a little on the drunk side. When I looked around, I was quite astonished. The whole church was empty except for the people getting ready for the evening service. It must have taken at least hours to pray over all the people and for everyone to leave the church. People always hung around after the service to mingle. But it seemed like I was only down for a few minutes.

I decided to test things out. I bend over forward to touch my toes. No pain! I twisted and turned to the right and the left. No pain! I jumped up and down. No pain! My daughter Christina came and embraced me, with both of us crying, knowing that God healed me. I then heard the Holy Spirit say, "Start running!" I called out to my daughter and said, "Come on." She replied with, "Mom!"

I began running around in the sanctuary. The faster I ran the more I was filled with the power of God. I was running everywhere. I ended up running to the top of the bleachers where we sang. When I got to the top, it felt like something exploded in me. I just began to sing and pray in the spirit. The more I did the more I was filled with a joy I never knew. I eventually came down and saw that my praise leader had witnessed everything. My daughter and I went to gather my walker, my back brace, and my pillow. I grabbed the walker and through it across the floor as if to throw it in satan's face! We left the church in my beautiful car, and I drove home with absolutely no pain.

When we got home, Jesse and Esther were at the pool which was right across from us. They saw me get off my car without my brace and walking around normal. They called out and waved us over, so we went over there. They asked me what happened so, I gave my testimony about how God healed me. They were in absolute shock, but so happy for me.

I decided to go back to the evening service, so that I could sing my praises and give thanks to the Lord. I walked in and the choir was already practicing, but they all turned to look at me. I took my place on the bleachers where I always stood to sing. My friend hit me with her elbow, and asked, "where is your back brace?" I smiled and proclaimed that I was healed! After the song was over, our worship leader who was on the other side and couldn't see me asked, "Is Jasmine here?" I jumped out of the bleachers, and yelled out, "Here I am!" He said with great enthusiasm, "Give them your testimony girl!" I was more than happy to do that! As I gave my testimony about what God had done, half the choir was praising God and the other half was crying because they saw me lying in my hospital bed during the times, they came to bring me food or pray with me in my apartment. They knew I had a long road ahead of me, but there I was standing in their presence fully healed. God was faithful to heal me, like I believed He would! No more pain, no medication, no limp, and no messed up back! Praise God!

That evening, I got on my knees to thank and give my praises to God. While I held my hands out in worship to Jesus, my Savior and Healer, my hands began to burn and tingle. I heard the Lord say, "I have anointed your hands." My desire to pray for the sick became even stronger.

For two weeks straight, God sent people my way to pray for their backs. I was on a spiritual high that felt like I was floating on air. Because of my healing and all the witnesses that were at the healing service, many people's faith was restored, and they were encouraged not to give up hope for their own healing miracles. Some people said while I was

praying for them, they could feel heat coming out of my hands. Some said they're backs felt better and the pain was gone. Others said they could feel warmth all over their body, while others said they felt like they were going to fall over. I told them it was the power of the Holy Spirit and I give all the glory and honor to Him who sits on the throne.

# This is my Commission:

(Prophesied over me as a personal word from the Lord)

*"The Spirit of the Lord God is upon me, Because the Lord has anointed me to preach good tidings to the poor; He has sent me to heal the brokenhearted, to proclaim*

*liberty to the captives, and the opening of the prison to those who are bound; to proclaim the acceptable year of the Lord, And the day of vengeance of our God; to comfort all who mourn, to console those who mourn in Zion, to give them beauty for ashes, the oil of joy for mourning, the garment of praise for the spirit of heaviness; that they may be called trees of righteousness, the planting of the Lord, that He may be glorified."* (Isaiah 61:1-3)

## There Goes Another One

When Manuel graduated from high school, we had a graduation and going away party for him at the same time. He had joined the military and was to report for basic training the following day. I remember dropping him off at the recruiter's station. I gave him a hug and told him I loved him. As he walked off with his bags, I started to cry. One of the recruits saw me and asked if I was Ok. I nodded yes,

thinking, "There goes another one." I walked back to my car, praying for him.

Fortunately, he was trained in our very own city. After graduating basic training, he was off to tech school where he would graduate again. God had a plan for him before he was in my womb. Not only does he serve God, but he served his country as well, while putting his own life in danger. I am so proud of him.

He married the love of his life, Sheila. I knew God had placed a special blessing on their marriage because they saved themselves for their wedding. They were high school sweethearts and made a promise to God that they would wait until they married. They kept their promise, God honored them for it, and you can see the manifestation of His special blessing in their relationship. This is the God we serve. He is faithful and takes delight in blessing His children!

I got to attend his high school, basic training, and tech school graduations. All healed, whole, no limp, and without any pain! To include his wedding day! What a mighty God we serve!

# Chapter 15

# What Happens When You Don't Wait On God?

## The Biggest Mistake of My Life!

**Mistake definition**: (Miriam-Webster) An action or judgement that is misguided or wrong: an error in action, opinion, calculation, or judgment caused by poor reasoning and carelessness, insufficient knowledge, etc.

**Mistakes usually cause some degree of pain, loss, or struggle. And because of mine, I experienced all the above and a lot more!**

I was still attending my church on the Northeast side of San Antonio. I have been there for about nine years. One day the enemy of my soul, brought a weapon against me that would tarnish my reputation, put an end to my ministry work and ignite a hellish nightmare that would threaten my life. This weapon came in the form of a man.

I was serving on our praise and worship team at the time. Worship is a passion of mine. We were having practice on Wednesday night. All of us were in formation and in our assigned places, when a nice-looking, very well-dressed man showed up to join us. He seemed very quiet and reserved in the beginning of his sessions with our team. During the next few weeks, we started talking to each other and eventually started dating. I had my twelve-year-old youngest daughter, Christina, still living with me. At that point, I had been a single mom for 11 years. During those years, I prayed for a Christian husband and the one God wanted me to have.

My daughter and I were living with my brother Brian, his wife Yamileth, and children. We moved out of our apartment because it was far from my work and there were too many shady people that started moving in around us; to include a satanist, right across from our apartment. I didn't feel it was safe anymore. Besides that, I had to say goodbye to my "Big Brother" Jesse and my close friend Esther, just a few weeks prior to that. He got stationed somewhere in Missouri and had to pack up and leave. It was really sad for us. We were going to miss them so much. We promised each other to keep in touch. I really cried when my friends left. Esther had become a sister to me.

I am going to call this man Lobo, which means wolf in Spanish. During the dating period with him, he would take me to expensive stores. He would have me try on extravagant clothing, he would have me pick out beautiful bedding sets, and even look at high-priced jewelry. After our shopping spree, he never bought anything. He would just leave the basket, walk away, and say, "Well, I would buy that for my wife."

Lobo would always take me and my daughter to expensive restaurants and just promise the world to us. He presented himself as having lots of money, he was always very well-dressed, drove a nice vehicle, and had a very well-paying job. Lobo made himself to be a very distinguished and important man.

One night while visiting at his apartment, we were standing on the balcony and I heard a voice say, "This man is your husband." I assumed it was the Lord. I turned around and told him what I heard, and he got a weird smile on his face. Then he hugged me.

The next few months kind of flew by. During this time, I noticed some red flags about Lobo. If I didn't call him back right away, he would get upset and sort of accusatory. He didn't like it if I went somewhere without him. If I spoke to another male friend at church, he watched me and told me about my body language, as I spoke to him. What? I found out from my best friend at the time, that she too had dated this guy for a couple of years. She never brought it up until she found out I was dating him. She informed me of his very aggressive behavior towards her. When she broke up with him, he insisted on taking back everything he bought her as a gift. To include a washer. She also told me that during a picnic she attended at one of the leader's homes, he was also there. He ended up throwing a drink in her face, twice, and proceeded to try to strangle her. A friend jumped in and threw him to the ground to stop him. Some of the guys had to escort him away. Even though I was being shown warning signs, I chose to ignore them. I thought to myself that I should give this guy the benefit of doubt, since it was in the past. Normally, I know I would have run the other way, but I didn't know I was under some sort of demonic trancelike hold.

After much consideration, and a few weeks later, I decided that I was going to take a break from this guy. I wrote him a letter asking him to give me some time to think things over. I gave it to him after practice on Wednesday at church. I just remember him saying, "Don't do this to me now." As I walked away, I told him, "You need to respect my wishes."

It was only a few days later when he began calling me and leaving messages. I should have just ignored him, but I got caught right back into the relationship. I honestly don't remember the rest of the next two months. We ended up going to a jeweler and buying wedding rings. Then I started planning a wedding. We only dated for four months. When we got to about a week before the wedding, we decided I should move in with him, since we were going to be married anyway. I figured I had imposed on my brother long enough. I had no intention of having sex with him before we got married, but the devils plan overruled my self-will. I was sleeping on the couch, and something scared me. I felt something evil in the room. I called out to him, but he didn't respond. When I went to his bedroom, he said, "Hop in. I knew this was going to happen." I didn't know what he was talking about. He kissed me and I fell into immoral sin. Exactly what I didn't want to do.

His parents and family members came into town for our wedding. We all met at the hotel they were staying at and had cocktails. His parents treated everyone to a very expensive dinner and presented us with a wedding gift. It was a check for $2000. I never saw a penny of it.

The pastor who had mentored me in the spiritual gifts for five years was the one who married us. I had spent all my savings on our wedding because I wanted it to be nice. Lobo never offered to pay for anything. I paid for the cake, the engagement and wedding photos, all the floral and table decorations, my veil, my bouquet, the bridesmaid's bouquets, the boutonniere's, my shoes, my wedding dress, the guest book, the wedding invitations, and the limo. We had the wedding reception at our church venue, so it was free. I did a lot of the decorating, as that is one of the talents I was blessed with. The wedding itself was beautiful, thanks to me.

When we got to the reception, I informed Lobo that he was going to have to pay for the caterer and the DJ because I ran out of money. He got really upset! His faced contorted to this very angry look that made me step back. I was in shock. I never saw him act like that before. He was forced to pay because I could not. I thought, he could just use some of the wedding money gift from his parents, so why get angry?

After he got over his anger at having to pitch in for our wedding, he relaxed a little and I continued to enjoy my family and friends. He didn't have any friends there, just his family. I wondered why he didn't invite anyone from his workplace.

Next came the honeymoon. We went to the Caribbean, and it was just beautiful over there. I don't know how he paid for it, but he had it planned already. Unless his parents paid for it because they were well off. Everything seemed normal enough. I got to go parasailing and snorkeling. If I wanted to do anything else, he said he didn't want to have to spend any more money. We ate the free meals and drank all the free drinks. Other than that, I can't remember the honeymoon night or any of our nights together. It wasn't because I was drunk. I have never been big on drinking. How strange that is! We were there for seven days, and I have absolutely no memory of the nights that were supposed to be meaningful. Not one of them!

So, now the honeymoon is over and as soon as we get back home, all hell breaks loose! The yelling begins, the accusations, the uncontrollable rage, the demands, and even him trying to isolate me from my family and friends. I was instructed to tell them that they couldn't come over unless they called first, and he was there. I did not agree to this, so he went into a rage of anger. He would get so ravenous, that his body would shake. One time he was yelling at me, and I literally saw a demon in his face. I got chills of terror all over my body and thought to myself, "Oh my God! What did I get myself into? I married satan's spawn from hell!" I didn't want to look at his face, so I ran to the couch and sat down with my legs curled up and my hands covering my head, while repeating the name of Jesus. He kept demanding, "Looook at mee! Looook at meee!" I just couldn't! He finally gave up and slammed the bedroom door shut. I slowly let my legs down and uncovered my head. I was still shaking in fright. I must have just sat there for a couple of hours. When he came back

out, he was talking so sweet to me. Like nothing happened. I
was in disbelief.

Lobo was so self-indulgent and self-centered. I had taken my daughter's bridesmaid dress to the cleaners because it got a small stain on it. It was only four dollars, which I used her child support on, but he went into a tantrum about it. He yelled, "You should have thrown the dress in the trash instead of wasting my freaking money on it! (I did change his exact word, because I don't use that type of language) You should feel really STUPID for doing what you did!" He yelled it in front of my daughter and made her cry. Yet, he would spend at least thirty dollars a week to have his shirts steamed and pressed.

Lobo would take his car to get washed, but he would leave mine dirty. I never had any money on me because if I did, he would accuse me of stealing from him. He would tell me that I was evil and so was my daughter and we needed to be delivered.

He would get up and go to church, but he wouldn't wake me up to go with him. This was very unusual, as I am a very light sleeper. Normally, I would have woken up just by him getting out of bed. It wasn't long before I got introduced to his snoring that was not normal. I am not exaggerating when I say that he sounded like, some sort of animal that was howling and growling in torment at the same time. It was so loud it hurt my ears. I would go to sleep with my daughter, but it was still so loud. We put earphones on and covered our head with a pillow. He would get so angry at me and scream, "You will never sleep with your daughter again!" He would scream even louder at me saying, "I have slept with HUNDREDS of women and not one of them ever complained!" I thought to myself, "Yeah. They were probably drunk or on drugs."

One day he left his computer opened and he had all these pictures of women barely wearing anything in a very

267

revolting position. My mouth dropped, as he was supposed to be a Christian. I asked him to delete them. He was hesitant but did it anyway. That was just on the desktop page. I couldn't even imagine what he had hidden inside his folders.

To my surprise, I received a rebate check in the mail for some sort of child credit that was passed. It was over five hundred dollars. Of course, Lobo drove me straight to the bank to deposit it. He had an evil smile on his face. When I looked on the account the next day to buy something for myself, he had spent every penny of it to pay off his credit card that he had before we met. I was so angry! He was so selfish and greedy!

I began to go to marriage counseling. The same pastor that married us, is the one doing the counseling. I convinced Lobo to go, but everything they asked him to do, he didn't do it. He would lie right in the pastor's face. I wondered if this was just a waste of time.

When Lobo came home from work, he wouldn't greet me. He just came in with an angry face, so I just left him alone. If I was watching tv, he would change the channel, even if I was at the end of a movie. He didn't care. He did exactly what he wanted to do because it was HIS apartment and HIS tv. He frequently went out and brought food home, but only for himself. Who does that? He would get extremely bad headaches, so I would try to help him relieve the pain with cold towels on his forehead. I noticed that he was always inhaling a bottle, but he said it was for allergies. And that is what the bottle said.

One day when my daughter opened the door to her bedroom, it accidently hit the wall and made a small hole. She got so scared that I had to calm her down and tell her it was just an accident. When Lobo got home, I explained what happened, but he wasn't hearing it. He got enraged and started yelling at my daughter. He accused her of doing it on purpose, and when he started cursing, I said, "Hey! I don't talk to my children that way" He turned his focus on me, which was good, but then he turned again to my daughter and screamed at the top of his lungs and pointing, "You gooo to your roooom!" I began to yell at him and tell him that he was not to treat my daughter that way. He came at me like an angered bull. I knew he was going to hit me, so I backed off around the table and kept going around, as he followed me. He stood there accusing me and my daughter of all these ridiculous things. When he ran out of things to rage about, he left to go to the store. I looked out the window to make sure he was gone. I called my daughter out of her room and told her, "We're out of here! Grab enough clothes for at least three days." She packed her backpack, and I grabbed an overnight bag. I no longer trusted leaving my daughter alone with him. I went to my brother's house to spend a couple of days there. I called the pastor to let him know I left. When Lobo got back from the store, he saw that we were gone, so he started calling me and leaving messages. I waited until the third day to call him and ask if we could go get some clothes. Of course, he said no. I went the next day when I knew he was at work, but discovered he changed the locks. He also had an alarm system installed. I told management and they forced him to change his locks back to theirs. Now he knew I was trying to get in, but even though I had a key, he had the alarm. I think it was about the sixth day that my pastor talked him into letting us go get some more clothes. I took several friends with me and got as much of my belongings out of the apartment that he allowed me to take. He watched me like a vulture. I got most of our clothes, all my jewelry, and all my daughter's belongings. Someone had grabbed some towels from the bathroom that were pink.

They thought they were mine. When he saw them, he yelled out, "Those are mine!" I immediately got them and said, "They thought they were mine because they are pink." I wondered why he had pink towels. I also wondered why he had so much stuff in boxes that were old. Boxes of female stuff. Things that seemed to be hoarded, belonging to women. Before I left, he threw a medical bill at me and said that I needed to pay it. It was over four hundred dollars that belonged to him. I just threw it back on the porch.

A few hours went by when my phone rang. I was pre-occupied and didn't look at the caller id. I just picked it up and said hello. Uhhhh! I heard the dreaded voice begin to accuse me of stealing his grandmother's glass bowls. I replied, "I did not take any bowls!" "Yes, you did. You're nothing but a thief!" he howled back. Then out of nowhere, he changes his voice to a calm, "Why don't you come back home?" I said, "NO!" His voice literally changes to a scream, "YOU COME HOME RIGHT NOOOW!" I quivered my voice and said, "Oh, ye- yes master!" (Three seconds of silence) Then I continued with, "NOT!" I hung up on him. I powered off my phone because I was just sick of his obscene, filthy, and vulgar phone calls.

Lobo began to tell lies about me at my church. I was asked to step down from the praise and worship team, I was no longer allowed to pray for people at the altar call, and I was told to stop all ministry work that I was involved in. My pastor called and asked me about an adulterous affair that I was being accused of. What? This pastor, who mentored me for five years and whom he had me teach a class for him, should have known my heart. He should have known it was a lie. Not only that, but he also began to accuse me and my daughter of things we never did. Are you kidding me? I have been attending this church for nine years. He took the side of this liar, whom he only knew for three months! None-the less, I kept going to counseling because I wanted to do all the right things a Christian wife is supposed to do, and I was told I needed to keep seeing him.

I ended up getting an apartment for myself and my daughter. I called the child support office and changed my address, so that my checks would no longer go to his address. A friend of mine gave me a twin bed and another friend gave me a glass table and chairs. I was given an old dresser and a chase lounge chair. I was using my credit card to buy dishes and utensils. I also bought myself a desk and a computer so that I would be able to take care of my everyday business online.

I got a job at a tax office. One of my closest friends worked there as well. She called one night telling me that Lobo called her and asked her how she knew me and what was her relationship to me. He was calling everyone on one of my cell-phone bills, demanding that they give me messages and trying to find out where I was. He was relentless about his phone calls and voice messages. If I didn't answer back, or call within minutes, he would get irate and leave sadistic voice mails. One minute he would say in a sickening soft voice, "Why don't you let the Holy Spirit lead you into coming back home to be the wife you are supposed to be?" The next second it would be, "Yeah, your nothing but a used-up whore!" I swear he was possessed by demons!

It must have been about the third month of being separated when I got a phone call from one of my brothers. He told me he was on his way to visit me. A little while later, there was a knock on my door. I thought it was my brother leaning on the rail. I saw his back and the shirt he was wearing. My brother wore nice shirts. When I opened the door, to my shock, it was Lobo! He pushed the door in and immediately started searching the apartment, asking who I was living with, pertaining to another man. His eyes were enlarged and focused. He looked like a roaring lion ready to devour anything in his path. He started with my living room and went into my bedroom. He turned around and headed to my computer. When I yelled out that it belonged to my brother, he stopped. I thought he was going to destroy it. Again, he went into a rage yelling at me saying, "Oh, look at you with all this stuff! And there you are telling everyone that you have nothing! Oh, poor you!" I don't know where he got his information from, but I hadn't spoken to anyone of what I had or didn't have. Except my pastor. My friends who helped me, knew I had nothing when I got my apartment. I pushed past my fear and asked him how he found me. He said with a devious smile, "I am very intelligent. I have connections." After he said this, I saw him moving towards me like a snake. I gasped when I saw this. I had to have seen this in the spirit. He then said, "I'm a Chameleon. I can become whoever I want, at any time and place that I want to, whenever I need to."

## Chameleon definition: (Miriam-Webster)

**1.** a small slow-moving Old-World lizard with a prehensile tail, long extensible tongue, protruding eyes that rotate independently, and a highly developed ability to change color.
**2.** A person who often changes his or her beliefs or behavior in order to please others or to succeed.
**3.** One that is subject to quick or frequent change especially in appearance.

After this disgusting description of himself, I told him he needed to leave. He refused and plastered himself down on my chase chair after locking the door. He glared at me with these eyes full of defiance, which seemed to be turning black. I had seen his green eyes turn black before, during his rage sessions. I knew he had intentions of hurting me. Oh, the evil I felt in that room! My heart began to race in fear. The tiny hairs on my arms stood up. I grabbed my phone and dialed 911. As I called on the name of Jesus, he jumped up like a kangaroo that just got bolted with a high electric charge. He ran out like a coward. Thank God my daughter wasn't there.

My brother showed up while the police were still there. He was scared at first, thinking Lobo had hurt me. Then he wondered how he found out where I lived. He stayed with me that night to make sure Lobo didn't come back.

From then on there were numerous police reports on him. He refused to leave me alone and began with his threats. He prohibited me from getting the rest of my belongings that were in the garage. He used them against me saying, "If you don't go meet me somewhere, I'm going to throw them out on the sidewalk or in the trash!" If I didn't call him back, he would threaten to cancel my car insurance. I met him once in a public place, just so that he could yell at me for changing my address and demand that I give him my child support, because I owed him my check. I didn't understand how he knew that I changed my address. I don't know why, but I could never get one step ahead of him. It was as though he knew my every move.

I asked the pastor to talk to him and see if he would let me get the rest of my things. Lobo agreed but said that he was going to call the Sheriff, so that he could be there to watch me. Seriously? I had to wait for the weekend when he

# Ushering In Your Spouse

was off work. I decided to try and get them while he was at work one day during the week. My sister had a truck, and we went to the office manager and explained what was going on. She told me that he didn't have the right to hold my things hostage and since my name was on the lease, she opened the garage for me. My sister and I loaded everything that was mine, as fast as we could unto her truck. I did notice that most of my expensive items were missing. He had taken them out and had them in his apartment. We jumped into the truck and fled the scene of the crime laughing at the thought of what his reaction would be when he opened the garage. I finally got some victory over the enemy's camp! When the weekend came around, I got a phone call from Lobo stating, "I have a sheriff coming by in the afternoon and you BETTER be there to get your things." I replied and said, "No need to bother. I already got what I needed out of the garage. Yup! The office manager let me in!" He got very quiet, then before the violent storm could hit the phone line, I hung up on him. Phone calls began, but I just turned my phone off. When I turned it back on hours later, sure enough, a bombardment of psychotic voice messages filled my phone. I didn't delete them so I could have them as evidence if I ever needed them. I should have used the Sheriff to get my expensive things out of his apartment, but when you are in a situation like this, you don't think clearly.

One day he called me 99 times in a row, like he had absolutely nothing else to do in his life. I called the police to file for harassment. The phone rang and showed the 99th call. The police asked, "Is that him?" I answered, "Yes." So, he picked up the phone and said, "Lobo, this is officer _____." The coward hung up on him. I explained to the police officer that Lobo kept harassing me and showing up uninvited. He told me there was nothing they could do unless they saw him on the property. I went to the police station to try to get a restraining order, but the police told me that he couldn't grant me one because I wasn't stabbed, bruised, or bleeding. I said, "But that is what I am trying to avoid!" He sympathized with me and said he was really sorry, but he had to go by the rules.

Soon after that, while I was working, that demon showed up at my job. My friend frantically ran to tell me that he was in the front. He had a crazed look on his face. I ran to the back office to tell my boss. He told me to say there until he left. They called the police. He found out where I worked and began harassing me, breaking into my car, and stealing things. I was afraid to go to my car at night. I was being stalked all the time now. I was afraid of going outside. I was afraid to leave my daughter alone because I knew if he had the chance, he would hurt her, just to hurt me. One day he showed up banging on the door. I told my daughter to call the police. I called him around to talk to him off my balcony. I played it cool and kept him in conversation until the police arrived. Boom! They caught him! Lobo wailed in anger shouting, "You see what you teach your daughter?" Of course, I'm going to teach my daughter to call 911, when you have a maniac pounding on your door, who believes he is above the law. He was escorted off the property and advised never to go back. The police wrote out yet another report, but this time there was record that they caught him on the premises. Of course, that didn't stop him. He showed up three more times right after that. My life was hell with him in it.

One day, as I was laying prostate on the floor and crying out to God in tears and desperation, I shouted, "Lord, what I should do?" He answered, "Get out!" There was an urgency in His answer. I knew I had to get out of this demonic and

dangerous relationship.

*Beware of false prophets, (men) who come to you in sheep's clothing, but inwardly they are ravenous wolves.* (Emphasis mine) (Mathew 7:15)

As I lay there in my closet, I asked God to forgive me for not even asking Him if I should marry this man or not. You see, I had two other men in my life, who had both pursued me for six years. They wanted to marry me at different times during my eleven years of being a single mom. One was a marine who was ten years younger than I was. He was very handsome and had green eyes. The other was also, very good looking with blue eyes. He was six years younger. I always attracted younger men. Maybe it was because I had always looked younger than my age. I suppose I took after my beautiful mamma. She aged very gracefully and had youthful, flawless skin. No one ever believed she gave birth to thirteen children! Getting back to the other men, I really didn't have to argue with myself about them. I wasn't in love with either one. And yes, I fell into sin with both, just as I did with my ex-boyfriend. These two were before my boyfriend. But with them, I knew they were not saved. So, when the time came, and I was ready to let go, I asked God to remove them out of my life. He was faithful in answering my prayers.

I repented for marrying Lobo. As tears flowed down my face, I knew it was my fault for not getting confirmation about this man. Yes, I clearly heard that voice tell me that he was my husband, but it wasn't the voice of the Lord. It was the voice of the devil, to deceive me. I should have known better. Every time a man would try to come into my life, I would ask God if he was not my husband, to get him out of my life and send him far from me. The Lord was always faithful. I didn't ask this time. I guess I just got caught up in the excitement of planning a wedding. I knew deep in my heart that I didn't have complete peace. I honestly could say that I never loved him. It was as though I was in some sort of trance that held me captive in lies. You see, if you want something bad enough, you convince yourself that it is truth and from God. One of the biggest weapon's satan has against us is deception. If he can make us believe a lie is the truth, then he succeeds and a doorway to hell is opened up into our lives, especially to take you off course with God.

*When he speaks kindly, do not believe him, for there are seven abominations in his heart; Though his hatred is covered by deceit, His wickedness will be revealed before the assembly.* (Proverbs 26:25-26)

Even after we were married, I would look at Lobo and ask, "God, Shouldn't I be attracted to my husband?" You know what? I didn't love him, I wasn't attracted to him, and I was miserable, for the fact that he was NOT my husband! He absolutely was not the man I had been praying for. The enemy wants us to settle for way less than what God has for us. And if he could use that person to destroy you, he will!

*The thief does not come except to steal, and to kill, and to destroy.* (John 10:10)

Lobo would take showers and only wash his private part. Nothing else. He would not brush his teeth. He had at least 10 bottles of the same cologne under his cabinet. One time, reached up to his face with both hands and had touched the back of his ears. When I pulled my hands away, there was such a gross stench! I looked at the back of his ears and there were these layers of deep crevices that had accumulated old gunk in them. He just smiled and said, "Yeah, It's pretty gross." I gagged and went to wash my hands very vigorously to try to get the horrible smell off them.

## Divorce Papers

I continued to ask the Lord for direction. I prayed for protection for myself and my daughter. I was alone at home, as my daughter would go and stay with her dad every other weekend. There was a knock on my door, and it was a constable. I opened the door and he handed me a brown envelope and said, "You've been served." In his presence, I opened the envelope, and it was divorce papers! I yelled in such joy and said, "Thank You Jesus!" I was so happy that I hugged and thanked him. He just looked at me and said, "You are the third person to react that way today!" Then he left. I truly had something to celebrate! When I looked at the date of when he filed, it sickened me to no end. I literally wanted to throw up. He filed for divorce on Valentine's Day. He had called me on that very day to ask me out on a date. After the realization of how sick this man was, I focused back on the joy that the divorce petition was filed, and I didn't have to pay for it. I would be legally and spiritually detached from this union that came from hell!

Enough was enough already. I called my sister to meet me at Lobo's apartment so that I could get the last of my belongings. I told her that I would call the police so that they could escort me in. When the police officers got there, I explained to them all that had been going on. They looked at me and said, "We know exactly who this guy is. He called us to file a complaint against you for harassment and doing sneaky things behind his back." My jaw hit the ground! What? They proceeded to tell me that they didn't believe him. They were the same officers who had to escort him away from my premises. How embarrassing for him that the police knew he was a liar. My sister got there with her truck. The officers knocked on his door and told him to stand back so that I could collect my belongings. If looks could kill! They stayed in the living room with him to make sure he didn't stop me. I got back my expensive leather recliner, (it wreaked of cigarette smoke) my lovely couch, my nice candle holders, my curio cabinet, some boxes with my porcelain angels, and I also grabbed the nice jewelry box that he had bought me as a gift before we were married. That was the only thing he bought me. I think it was to lure me in. The last thing was my Ethan Allen desk that I bought from the same sister that was helping me. When we were taking it out, he growled, "That's mine!" My sister told him she sold it to me before we met. The officer held him back until we were out the door. They made a report and I thanked them again for helping me out. Another victory over the enemy!

We were now in May, and I kept going to counseling, but so did he. We went at separate times to the same pastor. I also, went to a different church service so that I didn't bump into him. After the second service was over, a very close friend of mine came running to me as white as a ghost. She grabbed my arms and frantically said, "Oh My God, Jasmine! I just ran into Lobo, and he tried to hug me and say hello. I never felt so much evil in my entire life!" She was literally shaking in fear! I grabbed her hand, and we ran out of the sanctuary.

I tried to stay busy with my job. When it was time to

leave, my boss would walk me to my car. I made sure to lock my doors before leaving the parking lot. I was always checking my mirrors to make sure I wasn't being followed. My heart would race in panic mode, as I got off my car and hurried as fast as I could to get inside my apartment to safety. I was losing sleep at night. Any noise I heard, made me jump up to look out my window in case Lobo tried to climb my balcony. I had laid a large board across my balcony door to block it from being slid open. I also had a huge knife under my pillow. I laid wide awake with no sleep.

My attendance at church continued as I could feel people staring at me and I knew they were talking about me behind my back. Some of these were supposed to be my friends. One of the ladies who went to the singles group I had been attending, approached me, and started telling me something about my consequences for me "looking for a husband." I said, "I wasn't looking for a husband." She then turned around and raised her voice at me in a stern tone and said, "You bought a wedding dress!" She walked away without waiting for my response. I just thought, "She has no idea what she's talking about." I know I had explained all this to another friend.   Another one who was with me when I bought the dress knew, but apparently one of them was telling the story in gossip form.

Yes, I did buy my wedding dress. I had my dress hanging in my closet for about three years. I was invited to go to a wedding event with my friend, Sharon. They were going to have all kinds of wedding vendors there. My friend did weddings, so I thought it would be fun to go. Our senior pastor had just given a sermon about taking a step of faith. If there was something that we were believing God for, then

we needed to take action in our faith. So, I told my friend that
I was going to take a step of faith and look for my wedding

dress, knowing that God had a husband for me one day. When we got to the venue, there was much excitement in the air. We came across several vendors who had wedding dresses on racks. Both of us began to look through the racks, as she too wanted to get married. We must have looked at hundreds of dresses. Nothing was grabbing my attention, but we were having so much fun! I prayed and asked Father God to pick out my dress for me and let me know which one it was. When we moved on to the next vendor, we began our search again. Then, as I pulled one dress out for a better look, my heart leaped. This dress was so stunning, elegant, and graceful. It was exactly what I had envisioned. I then heard a voice say, "This is your wedding dress." I showed it to Sharon and told her I was going to try it on. It was a perfect fit! A size six, to be exact. I looked at the price tag, and it was over a thousand dollars. The sales lady told me they were having a special on all the dresses they sold at the event. I got a remarkable discount, paid for the dress, and felt so blessed and grateful. So, my beautiful, *Faith Dress* hung in my closet for three years. Remorsefully, I wore it to the wrong wedding, with the wrong man. If ONLY, I had asked God!

Before one service, a very sweet elder lady came to my side and put her hand on my shoulder. She blessed me and said to ignore the whispers behind my back. Those were the kindest words I heard in a long time. I couldn't hold back the tears, as I held on tight to my Savior. He was my rock and my strength.

*You shall hide them in the secret place of Your presence, From the plots of man; You shall keep them secretly in a pavilion, from the strife of tongues.* (Psalm 31:20)

# Divorce Court

The day finally came! It was time for divorce court! Yaaayy!! I had hired an attorney to represent me. He made promises of getting most of my money back from the wedding. When the judge entered the room, I got the impression that he was a hard man with little compassion. Sure enough, I was right!

Lobo's attorney began with false accusations against me and had a binder with checks that I supposedly wrote. They were asking for everything we got from the wedding, which he already had kept, except for 2 books and a vase that my friend gave me. He also wanted my ring back. How rapacious (aggressively greedy) and ridiculous at the same time. After they were done making their demands, it was my turn. The judge turned to us, and I looked at my lawyer who just stood there and didn't say a word! He just waved his hands in the air and looked down at the ground. What the heck is going on? I literally had to defend myself. I told the judge everything that Lobo did, I brought the police reports with me and all the evidence of his threats and disgusting phone calls. I had a few witnesses waiting outside the courtroom as well. I told of all the expenses I paid for the wedding and how I was forced to give him my child support checks. When I was done, the judge said to me, "Those are serious accusations. Do you have proof?" I declared, "Yes, your honor, I have proof and witnesses outside." To my disbelief, he ignored all that I said, and just told Lobo that he was going to have to pay me for having to get a lawyer to defend myself. It was $1500. The judge told Lobo that my ring was a gift and that I was allowed to keep it. He began to have a hissy fit, so his lawyer began to blurt out how his client shouldn't have to pay a red cent but, the judge slammed his gavel down and said, "This marriage is dissolved." I just smiled immensely, lifted my arms in praise to God and said out loud, "Thank you Lord!" As I walked out of the courtroom, I could feel the daggers piercing through Lobo's eyes, as I believed he was literally trying to stab me in the back with them. As for the cowardly lawyer, I just walked away from him when he tried talking to me. I never wanted to see any of them again. I left the courtroom with a huge burden lifted off my life. Oh, how happy and grateful I was that day.

## After the Divorce

It was almost a year to the day when I entered into a marital contract with an egotistical, self-infatuated, coward from hell to the day of divorce. I decided to trade my vehicle in for another. Even though I was divorced from Lobo, I knew it was just a matter of time before it would get vandalized by him. I only had one more month and it would be paid off. The Lord had blessed me with my beautiful blue green Cavalier. I loved it. I went back to the same dealer, and they gave me an excellent trade in price. It still looked brand new. I got a small SUV. A few days later, I drove it to my spiritual mom's house so that she could pray for me. While I was there, her phone rang and whoever it was asked for me. I thought it was one of her daughter's, so I answered the phone. When I said hello, A wave of horror gripped me as I heard this familiar evil voice on the other end saying, "Yeah, now that I know what you are driving, you're going to reap the hounds of hell!" How did he know I got a different vehicle? How in the world did he know where I was or the phone number?

A few days went by, when I was leaving early in the morning to run some errands. It was about seven a.m. As I approached my vehicle, my heart sank as I beheld the sight of all four tires that had been slashed, to include my spare. I called the police and told them I believed it was Lobo. Since I didn't have proof, all they could do was make a report. They didn't have security cameras. I called my pastor and told him what happened. I told him about Lobo's phone call, but he didn't believe me. I called one of my brothers to ask him to take me to get new tires. I was crying and he got very upset. After I got the new tires put on my vehicle, I went straight to the pastor's office with proof of all the sickening voice messages. He listened to them and afterwards said with a nonchalant voice, "He's just yelling." Are you kidding me? Did you not hear all the vulgar language and all the threats? I was so infuriated! As I was leaving, I ran into one of the leaders that held a Divorce Care class. She was trying to comfort me because she was one of the few who knew the truth of what was going on. She informed me that Lobo had joined her class and was making himself out to be the victim of an abandoned and abused husband. Unbelievable! She was very in-tuned to all his lies. She told me, "Jasmine, Lobo is a very sick person. He is a narcissist." I asked, "What is that?" This is what she described him as: "He has an excessive interest and admiration of himself. He believes his existence is an immaculate gift to others who should recognize and admire him for it. Narcissists think the world revolves around them. He enjoys getting away with violating rules. They are overly self-involved, and often vain and selfish. He believes that he is very important and classifies himself with a regal status. He believes that he is entitled to anything he wants. He excels in lying and playing with emotions." I cried out, "Wow! You have described exactly who he is!" She must have memorized that description because when I looked it up, that is almost exactly what the dictionary said. My tears dried up and she gave me a big hug.

Then she warned me and said, "Jasmine, you must be very careful of him!" I drove back home and just sat there and cried. My brother Brian whom I lived with before, called very concerned about what happened. He told me that I was going to have to leave the city, or Lobo was going to end up hurting me. I knew, that because of this man's deep connection with satan, he was very capable of hurting me. Even though I knew God would protect me, I still had to use wisdom. I found out that Lobo had fled his hometown for crashing his car into another man's vehicle because he was dating his ex-girlfriend. I also found out by my pastor that he was snorting liquid opium and refused to stop. That was the supposed allergy medicine bottle and why he was always getting headaches. OMG! He actually went to the hospital to have his head checked and used that as an excuse to try and get me go to the hospital to see him. And the pastor had the nerve to call me to ask if I would go. What a chronic liar! And yes, there was definitely something *wrong* with his head. And no, I did not go.

My brother told me to go stay with him where I would be safe. Within two hours, my sister, two brothers and a trusted friend moved me out of my apartment. I did not tell the office that I was moving out. God gave me peace about letting my daughter go stay with her dad. She was only twelve, and this was a critical age, but God gave me the peace that surpasses all understanding and let me know she would be safe and ok. I cried as she put her belongings in the truck and watched her and her dad drive away. I knew God would take care of her. Now, I had to go to a safe place for myself.

*I will love You, O Lord, my strength. The Lord is my rock and my fortress and my deliverer; My God, my strength, in whom*

*I will trust, My shield and the horn of my salvation, my stronghold. I will call upon the Lord, who is worthy to be praised; So, shall I be saved from my enemies.* (Psalm 18:1-3)

I put all my furniture and kitchen appliances in storage and packed my suitcases with my clothes and personal belongings. I had given all my food to my ex-husband and some other items that my daughter wanted. I was now free to go wherever God's plan would take me. For now, that was with my brother. He is an ex-Marine and expert sniper. I took comfort in knowing I was in a much safer place. I could barely fall asleep that night but managed to get a little rest.

# Chapter 16

# The Betrayal

The next morning after waking up from little sleep, I felt like there was something that I needed to do. I brushed that thought aside and had a nice breakfast with my brother and his family. It sure felt good to know that I was in the comfort of love and support. I thanked them so much for taking me in again. My brother was telling me that he wouldn't recommend me going anywhere by myself. As we continued
our conversation, I just remembered what it was that I

needed to do.

I excused myself and went to my room to make a private phone call to the pastor. I had no intention of divulging any more information to him. I remembered that Lobo mentioned something in the courtroom that he couldn't have possibly known. When the pastor answered hello, I asked, "How did Lobo know about the situation that I discussed with you, when you were the only person, I told. He brought it up in court." I heard a deep silence come over the phone for a few seconds, then he said in an angry voice, "It doesn't matter!" He kept speaking, but everything seemed to zoom out and my ears began to ring. I was now thrown into a whirlwind of every emotion you can imagine. I had been set free out of one nightmare, just to be thrown into another. All this time, it was my pastor whom I had trusted in confidence for years with all my personal feelings, everything I was going through, and my plans to get ahead and away from Lobo, who was feeding it right back to the ears of my nemesis!

My heart was racing so hard! I felt as though it were a Trireme warship at full speed and all the oarsmen in full force with each pound of my heart, getting ready for the ramming collision upon the enemy. My mind was filled with confusion and a thousand questions at the same time. I was swept into a tsunami of uncontrollable hurt, anger, and disbelief. The truth and reality of where this source came from was too much to bear. I had slammed the phone down, just as I was thrust into a turbulent force of betrayal!

It must have been hours before I came back out of my room. I don't know if I fell asleep because I was so tired, or if the shock of it all, just knocked me out. When I woke up, I immediately changed my number. Every memory of how

Lobo knew my next move, how he found out where I lived, where I worked, my change of address for child support, my new vehicle, to all the details he knew, fit into a perfect puzzle that all led right back to the pastor of betrayal. WHY???

## Betrayal: (Miriam-Webster)

**1.** Violation of a person's trust or confidence, of a moral standard

**2.** Revelation of something hidden or secret

**3.** To deliver or expose to an enemy by treachery or disloyalty

**4.** To disappoint the hopes or expectations of; be disloyal to: to betray one's friends.

**5.** To reveal or disclose in violation of confidence: to betray a secret.

*The words of his mouth were smoother than butter, but war was in his heart; his words were softer than oil, yet they were drawn swords. (Psalm 55:21)*

*Even my own familiar friend in whom I trusted, who ate my bread, has lifted up his heel against me. (Psalm 41:9)*

*When Jesus had said these things, He was troubled in spirit, and testified and said, "Most assuredly, I say to you, one of you will betray Me." (John 13:21)*

I can't describe the emotional paralysis this unfathomable betrayal caused me. I just shut down my mind and buried all the pain into a deep abyss. If Jesus was betrayed by his own disciple, most assuredly we as His children will be betrayed as well.

# Chapter 17

# Fireworks in Florida

After being in a state of mental and emotional paralysis, it was probably early afternoon when I had finished praying.

I joined my brother and sister-in-law in the kitchen. I didn't mention what happened because they were already concerned for me. We were just hanging out when my phone rang. It felt strange not to have to worry who was on the other line. My daughter Angela called and invited me to go for a visit to see my son-in-law, Armando, who was attending

tech school at Hurlburt Field in Destin, Florida. Armando

would be graduating later to be a TACP (Tactical Air Control
Party) in the United States Air Force. I immediately said
Yes! I desperately needed to clear my head and do something
fun with my family. It was the fourth of July weekend, so
this was perfect.

I packed a bag and headed to my daughter's house,
where I would park my car and ride with her and one of her
besties, Monica Dickson, who grew up with her and calls me
mom. Her mother in-law sat in front and Monica sat in back
with me and my grandson. Tre, who was around 6 years old,
sat in the middle. This was almost a twelve- hour drive, but
I was just happy to be getting away for some relaxing and
quiet time.

There was the usual, pit stops for eats, bathroom
breaks, and driver trades. The hours seemed to be
accumulating for a while when we finally arrived at our
destination. We were blessed to be able to stay at
Armando's cousin's house, instead of having to pay for a
hotel. It was really nice there. Since we were so close to the
beach, we decided to drive there, park the car, and get off to
enjoy the sand and water. I remember thinking that I had
never seen such a beautiful beach in my life! The sands
were of trillions of stunning white quartz particles that
seemed to be a never-ending coastline. As I sank my feet
into the cool refreshing sand, I just stood there to behold
the beauty of this massive emerald ocean. I could feel the
ocean breezes that seemed to come from every direction
caressing my face. Did I even dare to put my feet in the
water? After about fifteen minutes of just standing there
enjoying the winds of freedom, I slowly walked to the
water's edge and stepped into the blissful waves. As they

came wave after wave, I felt as though God was washing my feet in His peace. Tears began to flow down my face. "Lord", I whispered, "Have Your way in my life! Help me Holy Spirit to know what Your plan for me is from this moment on. I love and trust You!" A strong gust of wind came suddenly and dried up my tears. As I looked up into the sky, I noticed these clouds that seemed to be dancing as the wind carried them to and fro. The sun was stunning as it showed off its rays through the heavens blanket of beautiful hues of blue.

My attention was taken back to my family, as we were going to have lunch together. There was a very nice boardwalk with quaint shops to explore. We found a restaurant that had a joined gift shop. As we waited for them to prepare a table for our party, we had fun taking family photos and selfies with each other. We enjoyed cocktails and then were escorted to our table. The food was delicious, but the company was even better. After our meal, we all got up to go shopping at the different beach shops. It was so much fun hanging out with my family. I thanked God for giving me this special time with them.

The early evening came as Angela and Armando got ready to go to a BBQ they were invited to. His mother and my grandson were going too. That left me and Monica. We decided to go have dinner together and enjoy each other's company. She is one of my "adopted" daughters. There's about five that have grown up with Angela. So, out the door everyone goes.

Monica and I chose a seafood restaurant that was right on the beach. I don't remember the name if it, but it was so perfect for that night. As we walked in, it definitely captured the ambiance of a very cozy coastal place. We sat by the window, which overlooked the beach. The windows were long and had some sea green, antique looking shutters that were

opened. Some lights surrounded the shutters, giving them a

glow about them. We felt the gentle night winds flowing into the restaurant.

The waitress came to take our order and I believe we both ordered the biggest seafood platter they had to offer. We
were going to be there for a while. We also ordered frozen drinks to enjoy while waiting for our food. As we looked outside, it was sunset. There were colors of red, orange, yellow and pink that fused together making a gorgeous tapestry of artwork. The ocean took on this canvas of radiant colors, as the sun duplicated its beauty making it look like waves of rainbows flowing in layers as it intermingled with the soft splash of its white foam. We sat there mesmerized at this captivating scenery.

Our food came and we blessed it to nourish our bodies. We were ready to engage in this seafood feast. Right after we held up our glasses to toast to our evening, an explosion of fireworks began to fill the skies. We turned and looked at each other with astonishment. We were now being serenaded with an eruption of enormous glittering sparkles, outbursts of bright brilliant colors, and a dazzling performance of falling incandescent lights. As the waterless fountains in the air continued to outpour colors of grandeur, the sound of their booms and crackling, resounded into the night sky. We couldn't believe what a spectacular demonstration of fireworks we got to witness, but it still couldn't compare to the miraculous sunset behind it all. I believe that the Lord had orchestrated this breathtaking finale just for us. It was just so surreal. Monica and I just sat there and enjoyed the rest of our delectable dinner. This was the perfect memorable ending to our evening. I will always remember this Fourth of July weekend.

You know the old saying, "All good things must come to

an end." Well, I don't believe it. I believe God was showing me the beginning of a new season in my life that was going to be filled with the unexpected and excitement. I didn't know what was going to happen when I got back home to my brother's house, but I know God had a plan.

The next day, everyone gathered their belongings for the trip back home. I decided to call Christina to let her know where I was. She didn't have my new phone number yet, either. I heard the phone ringing and almost hung up, but at the last ring I heard, "Hello." I said, "Hi Punk!" (Her nickname) All I heard in a frantic voice was, "Oh my God, mom! Your alive!" She really sounded scared. I said, "Of course I am." She began to tell me that Lobo had called her at four o'clock in the morning and left a voice message yelling at her saying, "YEAH, YOU BETTER CALL YOUR MOM AND SAY GOODBYE, CAUSE SHE'S DEAD!" She thought he had done something really bad to me. When she tried to call Angela, she didn't get through. I reassured her that I was fine and that I was in Destin, Florida with her sister and family for a visit with Armando. I told her to block Lobo's number so that he couldn't call again. I promised her I would keep in touch and let her know my whereabouts. Then I apologized for that demon, scaring her the way he did. I didn't know that Lobo had his own evil fireworks going on in his sick head.

Right after I hung up with her, my phone rang. I had only given my new number to my family and my best friends. I didn't have time to add everyone's contact name, so I didn't know who it was that was calling. When I answered, it was my "Big Brother." I hadn't spoken to Jesse or Esther for a couple of months. They knew what was going on with Lobo and they would pray with me. I had just texted them my new phone number, right before I left. "Hey Jesse, good to hear

your voice. How's Esther?" I asked. He told me that she was

about five months pregnant now and that she was nervous because he was about to get deployed in a few weeks and didn't know how long he would be gone. He asked how Christina and I were doing. I told him what happened and that I had to let Punk go live with her dad so that she would be safe and that I was staying at my brother's house for now. "Well, then let me tell you the reason for my phone call," he said. "Esther is very nervous for my deployment. This is my second one here and she's scared. We don't have family here, but she doesn't want to go back home. She wanted me to ask and see if you would be willing to come stay with her. You can get a job on base, and she would have watched Christina for you, but now she doesn't have to. You can stay here as long as you want and not worry about paying rent. Even when I come back. What do you think?"

Wow! I didn't even have to figure it out. God already had a plan for me! I blurted out, "Yes! Thank you, Jesus!" I told Jesse I would leave as soon as I got back home. All I had to do was throw my already packed suitcases in my car. He handed the phone to Esther. She was so excited and grateful. "Oh, thank you Jasmine! You don't know what this means to me. We can't wait to see you!" she exclaimed. I said, "You have no idea what a perfect timing this phone call was, so thank you and Jesse. I'll see you both soon!" She gave me the address to their house that was right outside the base. I would just put it in my GPS when I was ready to leave.

When I got back inside, I told everyone what happened with Christina. They were all in shock that turned into anger. But then I told them what God did. God was sending me to a safe place, and I would be just fine.

We left Destin and as soon as we drove up to my daughter's driveway, I kissed and hugged everyone goodbye and asked for prayers for a safe trip. When I arrived at my

brother's house, before I could tell him my story, he began to tell me his. He reported that Lobo had been circling his house at three and four a.m. My brother lives on kind of a cul-de-sac. He has trouble sleeping at night, so he will usually look out his window to make sure everything is ok.

Well, the first night I was gone, he said Lobo drove by very slowly several times. He must have tried to find me at my apartment and management must have told him I left. He knew where my brother lived because that is where I lived before. The second night, my brother was waiting for him. He said he came driving by slowly again and stopped for a few minutes. My brother said to me, "I have no problem protecting my family from someone who is trying to hurt them. Lucky for him, he didn't get off the car and step into my property. If he comes by again tonight or rather early morning, he better be prepared to meet his fate!" I was in dismay and fear at the same time. I told my brother what he said to Christina. He was then, more than convinced that Lobo was out to fatally hurt me. I knew this was true, but I told my brother that I was going to go live with my friends, and I didn't want to be the cause of bringing any danger to his house and family. He warned me not to tell anyone where I was going, except my family. We hugged each other and I hugged my sister-in-law and nephew's good-bye. Brian helped me put my bags in the car and then we said our goodbyes. I drove off with tears in my eyes, as I am very close to him and Yamileth. As I drove out towards my new destination, I also knew I was driving away from my life

here. I was literally having to do a disappearing act. I left my church, my job, my friends, and my twelve-year-old daughter behind. I would be able to talk to my little "Punk" (Christina) later. That was and still is her nickname for me.

A fourteen-hour drive, but I knew I would not be alone

on this adventure. God would be with me all the way. I had plenty of time to pray, listen to praise music, and focus on what God had in store for my future. Thus, a new chapter in my life began.

# Chapter 18

# Knob Noster, Missouri The Next Chapter

I arrived in Missouri with a sense of great anticipation and expectation. I don't know exactly what God had in store for me, but I know it was good. I felt this was a new beginning for me. The drive through Missouri was very peaceful. It looked like there were forests of green trees everywhere. I saw some signs for state parks, lakes, and rivers. There were horses, cattle, pigs, and other various livestock that captured

my attention in the fields that I drove by. It certainly had that very country feeling, but it all felt so fresh. There were long winding roads and some farmlands off in the distance. When I got to Knob Noster, it had an old town appearance with some really cute boutiques and businesses, making it feel all local. I thought to myself, "I think I'm going to like it here." The next thing I saw was in the air. It looked like a big black bat flying above. I never saw anything like it.

I called Esther to let her know that I had arrived. When I drove up to the house, she came out to greet me. I rubbed her baby bump and then we hugged for a long time. It was something that we both needed. As I entered her home, she led me to a bedroom that I would call my own for as long as I needed. We got reacquainted with one another, as it had been almost a year since I had last seen them. Jesse was still at work when I arrived. Our conversation must have gone on for a couple of hours, while we sipped on some warm tea. She must have noticed I looked tired and asked if I wanted to take a nap before dinner. I nodded my head yes and gave her another hug before I went to rest after that long drive. I let my family know I arrived. Before I fell asleep, I thanked God for getting me there safely.

When Jesse got home from work, I was still asleep. I had a dream that I was at a huge stadium. I was praying over people to get healed. I briefly woke up to the sounds of pots and pans. I went back to sleep and my dream continued. This time, I was doing warfare against the devil, who was trying to stop me from praying over people because he didn't want them to get healed. I kept saying, "Devil, I rebuke you in in Jesus's name! In Jesus's name!" I woke myself up from the sound of my voice. I wondered if they heard me in the kitchen. I laid there for a few minutes, then got up. I slowly snuck into the kitchen to find Jesse's back facing me. He didn't hear me, so I signaled to Esther not to say anything. When I got close enough, I yelled out, "Hey big brother!" I startled him and made him jump. We all laughed and then I hugged him. He said, "I should have known better!"

During dinner, Jesse briefed me on the dos and don'ts around the base. Their house was about six blocks away. He explained the big black bat I saw, was a B-2 Stealth Bomber. I thought it was pretty cool looking. He told me about some of the history of the base and that he would give me a tour the next day. We all sat outside on the swing they had in the front yard, as we enjoyed some ice-cream for dessert. When the sun went down, we all went inside and went to bed. I had a nightmare that Lobo found me and was coming at me to hurt me. I woke up with my heart pounding hard. I was so scared, even though it was just a dream. I had to put my nightlight on. I had a hard time falling back asleep. After I prayed, I dozed off.

Jesse was off work the next day. During breakfast, I shared the nightmare I had. I told them it felt so real and that it really scared me. He showed me where they kept a weapon for security purposes. He bought it for his wife for when he was deployed.

We all hopped into his car, and he made sure I carried my ID and car insurance, so that I can get a pass with him as my sponsor. As we approached the entrance to the front gate, I saw a big sign that read, Welcome to Whiteman Air Force Base. We veered off to the right to go to The Welcome Center building. Jesse took me in to get a visitor pass. Since he did not live on base, it was only good for three days. This would allow me to drive on base without them. We drove to the gate and handed the MP (Military police) our ID's and my pass. We first drove around the base so that I could see where all the main buildings were. It was a very nice base.

There were a couple of lakes with walking trails. I saw a gazebo right off the lake and thought, "That would be a nice
place to spend quiet time with the Lord." I was then taken to the shopping area of the base. There was the main Base Exchange with the food court. There were different little stores and booths that made up the rest of the shopping area
 inside the huge foyer of the building. They also had a military clothing sales store. They had everything you could possibly need. After the grand tour, we went home and Jesse helped me fill out applications online, for a job on base. I was praying for a job so that I could start to work right away.

Only two days later, I got a call for an interview. I got hired for a part time job on base, at the Shopette, which was their gas station. They needed someone to work the night shift, so I took the job. After I got my badge, my boss told me that all I had to do was show it at the gate and I would be allowed on base. Thank God! I would start training the following week. In the meantime, I helped Esther with any preparations she needed for the baby. I painted the nursery for her. She was having a baby girl, so we went all girly in her room. I put the crib together for her since Jesse was at work and preparing to deploy. We went shopping together at the BX (Base Exchange) and bought the cutest clothes. She also drove me around Knob Noster, to show me around. We went to this little restaurant that I ended up loving. They served the best sandwiches and soup ever. Not to mention their teas! We went into a thrift store that had some unique pieces of furniture. I knew I would be going back to pick up some treasures. When we got home, I offered to make dinner so that she could rest. After dinner, I enjoyed sitting outside on their swing. The neighborhood was quiet, and I liked watching people walk their dogs, bike ride, or hang out in

their front yards. I became friends with a couple of the wives

on that street. One was a police officer that lived next door. I
shared my story with her, and she told me that she would
make sure to keep a close watch on things. I gave her a
Photo of Lobo, so she could know what he looks like, just in
case.

After a week, Jesse got orders to deploy. He didn't want
his wife to go to the passenger terminal, where he and
everyone else would fly out. It would just be too hard on her.
His buddy would pick him up and take him. I promised I
would take care of her. We had to say our goodbyes, but
Esther and I would have each other. I was there to comfort
and pray with her. That evening, I had another nightmare.
Lobo found me and was determined to get to me. This time,
I was surrounded by people who were letting him get closer
and closer to me. He deceived them into believing that he
was a good person, despite me trying to warn them. There
was such evil in his eyes. Right before he got to me, I
gasped myself awake. My heart was racing again in fear.
All I could do was call on the name of Jesus. I felt God was
trying to warn me about him.

The next day, I started my new job. As I drove up to the
Military Police on guard, I handed him a picture of Lobo
and explained my concerns about him. The MP assured me
that this man would never get past their gates! He hung
Lobo's picture inside the entry control office's bulletin
board, along with a warning message that stated he was
not to be allowed on base. Lobo had served for a short while,
so I'm sure he would have found a way to try to get through
the gates. I thanked the MP and drove off to my new job.

I got off work in the wee morning hours. Between one
and three a.m. I was there for a few months, when I began

to ask God to open another door for me. I really hated the idea
of having to sell liquor to already intoxicated people, plus
selling porn magazines. Men were always hitting on me and

it made me very uncomfortable.

I started attending the church that Esther took me to. It
was a small non-denominational church, but I could feel the presence of the Holy Spirit in that place. It was called Antioch Christian Fellowship. The pastor and his wife were down to earth. This was the place God would use to bring me back to a place of healing and restoration. I would be taken to a journey with the Lord of a deeper and closer relationship with Him. It was going to cost me to learn hard things and to have to surrender my will and my ways. After what I had been through, I was willing to endure whatever it took to get me on the right path again. My heart was filled with anger, hurt, betrayal, pain, unforgiveness, and fear. All I wanted was to be happy and peaceful again, with my Lord.

I loved Sundays and always looked forward to going to church. God was already working on my heart. He told me that if I wanted to begin the healing process, I had to learn to forgive *all* the people who ever hurt me. I had to learn *true* forgiveness. I suddenly had a vivid vision of Lobo's face appear before me. I could see the piercing hatred in his eyes towards me. It felt as though I were being choked but managed to catch my breath between all the tears that were streaming down my cheeks. I said to God, "Lord, I don't want to forgive Lobo! You saw everything he did to me!" He gently reminded me of all the things we do to Him. What they did to His Son, Jesus. How He gave His only Son to die for us.

*For God so loved the world that He gave His only begotten Son, that whoever believes in Him should not perish but have everlasting life.* (John 3:16)

*But, if you do not forgive, neither will your Father in heaven forgive your trespasses.* (Mark 11:26)

God knows our heart; you can't conceal anything from Him. Again, I spoke to God and said, "Okay Lord. I don't want to forgive Lobo but, I want to be obedient to You. So, I am making the choice to forgive him because *I love You more than I hate him!* You are going to have to help me forgive him." This was extremely hard for me. I would say I forgive him, but then I would take it back. I would keep an account of all the bad stuff he did. Then I would say I forgive him, then I would take it back. It was, like I was playing yo-yo with God. This is one of the hardest things everyone must learn to do. The enemy doesn't want us to forgive. he wants us to harbor that unforgiveness in our hearts, so we can't move forward into the things God has for us. he wants that unforgiveness to turn into bitterness and hate! And that is exactly what happens in our hearts if we do not forgive. We put ourselves at risk hanging on to the anger and hurt. Our thoughts are plagued from the past. This puts us in a spiritual standstill because our heart is filled with a cancerous sickness. Unforgiveness brings sickness to our body. It literally has a physical effect on us.

*For the wages of sin is death, but the gift of God is eternal life in Christ Jesus our Lord.* (Romans 6:23)

Unforgiveness is a sin. satan uses this sin to destroy people's lives. Forgiveness is not for the other person; it is for us. Not only will God not move, but He also cannot move on our behalf, as long as we make the choice to hold on to unforgiveness. When we forgive, it releases God to begin His healing process in us.

If there is anyone reading this, and you know there is someone you need to forgive, please ask God to help you forgive that person right now, in Jesus' name. You will be set free from the sin that keeps you in bondage and control by the enemy.

Jesus died on the cross for all sins. We are all sinners, and we all need to ask Him to forgive us. Who are we not to forgive? It isn't worth going to hell for! Sin cannot enter the kingdom of heaven. If you don't believe me, look on Youtube for the testimonies of people who were taken to hell and brought back to bear witness of people who are suffering there for holding on to unforgiveness and to testify that hell is real. Please, I implore you. Forgive everyone who ever hurt or wronged you, or a loved one. I know it's hard, but God can help you do it. I promise when you do, a heavy burden will be lifted from you, and you will feel the freedom it brings. You too, will bear witness to the healing it brings to your whole being.

*If I regard iniquity (sin) in my heart, the Lord will not hear.* (me) (emphasis mine Psalm 66:18)

*For if you forgive men their trespasses, your heavenly Father will also forgive you. But if you do not forgive men their trespasses, neither will your Father forgive your trespasses.* (Mathew 6:14-15)

Months were going by as I continually sought-after God and His will for my life. Besides church and forming a close relationship with my Savior, I kept myself in shape at the base gym. There were also, a couple of lakes on base that I used to love to go to at night and spend time with God.

I used to have discussions with the Pastors wife who would give me good counsel and insight to the plans God had for me. We would pray together, and I loved her gentle spirit. She used to wear these pretty 60's vintage dresses and hats.

During worship time at church service is when I would really open up my heart to God and surrender my stubborn and willful ways. I would pour out myself to Him knowing that He cared about me. His love would penetrate my heart and soul and through His unconditional love and patience towards me, I was finally able to get to a place of true forgiveness towards Lobo. I know this in my heart because I was able to ask God to bless him.

*"But I say to those who hear, love your enemies, do good to those who hate you, bless those who curse you, and pray for those who spitefully use you." (Hurt or abuse you)* (emphasis mine Luke 6:27-28)

It was at this point that God began to release His healing power in my life. He began to soften my heart. My mind was no longer flooded with thoughts of revenge or playing the same offenses over and over again in my head. Little by little the fear that held and plagued me, left. I was able to leave the house and base without the fear of looking over my
shoulder and behind me to see if I was being followed. God helped me understand what His peace was.

*Do not be anxious about anything, but in every situation, by prayer and petition, with thanksgiving, present your re-quests to God. And the peace of God, which transcends all understanding, will guard your hearts and your minds in Christ Jesus.* (Philippians 4:6-7 NIV)

# An Open Door

There was a huge glassed in bulletin board at the BX (Base Exchange) that was used for announcements and job openings. I would go by from time to time to see if there had been any new jobs posted. On this particular day, I noticed there was a job opening at the Military Clothing Store. The second I read it, I said "Lord please let me get this job." I went to the Military Clothing Store and asked to speak to the manager. It was as though God opened the door for me because she gave me an interview right then and there. She asked me to fill out the application. She told me she had a few more interviews to do, but she would let me know if I got the job.

While we were speaking to each other, there was a connection between us. She was so nice. It turns out she too was a Christian. I got a phone call from her the next day to let me know I got the job! I gave praise and thanks to God for answered prayer. I would be getting more hours, work during the day and more pay. I know I had favor from the Lord. I immediately went to the Shopette to give my resignation. I was more than happy to leave that place. I would start my new job in just a few days. I treated Esther to a celebration
dinner. We were both so happy I didn't have to work at night anymore and I would be there with her. We planned to go
shopping the next day to send Jesse a care package and photos of her seven months baby belly.

## One Last Attempt

There was a knock on the door. It was one of the neighbors telling me that they got a phone call from a man and told them to tell me, to go answer their phone because I needed to know there was a family emergency. For a split second, I was going to go with them, but something stopped me dead in my tracks. My kids had my phone number, so

did my brother. I was horrified, as I pleaded with the neighbor
to tell the man that I no longer lived there and that I moved

away. I told them it was my ex-husband trying to find out where I was. She told me she would do exactly as I asked. I thanked her and closed the door. My heart was pounding really hard, but then I got angry and yelled out, "No! Devil you are a liar! I will not, live in fear!

*For God has not given us a spirit of fear, but of power and love and of a sound mind.* (2 Timothy 1:7)

It has been two and a half months since the divorce. I knew he wouldn't give up. He was actually calling all the neighbors around us who had a listed number. I don't know how he found out the name of my friend's street. I know Jesse's cell phone number was on my old phone bill, but he temporarily cancelled it when he got deployed. I found out later Lobo had called several others on our street that knew me, but they told him they didn't know who I was. I went to the security gate to notify them to keep an extra watch out for him. They told me not to worry. I told God I trusted Him to keep me safe and to keep Lobo far from me.

*I sought the Lord, and He heard me, and delivered me of all my fears.* (Psalm 34:4)

From that moment on, I never heard from him again. I pressed in even harder in prayer and surrender, so that God would show me what I was to do in order to continue moving forward with Him. God told me that I still needed to forgive
some people. The first one He showed me was the *pastor* who had betrayed me. Tears filled my eyes as I was forced to remember what he did to me. I had pushed it to the back

of my mind because I didn't want to face it. The feeling of betrayal encompassed me like a heavy blanket of darkness.

The hurt began to slowly crush my heart and I could feel the

pain throbbing with every heartbeat. My mind began to recollect the deceitful, breach of trust, and false impressions that this pastor tormented me with, which were stored away in a dark hidden dungeon. "Oh God, I can't handle this!" I

cried out. "But you must," He replied with such gentleness. "I need Your help, Lord." I said, as I was crying. "I am right hear with you, as I have always been," He said.

When you ask God for something, be ready to face the truth about yourself. It hurts! What hurt more was the pain this pastor caused because he knew my heart and I trusted him. He was my spiritual leader, and I was wronged by him in such a deep, personal, and spiritual way. If I could compare the pain, it would be no different than the stranger who raped me. Because this pastor *knew* me.

I could barely breath as I knelt before the Lord in such torment. I took all the pain, hurt, betrayal, and anger and laid it at the foot of the cross. I told Jesus, "I forgive the pastor. I don't want to carry all this agony in my heart anymore. Please take it far from me." I then proceeded to

forgive all the people at my church who had been judging me and talking about me behind my back. I felt another layer of

weight lift off that made me feel so much lighter. I felt a refreshing freedom come sweep over me. I was no longer bound to this debilitating and draining spirit that had attached itself to me. My tears of sorrow were now, tears of joy and gratitude for the love of my Father.

*Weeping may endure for the night, but joy comes in morning.* (Psalm 30:5)

*Therefore, if the Son makes you free, you shall be free indeed.* (John 8:36)

The next month was filled with the joy of my new job, my time in church, and spending time with my *brother* and *sister*. It seemed as though Jesse was only home for a little while when he got sent right back out to deploy. This was so hard on Esther. I shared in her tears and tried to comfort her as best a sister could do. I had no fear for Jesse's life, nor for any of my family. I knew they were kept safe. A lady had asked me once," Aren't you afraid for your brother's life? Or for any of your other family in the military? I would be terrified." I told her with boldness, "Not at all. God is always with them to protect them. My son says that he carries God in his pocket." She replied, "Well, you have a lot stronger faith than I do, that's for sure."

### Safety of Abiding in the Presence of God

*[1] He who dwells in the secret place of the Most High shall abide under the shadow of the Almighty.[2] I will say of the Lord, "He is my refuge and my fortress; My God, in Him I will trust."[3] Surely He shall deliver you from the snare of the fowler And from the perilous pestilence.[4] He shall cover you with His feathers, And under His wings you shall take refuge; His truth shall be your shield and buckler.[5] You shall not be afraid of the terror by night, Nor of the arrow that flies by day,[6] Nor of the pestilence that walks in darkness, Nor of the destruction that lays waste at noonday.[7] thousand may fall at your side, And ten thousand at your right hand; But it shall not come near you.[8] Only with your eyes shall you look, And see the reward of the wicked.[9] Because you have made the Lord, who is my refuge, Even the Most High, your dwelling place,[10] No evil shall befall you, Nor shall any plague come near your dwelling;[11] For He shall give His angels charge over you, To keep you in all your ways.*

*¹² In their hands they shall bear you up, Lest you dash your foot against a stone.¹³ You shall tread upon the lion and the cobra, The young lion and the serpent you shall trample underfoot.¹⁴ "Because he has set his love upon Me, therefore I will deliver him; I will [e]set him on high, because he has known My name¹⁵ He shall call upon Me, and I will answer him; I will be with him in trouble; I will deliver him and honor him.¹⁶ With long life I will satisfy him And show him My salvation." (Psalm 91)*

During my time at work, I met a lot of new people. Some I liked, some I didn't. I was in my season of being restored. The last thing on my mind was men. Wouldn't you know that the enemy would send them in to hit on me, ask me out, and try to entice me with their smooth talk. It was as if, I was wearing a neon sign that stated, *Single and Available*. I would reply back with irritation to some of them and ask,
"Isn't that a wedding ring?" they would say "So." Oh, how this disgusted me! It made me want nothing to do with men even more. All I cared about was my walk with God.

Someone had once told me, "I bet after what you went through, you never want to get married again." I replied and said, "No, all the more I want to get married. If the enemy tried to take me out with this last one, that only means my true husband is everything I have been praying for. I refuse to let the enemy steal the desires of my heart!"

*Delight yourself also in the Lord, and He shall give you the desires of your heart. Commit your way to the Lord, trust also in Him, and He shall bring it to pass. (Psalm 34:4-5)*

I was in constant prayer and seeking the Lord. I went to church every chance I had. If they had an extra service during the week, I was there. If they had special speakers come in that lasted a few days, I was there. All I listened to was Christian music. This helped me stay focused on my walk with God and reminded me of all the goodness of the Lord. My faith and strength in the Lord were at an all-time high. I felt in my spirit, nothing could bring me down.

There was a young man at church that I ran into after service. He looked to be in his early twenty's. I don't remember his name, nor do I remember how we got on the subject of marriage. I do remember him telling me, "You are going to meet your husband within a six-month period, and you will be engaged, but not for long." I just shrugged my shoulders and said "Really? That sounds good to me." I walked off, not taking to heart what he said, since I didn't even know him, other than casual greetings at church. I honestly didn't care anymore. I was in a place of being content with my walk and relationship with Jesus; nothing else mattered to me. My favorite time was in worshiping Him. I just wanted to be in His presence all the time. I knew that Jesus was and always has been my spouse since the moment I asked Him to come into my heart. He was all I needed. I depended on Him for everything. He is my true love! He loves me unconditionally and He accepts me just the way I am. He is the source of my protection, He gives me peace that I can't understand, He provides all that I need and want, He is my Savior, and I am His bride. Jesus is the One who died on the cross for me and took all my sins, sickness, and disease. He is the One who saved me and set me free! His love for me is perfect.

As you can see, the Lord is still at work in my life and is still by my side no matter what. Therefore, I have come to a place of being in complete peace and total surrender, commitment, and contentment, knowing that He is my everything. He is my spouse. My joy in this knowledge, is knowing how much He loves me. I know in my heart He does

have that husband for me. The one I have been praying for. Any day, any time, at any given moment, I know God will bring this amazing man into my life and he will be my perfect match. I am already *in love* with my husband because I am *in love* with Jesus. I know that he is going to be everything that I have asked God for.

It was one Sunday, in particular, that worship seemed to be more intimate than any other. I could feel the presence of the Lord so strongly, all I could do was stand there with my arms open wide. I felt wave after wave of His mercy, grace, and love penetrate through my body, to my soul, and then pummel into my spirit. I could barely keep my balance and thought I would fall out under His power, right there

where I stood. What a perfect song, "Holy Spirit Rain Down" for that intimate time shared with my Love. I did indeed *feel*

*His power fall*, as the song continued. I can't recall how long worship lasted, or the other songs that were sung. I was in a place of complete abandonment with my Savior, as *He hid me under the shadow of His wings.* The sermon was full of robust life as that is how the pastor preached. Always full of life. As the service came to a close, everyone was saying their goodbyes, or carrying on in conversations with each other.

I was in an ecstatic state as I walked from where I was sitting, to the front of the church to greet the pastors. I approached the pastor's wife and saw her husband talking to someone. I hugged her and we began speaking about how awesome the service was. I told her what I experienced, and she shared with me some of her own experiences. I was so in awe of how God draws near to us when we draw near to Him. The pastors prayed over me and then I left to go home and help Esther run some errands.

We are now in the month of November. It is very cold, wet, windy, and muggy from the rain the day before. I am running into work because it looks like it's going to rain again. I am covered in my long black coat. I have a scarf wrapped around my neck, but the wind is blowing so hard, it looks like someone is holding me back by the ends of my scarf. I'm trying not to slip and fall while running in my boots. I reach the glass doors as they open automatically, and I feel the warmth from the heaters in the building. I shake off the shiver from the cold outside and begin shedding my coat, gloves, and scarf. I walk into my workplace and see the smiling face of my boss as she greets me good morning. She said to me, "It's going to be a cold one!" And I say, "It already is!" I put my things in my locker in the back room and proceed to stock everything that our inventory was getting low on.

There were two other ladies I worked with. If one ran the register, the other would stock. We didn't all work the same day, but there were always two of us. I really loved my job. I was very good at it. I learned all the different ranks, uniforms, ribbons, patches, and accessories. It was all military clothing and a lot more that was sold in our store. We were always busy, someone always needed help, and we got to personally know a lot of the regulars. Time went by fast, and it was fun.

# A Glimpse of My Husband

One of the high-ranking officers who was one of our regulars, came into the store and said very loudly, "It's Snowing!" I thought he was joking. You see, we didn't have

a window to look out because we were attached to the inside
the huge foyer that led down the hall to the Base Exchange.

It was kind of a miniature mall. I asked my manager if I could run and look, because the last time I saw snow was back in 1985 when it snowed in my hometown. She let me go and when I went outside, I saw the most beautiful white landscape. I was so excited! The snowflakes were coming down softly and then a gust of wind came and swooped them up back into the air, while another layer of beautiful white flakes came to take their place. I stood there under the falling white crystals feeling that each one that fell was a blessing and gift from God. I held out my hands trying to catch some of them. It is astonishing to me to know that God created each flake different. Not one of them is alike. Just like He created us.

While I was under this beautiful covering, I had a vision. God showed me the back of my husband! I saw him with his arms crossed over on a table with his head resting on his arms. He was dark skinned and had a high and tight haircut. He was wearing a white undershirt and he had very broad shoulders and muscular arms. I thought to myself, "Oh. He looks like a boxer." I was excited that I got a glimpse of the back of my husband. My heart was stirred up for him and I began to pray for him.

The officer that had announced it was snowing was outside now, watching my excitement. Little did he know my excitement was of a double portion. I didn't have a coat on. I forgot to grab it, nor did I feel the freeze until he asked if I
wanted to borrow his weatherproof PT jacket. I said "Yes, please." As soon as I put it on, I ran to the white covered grass, laid down, and made a snow angel with my arms and legs. He laughed as I gave him back his jacket covered in snow. I thanked him and went back inside to finish my day. The angel I left lying in the snow was an imprint of a new

beginning, filled with the purity of God's love for me, along with all the blessings that were to follow. I was ready to fly!

*But those who wait on the Lord shall renew their strength they shall mount up with wings like Eagles, they shall run and not be weary, they shall walk and not faint. (Isaiah 40:31)*

# Chapter 19

# An Encounter With My Future Spouse

I remember it was a cold November day when the man I would marry walked into my life. I just didn't know it at the time. The register faced the front door, so we could see everyone who walked in. I heard him talking to a friend of his, saying that he had gotten orders to Germany. This sparked my attention because I had been there before, visiting someone at the time and I had prayed to God and said, "Lord, one of these days I would like to come back and actually tour this beautiful place." I was only there for about two weeks, but what I saw put me in awe of the beauty of God's creation.

After the word Germany came out of his mouth, I said to him, "Oh, you got orders Germany?" He looked at me and said, "Yeah, you want to go with me?" I thought to myself, "Oh, great, another typical ------- hitting on me."

He and his friend continued to shop the clothing store. They split up and he came around the counter to where I was standing. He started talking to me as he laid his head on his arm to rest. He talked about how tired he was after a long hard week, how he was separated from his wife for a year now, he had three daughter's and I don't remember much else. All the conversation kind of just faded away, as I wanted to know just one thing. I do remember asking him, "Are you Christian?" I didn't even want to be talking to him if he wasn't. He answered and said, "Yes, I am a Christian." He wrote his name and number on a piece of paper and asked if I wanted to get some coffee or go out somewhere, to give him a call. I just took the piece of paper and I put it away somewhere and forgot about it. I had no intention of calling him. There was absolutely no attraction towards this man for me. All I could remember about him, was that he had dark skin. After he and his friend left the store, I saw him walk down the foyer towards the BX and disappear. I thought nothing of it. God, however, had set up this divine meeting for the both of us. He would reconnect us at a later date and time. A time that I had no clue or inclination. Not a sign, signal, indicator, trace, or tip-off. This connection would take place ALL in His perfect timing.

I began folding a huge pile of BDU's (Battle Dress Uniform) and separating them by sizes. The phone rang and

as I answered, "Thank you for calling Military Clothing Sales, this is Jasmine, how may I help you?" Esther answers,

"Jasmine, I'm in labor!" I said, "Ok. Call 911 and..." Before I could finish my sentence, she told me she was already at the hospital, and they were putting her in a room. "I'll be there as soon as I can!" I replied. I went to the back office to ask my manager if I could leave because my sister was at the hospital in labor. Without hesitation, she let me go and told me not to worry about having to come back to finish my shift. She would let me make up the hours. How generous, she was.

I got to the hospital and found the room Esther was in. She was surrounded by nurses and her doctor. She was ready to deliver. She asked if I could stay with her, since her husband was deployed, and they said yes. I held her hand and prayed with her, while she began to push. After about the fourth really hard push, her baby girl was born. We both cried as she was placed in her mother's arms to meet for the first time. I was taking pictures for her, so she could show Jesse the birth of their daughter. She was beautiful. She had blue eyes with a lot of curly blond hair, like her mommy. She was named Emily Jane, after both their mothers. What a joy it was to share such precious moments with my sister. I so wished Jesse could have been there. Esther's mom arrived the next day and planned to stay for a couple of weeks to help her daughter. This was perfect since I had to work during the day.

December came along like a fairytale book. Driving from the house or off base, was always like a drive out to the country. I loved the snow and the cold air mixed with the hustle and bustle of Christmas. Roads and trees were covered in white crystals. The strings of lights that hung across the roads in the small towns, the big red bows fastened to the streetlights, and the decorated stores and coffee shops made it all look so picturesque.

There were people driving around with the tree they handpicked, tied to the top of their cars or the back of their pickups. You could see the stained-glass windows that glowed from the inside of the churches. All of this just seemed to be part of a fairytale story. I had no idea it was my own.

I just love Christmas time. My favorite scene is that of the Nativity. When I see the baby Jesus swaddled in cloth, laying in a manger, it reminds me of the great sacrifice He made for the salvation of the world. His birth, death, and resurrection were His sole purpose for coming to reconcile us to our Father. What a perfect and priceless gift He has given us. His life for ours!

Going to church on Sundays during this festive season seemed to magnify my yearning for the Lord's purpose for my life. Listening to the praise team and all the congregation lift their voices to the Lord was so delightful to my heart. Almost every song we sang, had a deep meaning and was pertinent to my life, thus far. It made me wonder if people were really singing with grateful hearts or just singing the words. Surely, God had touched their lives in one way or another. I was the last person to question the actions of anyone else. I pushed back those thoughts and went back into my intimate place with my Lord. Worship is my passion!

Christmas parties were spent with my friends from work. I even went to one with a male that turned out to be nothing. Just the enemy trying to lure me back into a sinful

life. December ended with me in prayer and gratefulness for all the things Jesus did for me.

A New Year, a new beginning! It was now January 2003. Esther and I, along with some of our neighbors brought in the new year watching the fireworks that the base displayed for all the military families to enjoy. Although the fireworks

can be seen from miles away. January brought in more cold-weather and more snow. Sometimes the snow would melt into a literal muddy slush. It reminded me of a drink called Mud Slide. I liked the refreshing cold air in my face and the fact that I got to wear sweaters and jackets. Yes, even boots! I never got to wear this clothing back in my state of Texas. It gets pretty hot there. Even though I missed my hometown and family, I still got to talk to my children on the phone and keep in touch.

The month went by fast as I continued to focus on my walk with God, doing the best I could at work, and trying to stay fit at the gym.

Men continued to come into my workplace and flirt with me, ask me out on dates, and pass their phone numbers that went straight into private file 13 (trash). They would try my patience, as I helped them get fitted with their uniforms. Some of them were as young as my son. All I could do was laugh on the inside. I had always looked much younger than my real age. Again, thanks to my mom who had the most beautiful complexion and looked amazing for having thirteen children.

# February

Another Sunday, February nineth, another day to give thanks and praise. For some unknown reason I felt exceptionally happy that day. It was Sunday before

Valentine's Day. Usual Sunday of praise and worship, preaching, and prayer. Always uplifting and encouraging. After-wards, I felt led to go speak to the pastor's wife. Her name was Carolyn. She always carried the sweet presence of

the Holy Spirit on her, which made her vintage clothing all the more stunning. We greeted each other with a hug and smiles. We asked each other the usual questions. How are you? How are things going? She asked how Esther and Emily were doing, knowing that Jesse was deployed. After answering all the questions with, things are fine, Esther and the baby are well, but it was too cold for them to come, and I was doing exceptionally well, I added this: "You know Carolyn, I have finally come to a place of contentment in my life. I don't care when God is going to send my spouse. I don't worry who he is or look around thinking if that could be him. I don't wonder how we're going to meet or where. I don't even care when we're going to meet. I am already in love with him, whoever he is. Right now, all I care about is God. My relationship with Him is the most important thing to me right now. I have come to depend on Him completely for everything that I need. He gives all my provisions, protects me beyond measure, and loves me without fail. He is all I need. Knowing how much He loves us, how He desires to answer our prayers, how He cherishes our time together, how He knows the depths of our soul........(tears flowing down my face), How can anyone long for someone else?" She wrapped her gracious arms around me and then pulled back with her hands on my shoulders and said, "You know Jasmine, don't be surprised if you meet your husband in a couple of weeks." I wiped my tears and said, "That would be nice." I walked away and joined my co-worker, who started attending church with me, as we went off to enjoy lunch together; this was our tradition after church.

# Sweetheart Day

Valentine's Day was filled with couples holding hands, shopping at the BX for heart-shaped candy boxes, balloons and flowers, cards, and gifts. I was off that day and was visiting all the little shopping booths that aligned the outside

section of the Foyer. What better excuse than to buy myself some chocolates.

I could have made this day sad for myself. Another year and another celebration spent alone. No one to hold my hand, no one to give me a kiss, no one to bring me flowers, no one to say I love you. Instead, I knew I had the greatest of love's walking right beside me. I had the most wonderful hand in mine, I had someone who was always there for me, good or bad times, I had a heart filled with unconditional love, which was pure and forever lasting. I had the one and only perfect man in my life, my Jesus, my spouse. I walked very proud that day!

# Chapter 20

# Our First Date

It was almost two weeks later February twentieth, 2003, on a brisk Thursday morning, that I am at work and see the same man that had given me his phone number, three months earlier, walk in the door. As soon as I saw his face, I cringed in thought and said to myself, "Oh, crap, I never called this guy!" He looked at me and as he did, I smiled and

asked, "Hi. You still going to Germany?" He said, "Yes. I told you, you have six months to figure out if you're going with

me or not." All I could think to myself was, "Why does he keep saying that? I don't even know him!" He and the same friend

that was with him back in November walked to the back end of the store to pick up a shadow box they had ordered.

He came around the counter again, where I was standing and started talking to me. He was in uniform, so I looked at his name badge. They only put the last name on it. It read Hartswick. Then I looked at his sleeve to see what rank he was. He was a Master Sergeant. Ok, I thought, He has been in for a while already. I started to look at him closely so that I could see what type of features he had. He was tall, dark skinned, and had very broad shoulders. He was clean cut, clean shaved, and had light brown eyes.

I found myself telling him, "I'm sorry I didn't call you; I misplaced your phone number." I really did forget where I had put his number. I know I didn't throw it away, like I did all the other ones. He wrote his number down again, slid it to me and said, "Here is my number again, call me, no excuses this time." I took the piece of paper and stuck it in my pocket. He and his friend walked out as they did three months ago. At that point, I still didn't know his first name. I reached into my pocket, looked at the paper and I thought, "Oh, his name is Thomas."

I continued my workday, thinking about the idea of calling this man. I argued with myself not to, then I talked myself into it by saying, "If anything, I could get a free meal out of it." So, I decided I would wait a day before I called him. It was Saturday morning on February twenty first. I was off that day and had nothing planned. It was cold with some snow on the ground. After much debating, I delved deep to cultivate enough courage to call Thomas. As the phone was ringing, I just took a deep breath and said, "Ok, Lord..." I heard his voice answer. "Hello" I felt like a schoolgirl calling her boyfriend. I proceeded with, "Hi. This is Jasmine. You said to call if I wanted to get some coffee or something." He said, "Hold on. Listen..." I listened to the sounds of a piano being played. I could almost feel the notes vibrating into the phone, as my heart began to melt." OMG! He was playing the piano for me! After he was done serenading me over the phone, he told me that he had written the music. "That was really nice, I said." He asked me what I was doing that day and I told him I had no plans. "Do you want to go out this evening?" he asked. I said, "Sure, come pick me up at my brother's house." I gave him my address and hung up.

I was a little nervous now. I was actually going out on a date! I remember wearing a black pair of dress slacks with a long sleeve white blouse. I wore black boots and the ever so soft black leather Lamb jacket my brother Christopher bought me. I remember he said he just wanted to buy me something nice. It wasn't my birthday, Christmas, or any special day. Just a beautiful gift from my little brother.

When Thomas came to pick me up, he drove up in a white minivan. Yes, I was looking to see what he drove. He came to the door and knocked. I opened the door and greeted him. Then I introduced him to Esther. I hugged her goodbye and went to the passenger side to get in. He opened the door for me. I thought, "Oh, a Gentleman." Our destination was Kansas City, Missouri. I had been there maybe twice, to go shopping at the mall, with Jesse and Esther. We went during the daytime, and it was a very nice scenic drive, so I was kind of excited to see what the mall and city looked like at

nighttime. The drive was just a little over an hour, so that gave us time to have a good conversation and get acquainted with one another. We carried on casual conversation for a little while. I found out he was half German, half Filipino. Hence the name, Hartswick. He could have passed for

Spanish, Hawaiian, or Samoan. He told me he got his dark skin from his mom who was Filipino and his size from his dad who was German with blonde hair and blue eyes. I then proceeded to tell him my tragic story and how I ended up living off base with my brother. He told me his story and how he had been separated from his wife for a year and that she too, was in the military. He told me more about his three daughters. He also shared how long he had been in the service and what his job was.

The drive seemed extra-long, as we finally approached the twinkling lights of the city limits. I was right. It looked so much prettier at night with all the different colored lights and Christmas décor. I rolled my window down to get a good breath in of the fresh cold air.

It was right about dinner time, so he took me to a very nice Italian restaurant, called Milano's. When the hostess led us to our table, Thomas pulled the chair out for me to sit. The food was splendid. We continued talking to each other with this sense of perceptiveness between us. I couldn't put my finger on it, but I was surprisingly comfortable with him. As if, we had known each other for a long time. We had a glass of wine and when we finished our dinner, of course, dessert. All I remember was this chocolate, chocolate mousse, more chocolate, and cake. It was ssssoooo good! It was meltable in my mouth. I remember trying to control my pleasure in this almost sinful dessert.

The atmosphere was very pleasurable. Soft music was playing, candles were lit on our table, and other people that surrounded us were keeping their conversations at a minimal level. I was very impressed with the way our date was going. After we were finished, he pulled my chair out for me. We walked towards the exit, and he held the door open. It was chilly and frosty and outside, so he helped me get my jacket back on. There were white lights hanging everywhere. They made the evening feel very tranquil. We started to walk across the street because we noticed there was an outside skating area. It was enclosed with a small brick wall and benches around it. The solid ice looked like a frozen hue of blue water with the reflection of the hanging lights over it. There were areas with a little snow and ice on the ground. I was trying not to slip and fall when Thomas held out his hand to help me. I put my hand in his and something about his touch made me feel like it belonged there. As we stood watching the skaters, he asked, "Do you want to skate?" I had to respond with, "I had a really bad back injury that needed surgery. I would be afraid of falling and injuring myself again." He said, "I'll hold on to you." As much as I was tempted, I had to decline. I was just enjoying everyone else that was skating.

I noticed that we were still holding hands when I turned to look at him. I just realized how tall he was. I was a whole 5 feet one and a half inches, and he was six feet tall. He was wearing a black dress shirt, a pair of jeans and a short black overcoat. Even in the gentle gust of winds I could smell his cologne. For some reason I was tuned in to the details of his features, that I didn't even notice before. I looked at his eyes and they seemed to turn hazel in the twinkling lights. Then
I noticed his lips. I thought to myself, he has really nice lips. They were full and his upper lip was perfectly defined. I just noticed; this guy is kind of handsome. As I was still in observance, it started snowing! The flakes seemed to be like magical dust flowing down from heaven. He must have noticed me looking at him. He reached his other arm around

my waist and kissed me. Oh, Lord...I got *"flutterbies!"* (Not butterflies)

Our evening ended with us holding hands, while the glorious snow surrounded our walk back to his vehicle. The drive home seemed to be shorter than the drive up. I remember we listened to music, talked, and continued holding hands. Something was stirring inside my heart, and I knew God was up to something. Thomas drove slowly into the driveway, parked, got off the van and helped me down. He walked me to the door and yes...another kiss goodnight. I felt like a barbie doll in his arms. My *"flutterbies"* seemed to be whisked away with a gentle breeze. I thanked him for a wonderful evening. He got into his van but waited until I got inside. My sister was already in bed. I'm kind of glad she was because I had the biggest smile on my face. I felt like I was floating on ice.

**That was the most perfect date ever!**

# Chapter 21

# The Revelations

**Revelation definition: (Oxford Dictionary)**

**1.** Surprising and previously unknown fact, especially one that is made known in a dramatic way.

**2.** The making known of something that was previously secret or unknown.

The next day, Tom (this is what I call him) called me and we

engaged in a very excited conversation about our date. We shared with each other how we both enjoyed it, then he asked me, "Would you like to go out with me again?" I replied, "Yes, I would, thank you." The next three days were filled with phone calls, visits, and dates. I don't know what it was, but it seemed like this whirlwind just came in and swept us both off our feet. By the third day, I knew that I loved this man. I knew that I was supposed to be with him and that he was the one I prayed for all those years. I just felt it in my heart. That was the work God was stirring up inside me. Remember that I wasn't attracted to him when we first met? Well, God made him attractive to me because he was my husband. Tom had even asked me, "Do you love me?" As strange and unusual as it was, "I told him yes!" He replied, "I love you too." We embraced and just held on to the moment we were in.

## Truth Be Told

Tom had a side job working for Pizza Hut, delivering pizza. He said he got the job so that he could hang out with his oldest daughter, Bailey, who also worked there. He would sometimes pick me up, so that I could keep him company while delivering pizza's on and off base. During these times he would really open up and tell me everything he felt I should know. He told me that the reason he was separated, was because he had an affair. He said he had asked God to forgive him, his wife and children, and even his church. They all had forgiven him. He was truly sorry for what he did. He
was being very honest and open with me. As he continued his confession, the phone rang. He ignored it. It rang again. He ignored it again. Then it kept ringing and ringing. I

asked him who was calling him. He said, with remorse, "It's her.
The woman I had the affair with." I am going to call her

Cozbi, which in Hebrew means liar/deceiver. He explained to me that she was a married woman with two boys. Cozbi had told him that if he told his wife, she would tell her husband, and they could then be together. Well, she never told her husband, so Tom felt like he lost everything for nothing. She kept playing him like a puppet, stringing him along, and causing more pain and damage in his life. This woman literally had the delusion to believe and tell Tom that it was God who brought them together. No, it was satan, using a jezebel spirit through this woman to destroy his marriage, his family, and his life. God would never destroy a marriage or family, much less two. The point is, it's been a year and she was still playing him for a fool. She played with him like he was a toy soldier. She messed up his mind and emotions.

He couldn't turn his phone off during deliveries. I sat there and listened to everything he had to share. He even told me that he was struggling, trying to get her OUT of his life. I told Tom that he was going to have to tell her to quit calling him once and for all. After his last delivery, the phone rang for the twentieth time. I told him to answer it. I could hear that she was extremely upset because he didn't answer his phone on demand. He interrupted her and said, "Look, I met someone, and she is my girlfriend now. I don't need you, nor do I want you in my life anymore. Stop calling me!" She became extremely irate because now, she lost control over him. She is a master puppeteer! He hung up on her and turned off his phone. This began an absurd number of voice mails, phone calls, and emails. All to which she tried manipulation, guilt, threats, and lies. Cozbi really poured out everything she could to trap Tom for life. There is so much more to this woman, but I won't get into all of this now.

## These are some of the traits of a jezebel spirit: (it can be male or female)

This seducing spirit is adept at using all sorts of manipulative tactics, especially flattery. The jezebel spirit is very evil and has been said to be like "the bride of satan." It will often work closely with a demonic network in order to conceal its presence and activities, so it can be difficult to identify and break free of. Some characteristics of the jezebel spirit in its outward appearance have been likened to narcissism *(Lobo)*

*https://truthinreality.com/2013/09/24/30-consistent-traits-of-the-jezebel-spirit/*

Tom dropped me off at home. He shared some more about his relationship with Cozbi. Again, he was very open with me and told me everything. He was humble, vulnerable, and very sorrowful. The night ended with a quiet goodnight.

## The Vision

As I entered my bedroom, I sat there and began to talk to God. I remember telling Him, "Lord! Are you sure this is the man I prayed for? He has a lot of issues!" He immediately showed me a vision of Tom in this bright shining armor. The body of armor looked to be made of a titanium and diamond mixture. It had such a brilliant, yet luminous shine to it. His helmet was attached to the armor, and it had a crown with seven points. I knew that the points represented the seven spirits of God. The beautiful crest on the crown was a crimson red cross that illuminated pure rays of light coming from the center of it. His breastplate was made of a translucent emerald jewel, divided into three sections, and outlined in gold that seemed to rhythmically move in a whirling motion. His shield was huge and made of a chromium steal alloy. It looked like an enormous amber stone was in the middle with flames of fire coming forth from it. Held in his hand was a sword made of the purest diamond, radiating iridescent colors of all kinds, and the handle was of lustrous pearl. I knew that it was God Himself who sharpened his sword. This is the best description of the vision I saw, with my limited vocabulary. I couldn't do it justice. God let me know after all was said and done, Tom would be a strong warrior for His kingdom. I said, "Ok God, I'll wait for that man." I fell asleep knowing that God was working in his life. I didn't share this with anyone for quite a while.

## The Rug

One day after a few weeks, Tom asked me if I wanted to see where he lived and have dinner with him at his house. I told him yes. He gave me his address, which was in Knob Noster. As he greeted me at the door and let me inside, I felt like I knew the place or that it was very familiar to me. I couldn't understand why. I had never been there before. I looked at the rug in the living room and there was a hole in it that seemed to be frazzled on the ends. It looked like a burnt hole. I asked him, "What happened there?" He said, "I don't know. It was there when I moved in." He had already started dinner, which was spaghetti and meat sauce. It smelled good. That became my favorite meal. He had a drink, then another. It was getting late, so I told him I was

387

going to go home before it got too dark. We kissed and said goodnight.

# The Lie Of Condemnation

As we continued to see each other, maybe another week went by when I began to be concerned about him. During the times he would have an early exercise or training in the morning, I would go see him at night. He would be drinking. This wasn't just a normal drink. He would have a bottle of Jack Daniel's every time I saw him. Sometimes he was rude and mean to me. I would leave, but he would always call to apologize.

I began to pray on his behalf. I asked the Lord to prepare Tom's heart to reveal the truth about his drinking. I knew what the cause of this destructive behavior was, but I needed the words to explain it to him in a loving manner. It didn't take long before I had the opportunity to talk with him. I went over one day after work for dinner. He greeted me at the door, and we sat down until the food was ready. He grabbed the bottle of Jack, but before he could pour his drink, I gently held my hand over his glass. I told him that I needed to share something with him. He hesitated, but then agreed to listen. I asked him, "Why do you drink?" He said, "I don't know, because I like it." I held his face in my hands and said, "When you ask God to truly forgive you for your sins, He immediately does forgive you and He doesn't remember that sin anymore." He said, "I know that He forgave me and so did my family."

*There is therefore now no condemnation to those who are in Christ Jesus, who do not walk according to the flesh, but according to the Spirit.* (Romans 8:1)

*For I will be merciful to their unrighteousness, and their sins and their lawless deeds I will remember no more."* (Hebrews 8:12)

"Yes, they did," I said. "But now you have to forgive yourself. Your mind is being filled with so many tormenting thoughts of condemnation. This is what the enemy wants. It's filling your thoughts with being a failure as a husband and father. This isn't true. The guilt, anger, and shame of that sin has already been washed away, but he wants you to think that it hasn't. That is why he keeps flooding your thoughts with guilt. And you drink to mask the pain and guilt away. You now have to forgive yourself!"

*And whenever you stand praying, if you have anything against anyone, (including yourself) forgive him, that your Father in heaven may also forgive you your trespasses.* (Emphasis mine) (Mark 11:25)

With tears falling down his face, Tom says this prayer with me.

"Father God, I come to you right now in my brokenness, knowing that You have already forgiven me of my sins. I make the choice now, to forgive myself. I render powerless, all the words the enemy has whispered into my ears. I release myself from the power of condemnation over my life. I thank You Lord, that I am set free from my sin, through Your blood and in the name of Jesus. Amen."

I held him in my arms until he let out a huge sigh of relief, wiped away his tears, and then said to me, "Thank you for praying with me." We ate dinner and I could see that his
countenance was more at peace.

I thanked God for this opportunity. If we were going to be together, then we needed to learn to share things that were going to impact our relationship. We also needed to humble ourselves before the Lord.

# The Introduction

I invited Tom to go to church with me. I told Esther I would meet her there, and whoever got there first, would save seats for the other. Service seemed to be extra special that day. I absolutely loved that we were worshiping together. As we held hands, I would look up at him from time to time and notice tears in his eyes. This brought tears to my own eyes, as I thanked God for bringing this man into my life. When he began to sing, I was moved by the sound of his voice. It was smooth and pleasing to hear.

As usual, the pastor preached a good sermon. He talked about restoration. It seemed as though this subject was chosen, just for me. It really touched my heart. I guess it touched Tom too, because he was holding my hand pretty tight and smiled at me with a look of gratitude. After the service, I asked Esther to wait for us, so that I could introduce Tom to the pastors. As we approached, Caroline and I met with our eyes and a big smile on both our faces. I told her, "You were right! This is Tom, the man I believe is the one I have been praying for. I met him exactly two weeks after you told me, "Don't be surprised if you meet your husband in a couple of weeks." "I told you!" she said. We had

a brief conversation with her and Pastor Harvey. They prayed for us, for guidance and blessings. We said our goodbyes with a hug.

# The House

A few days went by, and Esther got word that Jesse was coming home. There was much excitement in the air! I had to work the day he came home, but that was ok. It gave him and his wife time to be alone and he could meet his daughter. When I got off work, I hurried home to greet my brother. I was so thankful that God always protected him and brought him safely home to his wife, and now his child.

I began to tell him about Tom. I told him how we met, what rank he was and what his job was. I then told him where he lived and even about the burn mark on his rug in the living room. With a startled voice, my brother says, "Oh my God! That is the house I lived in by myself, before I brought Esther from her mom's house to live here." "What?" I said. I made sure to give him the address, just in case, but it was the exact house. He even said that the same burn mark was there when he had moved in. No wonder it felt familiar to me. My brother lived in the same house! I was taken back a bit with the knowledge that my brother, and the man I met and loved, lived in the same house. What are the odds of that happening? Only God knew the reason for that.

Tom came over to meet my brother. They had a lot to talk about. When Esther brought in their baby girl, Tom said he could remember when his girls were just as tiny, and Emily Jane brought back memories. I eventually met Tom's daughters. Bailey was the eldest, then Becca, (short for Rebecca) and Tori (short for Victoria). They were all beautiful, smart, and they could sing. It would take time for them to get used to me, since they weren't used to seeing their daddy with another woman besides their mom. I didn't

blame them. They loved both their parents and I know their separation was hard on them.

It began to bother me knowing that Tom was still legally married. I asked him if there was any chance of him and his wife getting back together, that I would gladly step out of the picture. I didn't want to be known as "the other woman", even though I met him a year after the fact. I loved him, but I needed to do what was right in my heart. He told me they were going to have one last lunch together to figure out their final plans. I said, "Ok. Just let me know what you decide to do."

The evening came quick. I was sitting on the swing in front of the house. Tom pulled up and got out of his van, still in his uniform. I said, "Well, what's the verdict?" "She said she's done," he replied. I felt myself let out a sigh of relief, even though I kind of felt bad. We sat there slowly swinging back and forth, as the cool wind caused us to cuddle up together. My phone rang. It was my eldest daughter Angela, calling to say hello. Tom laid his head in my lap while we caught up.

Time went on, as June was upon us. We continued to go to church together. The pastor from his old church invited us to sing at some of their services. Tom sang high tenor, and I sang soprano. I so, enjoyed singing with him. I felt a close and special connection between us when we worshiped together but, I was still bothered that he was still married. I told him that something was going to have to happen with his situation if we were going to continue with our relationship.

The next day, he called to inform me that his wife filed for divorce. It would only take two months for the divorce to be final since they had already been separated for a year.

I began to really press into what God wanted for me. I know that He showed me the vision of Tom in his armor, but I really didn't want to make another mistake that would cost me later. I began to have doubts about this relationship, but I thought it could be the enemy, trying to stop me from being with the spouse God had chosen for me. I already loved him, but I wanted to be one hundred percent sure.

## The Confirmation

I got into my room, closed the door, and really prayed fervently. I decided I would ask God something, just in my heart to Him, so the enemy couldn't hear me. You see, the devil can't read our minds. He can just watch our reactions, our behavior, and hear what we say. He uses our own words against us all the time. I wanted another confirmation that would seal this relationship once and for all. I said in my mind from my heart, "Dear Father God, I'm asking for another confirmation from You about Tom. I'm going to ask for something specific. If he ever asks me how to say queen in Spanish, then I will know without a shadow of doubt, he is from You." I concluded my prayer thanking my Lord for being a faithful God. I did not share my request to anyone. I kept it between me and God alone.

Tom was very busy getting ready for his PCS (permanent change of station) to Germany. During his busy times, I focused on my job. I hung out with Jesse and Esther
as much as I could, without feeling like a third wheel. I tried to find other things to do so that they could have some alone

time, since I knew marital time was precious; especially since he got deployed a lot. They needed to bond as a family.

Time seemed to be just whirling by. It was now July, and this day was such a beautiful day. Tom and I had a date night planned, as he had a little free time. He took me to a restaurant that we both liked. It was called El Tapatio's. As we were indulging in our delicious meal, I had just put a forkful of food into my mouth. I looked up, as he turned his attention to me and looked with intent into my eyes. As I chewed my food slowly, he asked, "How do you say queen in Spanish?" In astonishment, I swallowed my food, dropped my fork, and with disbelief, I said, "What did you say?" He answered, "I asked, how you say queen in Spanish because that is what you are to me. My queen." I took a deep breath and with this confirmation and revelation that could only come from God, I answered him, "Reina. That's how you say queen." Right there and then, I knew with all confidence and no shadow of doubt in my heart that Tom was the man God had chosen for me. He must have noticed my reaction because he took my hand in his and asked, "Are you ok?" "Yes, I am perfectly fine." I explained my prayer to him, and he was just as astonished as I was. I then had to ask him, "Why did you keep asking me if I wanted to go to Germany with you, when you didn't even know me?" His reply was, "When I first saw you, God told me that you were my wife." He then went into explaining to me that two weeks before we had first met back in November, that he got on his face before the Lord and prayed, "Dear Lord, I know that I sinned against you and I am not worthy to ask anything from You, but You are full of mercy and grace. Can You please send someone to me, who will love and accept me just the way I am? Can she be a Christian woman, petite, and Hispanic looking? Also, can she sing so that we can sing together?" He told me that he didn't know why he asked about a Hispanic woman because they weren't his *type*. Well, God knew what to put in his heart to ask for. God knew what his *type* truly was.

*Delight yourself also in the Lord; And He will give you the desires of your heart.* (Psalm 37:4)

# My List

You see, our desires must align with what God desires for us. I then shared with him the list that I made many years ago. I took a piece of paper and wrote down everything I wanted in my husband. I was very specific with God, as I believe He helped me write down what He wanted for me. I placed my list in an envelope and put it in my Bible and forgot about it for years.

**These were the things I asked for:**

Lord, I ask for a husband that:

**1.** Is a Christian with a heart after You

**2.** Is very strong to protect me

**3.** Is tall

**4.** Is handsome and I am attracted to

**5.** Can sing so that we can worship together

**6.** Does not drink

**7.** I won't have to raise anyone else's kids

**8.** Makes enough money that I can stay home and not have to work, only if I want to

**9.** Will love me just as much as I love him

**10.** Will only have eyes for me, his wife

**11.** Will love my kids and I love his, if he has any

**12.** Doesn't have a pot belly (yes, I actually put that on my list, but later on it didn't even matter to me because it didn't matter to God)

**13.** I will get along with his ex-wife if he has one, so that there won't be any drama between us

We were amazed at how both of our requests to the Lord, were very similar. Our dinner that night was filled with the awesome wonder of our faithful Father. After we shared our feelings, emotions, thoughts, and prayers, we realized that we were now, no longer dating, but in a *courtship.* (a period during which a couple develop a romantic relationship, especially with a view to marriage.)

During our remarkable courting from the month of June into the month of August, Tom just naturally began talking about doing different things when we get married. It just came so naturally, as if we had planned our journey together all along. Although it wasn't us, it was Abba Father. His divorce was finalized, so my heart was more at peace. Not because his wife divorced him, but because I was no longer dating a married man.

*"For I hate divorce!" says the Lord, the God of Israel. "To divorce your wife is to overwhelm her with cruelty," says the*

*Lord of Heaven's Armies. "So, guard your heart; do not be unfaithful to your wife."* (Malachi 2:16 NLT)

God wasn't saying that He hated divorce to cause condemnation to the spouse who was hurt in an unfaithful marriage, but it was a warning to the unfaithful spouse who was creating situations that could lead to divorce. Even though Toms wife forgave him, she had every right to divorce him.

*Jesus replied, "Moses permitted divorce only as a concession to your hard hearts, but it was not what God had originally intended. And I tell you this, whoever divorces his wife (her husband) and marries someone else commits adultery—unless his wife (her husband) has been unfaithful."* (Matthew 19:8-10 NLT) (Emphasis mine)

We were going to counseling at my church. My pastor told us that he normally required a couple to go to counseling for six months, but because Tom's PCS was coming up around the corner, he agreed to see us for what time we had. I mentioned to Pastor Harvey that there was a woman who refused to leave Tom alone. You see, Cozbi kept on calling him and leaving e-mails and voice mails. She was still trying to manipulate him into keeping a relationship with her. The pastor told Tom that he needed to block her phone number, block her e-mail, and sever any and all contact with this woman. Tom agreed. His heart meant it, but this demonic spirit called jezebel, who possessed this woman, was not going to let him go so easily.

# Chapter 22

# The Proposal

It was at the very beginning of August when Tom's divorce became final. Since our first date was at Milano's six months ago, he decided he wanted to take me there once again. We got to the restaurant and from the time we entered the doors, to the time we left, God poured out His favor upon us. Before we ordered our dinner, while toasting with a glass of wine, Tom pulled out a ring and officially asked, "Will you marry
me?" With tears in both our eyes, a trembling hand, and an excitement in my voice, I said, "Yes! Of course!" He placed

the engagement ring on my finger, and I gave him a big kiss

and hug that lasted a few moments.

We heard some clapping, and our waiter came over to congratulate us. We explained our story to him. It seemed other waiters and waitresses had been watching and listening. They catered to us like we were royalty. They explained that they loved our story and that they were excited for us. Anything we ordered or asked for, they went out of their way to serve us and make sure everything was perfect. We had a very expensive feast that night. Yes, I luxuriated myself in the chocolate dessert that I had pleasure in on our first date. When all was devoured with a sense of fulfilled gratification, we both sat back, sighed, and smiled at one another. We toasted with another glass of wine since they had brought us a bottle of their house special. We just sat there holding hands as we awaited the bill. I was admiring my ring, as it sparkled in the candlelight.

The waiter brought our bill over on a little black tray and handed it to my betrothed. Omg! It was close to $150.00! As Tom reached for his wallet, the waiter stood there smiling at us, then with an exuberant voice, proclaimed, "Dinner is on us!" We looked at each other, then looked at the waiter and in perfect harmony we both said, "What?" The waiter said they all enjoyed our conversation with them, they liked us a lot, and they were happy that we went back six months later to get engaged at their restaurant. We thanked everyone involved in making this night extremely special. What a fabulous evening. Thank You Lord, for Your favor and blessing!

August was like a roller coaster ride. Everything was going super-fast. I gave my two weeks' notice at work. I had to plan our wedding rather quickly. I needed to get our marriage license, help Tom pack, clean, and find a dress for myself and a suit for him to wear for our wedding. Jesse was still home, so he would be walking me down the aisle and Esther would be my matron of honor. Tom's friend Charles would be his best man. My children wouldn't be able to attend, but I knew they would be there in spirit.

Jasmine Hartswick

# Chapter 23

# Our Wedding Day

The day finally came! After praying, waiting, and believing, all those years for my true husband, I would finally be joined to him as his wife.

*"For I know the plans I have for you," declares the Lord, "Plans to prosper you and not to harm you, plans to give you hope and a future."* (Jeremiah 29:11 NIV)

We would be getting married at Antioch Christian Fellowship Church. Pastor Harvey would marry us. This was

going to be a very small wedding but filled with so much love
for one another and covered with the immense love of the Father. We would have some friends and family in attendance to celebrate with us.

Getting ready for my *Fairytale Day* was so surreal, I could hardly contain my excitement. I had gone to the hair salon in Knob Noster, and it took two ladies to curl all my hair. They had a special for a manicure and pedicure, so I took advantage of it. My make-up was already done, so as soon as I was finished in the salon, I could go home and get dressed. I had a very simple, but elegant long spaghetti strapped dress that I had worn to an event with my previous singles group. My leader had made a comment saying, "You look like a bride." Little did I know, I would be wearing this dress to my wedding. I didn't wear a veil. I asked the ladies at the salon to put some white baby's breath flowers in my hair that I took with me. I caught myself asking, "Is this really happening? Is this finally the day I have been praying for so long? My mind was racing, but my heart was dancing.

Tom and I drove to the church together. We had to be there a little early to go through a rehearsal with the pastor and give him our marriage license. Jesse and Esther would meet us there a little later.

As everyone arrived on time and people took their seats, the pastor and his beautiful wife announced that it was time to begin. I had chosen some instrumental violin music that was played by a prophetic musician. Her name was LaDonna Taylor, and her CD was called "Tis So Sweet." She had been at our church as a guest speaker when I first attended and as she played her violin, our ears were brimmed with sounds of music from heaven. I fell in love with the violin that day.

It was almost a year ago, but I had no idea she was playing prophetically for my wedding.

When the music began to flow, Jesse held out his arm, so that he could escort me down the aisle. We began slowly towards the front, and I was so happy to be walking down the aisle with him, since my dad couldn't be there. When we were about halfway to the front, I looked upon the face of this man, who was waiting for me at the altar. All my prayers, all those years and all the heartache I went through to get to this moment, flooded into my soul. I was overwhelmed with the promise that God so graciously kept. That promise was standing before me, *my husband*. He was tall, strong, dark, and handsome. He looked quite dashing in his new suite. Not only could he sing, but play the piano and the drums, as well. And of course, he was seven years younger than me. I was in an intense state of triumphant joy. I was about to be joined in marriage to the man of my dreams!

*Therefore, I tell you, whatever you ask for in prayer, believe that you have received it, and it will be yours.* (Mark 11:24 NIV)

As the music played softly in the background, we stood at the altar, holding hands, and looking deeply into each other's eyes. When the pastor began with the words, "We are gathered here together,"...It seemed as though the words were resonating through the church. I could hardly believe that this hour had finally come. As we repeated our wedding vows, the sound of our promises was like listening to a symphonic poetic recital. I was experiencing my own *fairytale*! Placing a ring on Tom's finger and saying those blissful words, "With this ring, I thee wed," filled my heart with the genuineness of my love as a wife, towards my husband. When Tom took my hand in his and exchanged the

same words to me, "With this ring, I thee wed." I could see the precious hand of Jesus in his, as they both placed the ring
on my finger. This was indeed a covenant marriage, not just with my earthly husband, but with my spiritual Bridegroom, Jesus as well. I felt so honored as a wife to Tom and bride to Christ. I could feel the presence of the Holy Spirit. I knew He was there to witness what He had joined together in marriage. I was beyond elated with gratitude, that I couldn't refrain my tears.

*Don't be pulled in different directions or worried about a thing. Be saturated in prayer throughout each day, offering your faith-filled requests before God with overflowing gratitude.* (Philippians 4:6 TPT)

We shared communion for the first time together as husband and wife. This made it so much more meaningful. We could now partake in this celebration of remembering what our Savior did for us when He died on the cross and reconciled us back to our Father, as we are now one with Him in marriage. We have the privilege to be able to eat of the Bread of Life and drink of His new wine, which is His new and everlasting covenant with us. Communion, with our Bridegroom, is such an honor!

After communion, our pastor prayed blessings over us and our marriage. He then declares, "I now pronounce you husband and wife." He turns to Tom and says, "You may now kiss your bride." He takes me in his arms and slowly lowers himself to meet my lips. We kiss each other with an ardent but gentle kiss. I then felt a ripple of flutterbies!

We were married on August sixteenth, 2003. After the ceremony, we were congratulated by our friends and family.

Then, we all headed to our favorite restaurant, El Tapatio's, where Tom asked me the secret question that was between me and God. "How do you say queen in Spanish?" It seemed like everything we did together was ordained by God. He led us into His perfect plan, our marriage.

We spent our honeymoon at the very quaint Mulberry Hill Bed and Breakfast in Pleasant Hill, Missouri. We of course, got the honeymoon suite. The canopy bed was decorated in a beautiful white Victorian style bedspread with pillows to match. On the white posts were white sheer linens that cascaded all around the top. There were a variety of gorgeous flowers in white, champagne, a very subtle beige and light pink that were clustered together, also draping in sync with the sheer linens. They had some chocolates and a bottle of champagne waiting for us. I couldn't comprehend as long as I had to wait, pray, and believe for my husband, that God made everything happen so quickly. I was so happy it didn't even matter how long I waited. It was as if God erased the time.

*But beloved, do not forget this one thing, that with the Lord, one day is like a thousand years, and a thousand years as one day.* (Peter 3:8)

When I saw my husband in his white undershirt sit down at a small table in our room and put his head down on his arms, I had a flashback. It was the vision God had showed me before, back when I was standing underneath the falling snow at work. The vision He gave me was of my spouses back,
when I thought, "Oh, he looks like a boxer." This was exactly what I was looking at in our honeymoon suite. The

vision God had showed me, was of my husband on our wedding

night. I just stood there in awe.

We had a very romantic wedding night. Soaking in the abundance of bubble bath in a jacuzzi, while sipping on a fluted glass of champagne, feeding each other chocolates, and just relaxing with each other was total bliss. Our intimacy was more than I could have ever dreamed of. There was not only our physical connection, but an emotional and spiritual one, as well. I truly experienced a holy union with my husband. I fell asleep in the embrace of my love.

*My beloved is mine and I am his.* (Song of Solomon 2:16)

*Therefore, what God has joined together, let no one separate.* (Mark 10:9)

I woke up the next morning cuddled up to my husband, who was still asleep. I raised my hand to look at the rings on my finger and rested my arm across his chest to feel the rhythm of his heartbeat. He let out a gentle sigh as he opened his eyes to find me smiling at him. "Good morning husband." I whispered. He replied with, "Good morning wife." He gave me a kiss and we got up to get ready to go downstairs to enjoy a very hearty breakfast that was already prepared and waiting for us to enjoy. There was a very charming boutique that was right outside the dining area. I went in and found this porcelain doll that looked like a bride from the Victorian era. Tom asked if I wanted it as a gift from him to remember our honeymoon. So of course, I said yes. I still have that doll to this day.

Eighteen days later, on September third, we were at Spangdahlem AFB in Germany. This was the beginning of our life together. When we were in flight, God reminded me of a prayer I had asked when I visited Germany the first

time, many years ago. I had asked Him if I could go back to tour the country. Then He brought another desire of mine when I was just a young girl and thought it would be cool to be a military wife. Amazing! God answered all my prayers and gave me a bonus package. I now, was indeed a military spouse and back in Germany where we would be stationed for not just one, but two consecutive tours, which were rare to come by. We would be spending the first seven years of marriage in Europe. What a miraculous dream come true. Only God could have established all this!

*Therefore, know that the Lord your God, He is God, the faithful God who keeps covenant and mercy for a thousand generations with those who love Him and keep His commandments.* (Deuteronomy 7:9)

*Let us hold fast the confession of our hope without wavering, for He who promised is faithful.* (Hebrews 10:23)

## Prayer

Father God,

As the men and women who are reading this book, await their own spouse, I pray that they will not waiver in their faith or trust in You. I pray they will continue to patiently wait upon You, as You prepare their hearts for each other.

May they take my testimony and use it to encourage themselves to believe and have faith that they too, can usher in their spouse. I declare and decree that if You did it for me,

You will certainly do it for them. I thank You Lord that Your

Word does not return to You void. I cover each person reading
this with the precious blood of Jesus. I cover their awaited marriage with Your living words of truth, promise, love, peace, joy, grace, favor, and protection. I speak Your perfect timing of union between them and all Your blessings over them. I render powerless all the plots, plans and schemes of the wicked one who would try to detain, hinder, block, curse, deceive, or stop them from their marital destinies, in the name of Jesus and with His blood. May they love and want You more than they want their spouse. I ask You Lord, to keep them under the shadow of Your wings, so that the enemy cannot come near them. May each one be willing to go through their own personal "preparation chamber" and be made pure and ready for their blessed wedding day. May they have a heart after You, first and foremost, as You are their perfect Bridegroom. I pray that they would seek You in the secret place and establish an intimate *bridal* relationship with You. When they do this may Your love for them, fill them to an overflow that would be poured into their marriage. I ask all this in the name above all names, the One who's love for us is unconditional, our Lord and Savior, Jesus Christ. Amen and amen!

**Be diligent and meticulous in your prayer's dear brothers and sisters! I love you all in Christ.**

# Chapter 24

# Jesus, Our First Spouse

The most important fact that you need to know, before getting married is this: You need to make Jesus your first spouse. He needs to be the foundation of your marriage.

It doesn't matter if you're male or female, Jesus must become your first love. He cannot be your *Bridegroom* if you are not saved. Salvation is covered in chapter nine. (My Testimony) He is and must be your everything!

You have to know within your heart that Jesus is the only One who gives you everything you could possibly ever need in your life. He is the only One that you can depend on, who will never let you down. He is the One who will forgive
you no matter how many times you fall and will be there to pick you up each and every time.

Jesus is the only One who will *never* keep an account on the wrong that you do in life once you repent. He is the One who accepts you just the way you are. Jesus is the only One who will fill any void in your life and make you whole. His love for you is so pure and so perfect. The love of your first spouse, Jesus, is the only love that is *unconditional*.

The joy of the Lord is your happiness. Nothing else in this world can fulfill this. When you live in this knowledge, allowing yourself to be totally dependent on Him, wanting Him and loving Him, then you are at a place where God can send the spouse, He has prepared for you. You Can *NOT* want a spouse more than you want Jesus! He is the One who will give you your earthly spouse. He will send them when He knows you both are ready.

## The Parable of the Wise and Foolish Virgins

*"Then the kingdom of heaven shall be likened to ten virgins who took their lamps and went out to meet the bridegroom. Now five of them were wise, and five were foolish. Those who were foolish took their lamps and took no oil with them, but the wise took oil in their vessels with their lamps. But while the bridegroom was delayed, they all slumbered and slept. "And at midnight a cry was heard: 'Behold, the bridegroom is coming; go out to meet him!' Then all those virgins arose and trimmed their lamps. And the foolish said to the wise,*

426

*'Give us some of your oil, for our lamps are going out' But the wise*

answered, saying, 'No, lest there should not be enough for us and you; but go rather to those who sell, and buy for yourselves.' And while they went to buy, the bridegroom came, and those who were ready went in with him to the wedding; and the door was shut. "Afterward the other virgins came also, saying, 'Lord, Lord, open to us!' But he answered and said, 'Assuredly, I say to you, I do not know you.' "Watch therefore, for you know neither the day nor the hour in which the Son of Man is coming. (Mathew 25:1-13)

## This next scripture is the very first one in the Bible that refers to Jesus as the Bridegroom.

John answered and said, "A man can receive nothing unless it has been given to him from heaven. You yourselves bear me witness, that I said, 'I am not the Christ,' but, 'I have been sent before Him.' **He who has the bride (church) is the bridegroom**; but the friend of the bridegroom, who stands and hears him, rejoices greatly because of the bridegroom's voice. Therefore, this joy of mine is fulfilled. He must increase, but I must decrease. (Emphasis mine) (John 3:27-30)

## Did you know the very first miracle Jesus ever performed was at a wedding?

On the third day there was a wedding in Cana of Galilee, and the mother of Jesus was there. Now both Jesus and His disciples were invited to the wedding. And when they ran out of wine, the mother of Jesus said to Him, "They have no wine." Jesus said to her, "Woman, what does your concern have to do with Me? My hour has not yet come." His mother said to the servants, "Whatever He says to you, do it." Now *there were set there six water pots of stone, according to the manner of purification of the Jews, containing twenty or thirty gallons apiece. Jesus said to them, "Fill the water pots with water." And they filled them up to the brim. And He said to them, "Draw some out now, and take it to the master of the feast." And they took it. When the master of the feast had tasted the water that was made wine and did not know where it came from (but the servants who had drawn the water knew), the master of the feast called the bridegroom. And he said to him, "Every man at the beginning sets out the good wine, and when the guests have well drunk, then the inferior. You have kept the good wine until now!" This beginning of signs Jesus did in Cana of Galilee and manifested His glory; and His disciples believed in Him.* (John 2:1-11)

This scripture represents what was going to happen. Jesus always used a symbolic or parabolic way of teaching. On the third day, a wedding takes place. The wedding represents the bride of Christ, the wine represents the shed blood of Jesus who will be the ultimate sacrifice without blemish. This is why Jesus told Mary, after she said, *"They have no wine."* He says, *"Woman, what does your concern have to do with Me? My hour has not yet come."* He hadn't shed His blood yet, the new and everlasting covenant, so the people at the wedding celebration had no *wine*. The people of the world had no *spiritual wine* yet. We as a people didn't have His precious blood to set us free. We didn't have our *Bridegroom* yet.

The third day represents Jesus's resurrection from death into eternal life, becoming a *Bridegroom Savior* for all mankind. The first miracle at the wedding represents Jesus showing us His *glory* for the first time. The Jugs of wine, represent us as His vessels. If He can take water and change it not just to wine, but the best wine, how much more change will take place in us when He takes our worldly lives (old

vessels/wine skins) and changes it, to a new spiritual life (new vessels/wine skins) filled with Him.

Changing the water into wine was a preparation for us to be in unity with Him. (Wine is a symbol of the Holy Spirit) A holy union. We become His bride and a miracle takes place when He, *ushers* us into an intimate, holy, bridal relationship with Him. Thus, He becomes our first spouse when we accept Him into our hearts, as Lord and Savior. We become the bride of Christ. The bride of Christ represents His church. (The body of Christ) So, what happens when we become the Bride of Christ? (His Church) Let's look at this scripture:

*"For as the body is one and has many members, but all the members of that one body, being many, are one body, so also is Christ. For by one Spirit, we were all baptized into one body whether Jews or Greeks, whether slaves or free and have all been made to drink into one Spirit. For in fact the body is not one member but many. If the foot should say, "Because I am not a hand, I am not of the body," is it therefore not of the body? And if the ear should say, "Because I am not an eye, I am not of the body," is it therefore not of the body? If the whole body were an eye, where would be the hearing? If the whole were hearing, where would be the smelling? But now God has set the members, each one of them, in the body just as He pleased. And if they were all one member, where would the body be? But now indeed there are many members, yet one body. And*

*the eye cannot say to the hand, "I have no need of you"; nor again the head to the feet, "I have no need of you."*

*No, much rather, those members of the body which seem to be weaker are necessary. And those members of the body which we think to be less honorable, on these we bestow greater honor; and our unpresentable parts have greater modesty, but our presentable parts have no need. But God composed the body, having given greater honor to that part which lacks it, that there should be no schism in the body, but that the members should have the same care for one another. And if one member suffers, all the members suffer with it; or if one member is honored, all the members rejoice with it. Now you are the body of Christ, and members individually. (1 Corinthian's 12-27)*

How amazing that our Lord had all this planned out before the foundations of the world. He was already crucified before we were ever born! Think of all the details, all the events that take place, and everything coming into perfect order according to His will.

Your own book has been written in heaven and you are at this chapter in your book, where you are seeking the one, He has for you. This is no co-incidence! He purposed me in my life to write this book, to help you in your own journey to prepare you for your own spouse. He blessed me with this gift, to share with you. So, as described in the above scripture, I am part of the bride of Christ, whom He is using to help the other members of His church. We cannot live our lives separate from each other. Everyone has a job to do. Everyone has a calling, and different gifts that need to be shared, to help each other out.

When we become the bride of Christ, the Holy Spirit *ushers* (draws) us into the bridal realm. Jesus is our first bridegroom, our *first spouse.*

*For your Maker is your husband, The Lord of hosts is His name* (Isaiah 54:5)

**His love is complete perfection, holy, and everlasting to everlasting!**

# Chapter 25

# What Is A God Ordained Marriage?

*So, God created man in His own image; in the image of God, He created him; male and female He created them. Then God blessed them, and God said to them, "Be fruitful and multiply; fill the earth and subdue it; have dominion over the fish of the sea, over the birds of the air, and over every living thing that moves on the earth."* (Genesis 1:27-28)

*And the Lord God said, "It is not good that man should be alone; I will make him a helper comparable to him." Out of the ground the Lord God formed every beast of the field and every bird of the air and brought them to Adam to see what he would call them. And whatever Adam called each living creature, that was its name. So, Adam gave names to all cattle, to the birds of the air, and to every beast of the field. But for Adam there was not found a helper comparable to him. And the Lord God caused a deep sleep to fall on Adam, and he slept; and He took one of his ribs and closed up the flesh in its place. Then the rib which the Lord God had taken from man He made into a woman, and He brought her to the man. And Adam said: "This is now bone of my bones and flesh of my flesh; She shall be called woman, because she was taken out of man." Therefore, a man shall leave his father and mother and be joined to his wife, and they shall become one flesh. (Genesis 2:18-24)*

## This is the first marriage instituted by God

God created marriage. The first marriage took place in the Garden of Eden at the beginning of creation. He created male and female, then joined them together as husband and wife. Marriage is ordained by God and was instituted by Him at the time of creation. Ordain means to establish and to institute something permanently such as a law. In this case, God was instituting marriage between a male and female. Adam and Eve were the very first couple joined in marriage by God. Marriage did not come from man, but by God Himself.

*And He answered and said to them, "Have you not read that*

*He who made them at the beginning 'made them male and female, and said, 'For this reason a man shall leave his father and mother and be joined to his wife, and the two shall become one flesh? So then, they are no longer two but one flesh. Therefore, what God has joined together, let not man separate."* (Matthew 19:4-6)

## Why does God take the husband and wife and make them one flesh?

Before they were joined as husband and wife, they lived separate lives. They were independent of one another. They each had their own way of doing things, their own way of figuring things out, their own lifestyle, their own agenda's, etc. You get the picture. Now that they are married, they are no longer two people living separate lives. They are two people living one life together. They become one relationship having the principles that God established for them to live by. (Which we will cover in another chapter) A marriage is a relationship that is so comprehensive and uniquely joined together, that only God can complete such a profound unity.

We become one with the Holy Spirit when we give our lives to Jesus and become the bride of Christ. Our marriage becomes a holy covenant that is so very intimate between a husband, wife, and God. When the husband and wife come together in physical intimacy, it is the greatest expression of their love for one another. They become one flesh through the Holy Spirt.

*But he who is joined to the Lord is one spirit with Him.* (1Corinthians 6:17)

On June 25th, 2015, Franklin Graham, son of William Franklin Graham, Jr., one of the most influential Christian leaders of the 20th century, made the following statement on his Facebook page:

The United States has ruled today that same-sex marriage is legal in all 50 states. With all due respect to the court, it did not define marriage, and therefore is not entitled to re-define it. Long before our government came into existence, marriage was created by the One who created a man and woman. "Almighty God" and His decisions are not subject to review or revision by any manmade court. God is clear about the definition of marriage in His Holy Word:

*Therefore, a man shall leave his father and mother and be joined to his wife, and they shall become one flesh.* (Genesis 2:24)

I thank you, Franklin Graham for words of truth!

**God ordained marriage from the beginning of time between a man and a woman. (God did not create homosexuals and it is not in our God given DNA)**

***Therefore, what God has joined together, let man not separate.*** **Mathew19:6**

God's original design for creating man, woman, and marriage was marred and made imperfect, as a result of human rebellion against our sovereign Creator. Along with everything else, because of the *FALL* every man, woman, and child has been born into sin. We inherit some form of brokenness and imperfection. So, the actual development of sexual preference, comes from that brokenness between us and God through sin. And the hater of our souls (satan) will steal our identities in Christ through lies and confusion. God created us in His image. That perfect image became distorted through sin. God cannot contradict Himself!

Franklin Graham told the truth and nothing but the truth. I too, share this truth in love and not in judgement. Only God can judge. There is scripture after scripture that testifies, manifests, and proclaims the infallible Word of God. One who argues, debates, fights, and twists the living Word (Jesus) is only doing so, to God Himself!

*Do you not know that the unrighteous will not inherit the kingdom of God?* **Do not be deceived.** *Neither fornicators, nor idolaters, nor adulterers,* **nor homosexuals,** *nor sodomites, (those who submit to homosexuals) nor thieves, nor covetous, nor drunkards nor revilers, nor extortioners will inherit the kingdom of God. And such were some of you. But you were washed, but you were sanctified, but you were justified in the name of the Lord Jesus and by the Spirit of our God.* (1 Corinthians 6:9-11)

*For the message of the cross is foolishness to those who are perishing, but to us who are being saved it is the power of God.* (1 Corinthians 1:18)

As with every sin, Jesus shed His blood for the forgiveness of ALL sin. Homosexuality is no greater sin than murder, (to include murder through abortion) lying, stealing, pornography, and so on. But make no mistake. **There are different consequences for different sins.** We are ALL sinners. We must love one another as God loves us, but hate the sin that God hates. All we need to do *as a believer,* is ask for forgiveness and repent of it.

**In summary, there is no mistaking, denying, or un-justifying what a God ordained marriage is. God created a man and a woman in His image and then joined them in marriage, as a husband (man) and wife (woman) to become one flesh with His Holy Spirit.**

*But people who aren't spiritual (People who are not saved) can't receive these truths from God's Spirit. It all sounds foolish to them, and they can't understand it, for only those who are spiritual can understand what the Spirit means.* (1 Corinthians 2:14)

# Chapter 26

# Attracting In Your Spouse: What Not to Do

I'm sure many of you who are reading this has heard about "The Law of Attraction" or also referred to as "The Secret." I have met a lot of proclaimed Christians who believe in this ungodly theory. This is a very carnal interpretation to give power and glory to oneself, instead of God, our Creator. This is what you should not do!!!

## What is the Law of Attraction?

(According to Wikipedia) In the New Thought philosophy, (A mind science religion) the Law of Attraction is the belief that by focusing on positive or negative thoughts, people can bring positive or negative experiences into their life. The belief is based on the idea that people and their thoughts are both made from "pure energy," and that through the process of "like energy attracting like energy" a person can improve their own health, wealth, and personal relationships.

People believe they can do this, totally on their own, without God! This can cause so many issues in one's life. Most believe that an idol is a statue or some other object. In reality, anything we make, use, or believe in to meet our needs that is not God or His word, is a false god. It becomes idolatry. Only God can meet every need in our life. I can't even comprehend how many false gods have been created by people all over the world, to include some Christians. God is our everything. *He is* our every need. *He is* our life!

*"I am the Lord your God, who brought you out of the land of Egypt, out of the house of bondage. "You shall have no other gods before Me.* (Exodus 20:2-3)

## Who discovered the Law of Gravity?

Any object having mass, attract other objects and this force of attraction is called gravity. This is a universal phenomenon. The law of gravitation was discovered by famous English physician and mathematician Sir Isaac Newton in 1680s. Its law of gravitation describes the universal force of gravity. ([www.whodiscoveredit.net/who-discovered-law-of-gravity/](www.whodiscoveredit.net/who-discovered-law-of-gravity/))

## This is a scientific fact. Gravity was created by God

## The Law of Attraction (the fake)

Now, just as with any other good thing that comes from God alone, satan comes in to *MOCK* what God created and turns it into something that is appealing, easy to follow, and looks like truth. Wrong! He took this Law of Gravity that was created by God and replaced it with a fake. The Law of Attraction.

The first use of the term, "the law of attraction," was in 1877 by a Russian philosopher and author named Helena Blavatsky. She published a book in 1888 that was called, *The Secret Doctrine*. Her writings and teachings were on world thought. At an early age she possessed what they called psychic powers. She attracted attention with her ability of producing psychic phenomena at will. (demonic powers)

In 1875, she was a co-founder of a movement called, Theosophical Society. (Wikipedia) any of a number of philosophies maintaining that a knowledge of God may be achieved through spiritual ecstasy, direct intuition, or special individual relations. Categorized by scholars of religion as both a new religious movement (New Age) and as part of the occultist stream of Western esotericism, it draws upon religions such as Hinduism and Buddhism. Theosophy teaches that the purpose of human life is spiritual emancipation and claims that the human <u>soul</u> undergoes re-

incarnation upon bodily death according to a process of *karma*. The principle of *karma*, wherein intent and actions
of an individual influence (*cause*) the future of that individual. Good intent and good deeds contribute to good karma and happier <u>rebirths</u>, while bad intent and bad deeds contribute to bad *karma* and bad rebirths.

## The Secret (copy-cat fake)

The Secret is a 2006 self-help book by Rhonda Byrne. It is based on the belief of the law of attraction, which claims that your thoughts can change a person's life directly. (Blavatsky's: The Secret Doctrine from1888)

"The Secret" also known as the "law of attraction," is the idea that because of our connection with a "universal energy force," our thoughts and feelings have the ability to manipulate this energy force to our liking. According to "The Secret," our thoughts and feelings attract a corresponding energy to ourselves.

**I am using a short excerpt of this article to shed some light on this "New Age" mind set.**

## The Secret Revealed

Article ID: JAS333 | By: Robert Velarde
This article first appeared in the *Christian Research Journal*, volume 30, number 6 (2007).

The Secret claims compatibility with Christianity, but it is anything but Christian. Jesus taught belief in transcendent, personal, holy God who is distinct from His creation. Human beings are fallen and in need of radical redemption that involves real repentance before God for sins committed against His perfect law, and through belief in the death and resurrection of Christ, His Son, who was a sinless sacrifice on their behalf. We are not perfect divine beings with unlimited potential.

**The foundation of "The Secret" is the law of attraction-an impersonal force that individuals can manipulate with their thoughts in order to achieve what they want in their lives.**

"It is," writes Byrne, "the law that determines the complete order in the Universe, every moment of your life, and every single thing you experience in your life...the law of attraction is forming your entire life experience, and this all-powerful law is doing that through your thoughts."

The worldview of The Secret is monistic pantheism (all is one, all is divine). Everything is interconnected energy. Our positive thoughts tap into this energy and produce positive results in our lives. Our negative thoughts, conversely, bring negativity into our lives. As a result, The Secret is in the precarious position of stating that experiences such as rape and child molestation are the result of the thoughts of those who have suffered such horrors.

**This belief is absolutely absurd!!!** Totally opposite of the truth!!! I myself was raped at the age of 23 and when I knew at the end of it all that the guy who raped me was going to kill me with his knife, I prayed the only prayer I knew at that time, which was *The Our Father*. My trust was in God, and He saved my life.

The guy let me go. Not once, did I ever have thoughts of being raped. And how can a child even have thoughts of something they know nothing about?

*satan, who is the god of this world, **has blinded the minds of those who don't believe.** They are unable to see the glorious light of the Good News. They don't understand this message about the glory of Christ, who is the exact likeness of God.* (2 Corinthians 4:4 NLT)

God gave us our life. We are to use that life according to His will and purpose for us. We were all created for a special purpose, unique to us. We will not know what our purpose or calling in life is if we do not know the Creator of all things. God created and controls the universe!

So, to put it bluntly, you either live for the world, (satan) or you live your life for God, who created the world, universe, and humans. People believe that they can control the created universe with their own thoughts and feelings? People ask and pray to the universe or creation, and totally ignore God who created it. God has many names in the bible. Universe and energy are not one of them. He created ALL things!

*In the beginning, God created the heavens and the earth.* (Genesis 1:1)

*The heavens declare the glory of God; And the firmament shows His handiwork.* (Psalm 91:1)

*Indeed, heaven and the highest heavens belong to the Lord your God, also the earth with **all** that is in it.* (Deuteronomy 10:14)

*And the Lord God formed man of the dust of the ground and breathed into his nostrils the breath of life; and man became a living being.* (Genesis 2:7)

The law of attraction (the secret) and the message of the Bible have a huge divergence between them. It is God who created the universe. He is the creator of all things and beings in the earth, above the earth, and below the earth. When you have a personal relationship with God, whatever you ask, He hears and answers your prayers in a vast assortment of ways and timing. What we ask must align with His word and will for us. The enemy of our souls can hear everything we say and use it against us! Since satan is the god of this world and dwells in the second heaven, he and his demons can appear as an angel of light and deceive people into believing lies as truth and truth as lies. This is called deception. (Lying, misleading, or otherwise hiding or distorting the truth)

Remember, it is God our Father who is the ultimate source of all our provisions and wants to give all good gifts to His children. *He is our universe!* God's presence, power, knowledge and love has absolutely no limits. He is omnipresent, (everywhere at the same time) omniscient, (all knowing) and omnipotent (having unlimited power; able to do anything and everything).

*Do not be deceived, my beloved brethren. Every good gift and every perfect gift is from above, and comes down from the Father of lights, with whom there is no variation or shadow of turning.* (James 1:16-17)

Our Father God loves us so much and only wants the very best for us. The law of attraction or the secret cannot give you a Godly spouse!

*If you then, being evil, know how to give good gifts to your children, how much more will your Father who is in heaven give good things to those who ask Him.* (Matthew 7:11)

**Know this:** satan cannot be everywhere at the same time like God. He doesn't know everything like God, nor does he have unlimited power like God. he relies on his fallen followers (devils) for everything. his demons have special assignments and powers they get from their master. Some of them monitor what we are doing and saying and taking that information back to him. Some of them speak lies, blasphemies, and condemnation into our ears and put evil thoughts into our minds. Some of them appear as angels of light and truth. Some of them can even perform miracles. They can even possess someone who is not a born-again believer. They can put curses and sickness on people. Some of them wage wars, conflicts, strife, divination, and on and on. This is only a tidbit of information on the powers of darkness. We as Christians, who know our identity in Christ, know that we have the power and authority to

dismantle, disengage, restrain, and break all the power of the enemy. satan isn't as big as he thinks he is. he only has

the power that people allow him to have. he wants people to believe that he is like God. To those who truly know who they are in Christ, he is but a useless looser, playing dress up dolls with his demonic *powerless* kingdom.

If you have ever believed or practiced the law of attraction or the secret, especially to get a spouse, now would be an excellent time to repent. Ask God to forgive you for believing a lie and putting your trust in something that came from satan. he is a false god and tries to make himself more powerful than he is. The only power he has is the power that

people give him by believing any of his lies. The only thing big about him is that he is a big LOOSER! he lost at Calvary and knows this.

*I have been crucified with Christ; it is no longer I who live, but Christ lives in me; and the life which I now live in the flesh I live by faith in the Son of God, who loved me and gave Himself for me.* (Galatians 2:20)

*But thanks be to God, who gives us the victory through our Lord Jesus Christ.* (1 Corinthians 15:57)

## Please take note of this!

There is a huge difference in being saved and living as a believer, than there is for those who are not saved.

*For the message of the cross is foolishness to those who are perishing, but to us who are being saved it is the power of God.* (1 Corinthians 1:18)

## What does this scripture mean?

Paul is dividing the world into two categories of people. Those who are perishing and those who are being saved. For the first group who are perishing, the reason the message of the cross is foolishness to them is because they refuse to accept the truth that Jesus Christ is the Savior of the world.

They will not allow the Holy Spirit to fill them with the truth, which will set them free. They are destined to live eternally apart from God. They will forever live a life according to the power of sin, having their ears deafened and eyes blinded to the truth. They will only go through life and its temporary provisions that come from their master, satan. Nothing lasts with him, except hell.

To those being saved, we are destined for an eternity of sharing in God's glory. Salvation is a life journey. It's a whole new supernatural world for us to live in. We are set apart from the rest of the world. The cross is the greatest and most powerful gift we could ever receive. We inherit all the blessings, favor, power and authority of our Savior, Jesus, because we are joint heirs with Him. We get to live life, not just go through life, more abundantly and filled with the riches of His glory hear on earth. And then, eternally with Him!

# Chapter 27

# Steps You Should Take Before Getting Married

**1. Self-examination:** the study of one's own behavior and motivations *(Collins Dictionary)*

First of all, you need to take a good look at yourself. Are you living a life that is pleasing to the Lord? If you are not, ask God to search your heart and tell you what areas you need to work on, in order to clean them up.  If you already know the answer, then allow the Lord to help you get aligned with Him and His plans for you. Ask Him for your own *Preparation Chamber*. Remember, you don't want to bring a lot of baggage into your marriage.

**2. Addiction:** The fact or condition of being addicted to a particular substance, thing, or activity. (Collins Dictionary)

Second, if you have any type of addiction, whether it be drugs, alcohol, looking at porn, food, sex, or anything that keeps you in bondage, the first thing you need to do is to ask God for to forgive you and to deliver you from such things. The only true source of deliverance can only come from God. Why? Because He is your deliverer. Jesus died on the cross and took every addiction upon Himself, so that you could live free from them. His blood sets you free.

*And since we now have a magnificent High Priest to welcome us into God's house, we come closer to God and approach Him with an open heart, fully convinced that nothing will keep us at a distance from Him. For our hearts have been sprinkled with blood to remove impurity, (addictions) and we have been freed from an accusing conscience. Now we are clean, unstained, and presentable to God inside and out.* (Emphasis mine) (Hebrews 10:22 TPT)

Ask Him for deliverance from anything that keeps you in bondage. This could include social media, tv, and even your phone. I know God can perform instant miraculous deliverance. It happened for me. However, not everyone

460

receives their deliverance in the same way. Your first step is to go to God. Humble yourself before Him and ask for help.

After you have done that, follow up with getting help from your pastor, an addiction program, or books that would help. But stay away from the very things that will tempt you into going back to that sin. There are so many programs and resources to help you conquer your addiction. Jesus is the first and most powerful way to start.

*Like a city whose walls are broken through, is a person who lacks self-control.* (Proverbs 25:28 NIV)

*Watch and pray, lest you enter into temptation. The spirit indeed is willing, but the flesh is weak* (Matthew 26:41)

*As a dog returns to his own vomit, so a fool repeats his folly.* (Proverbs 26:11)

# Here is a sample list

## Addiction:

**1.** Drugs or alcohol

**2.** Pornography

**3.** Food

**4.** Sex

**5.** Gambling

**6.** Social media

**7.** Television

**8.** Shopping

# Make your own list:

1._____

2._____

3._____

4._____

5._____

6._____

7._____

8._____

# Prayer

Dear Lord,

Forgive me for allowing _____ to control me. I repent of my addiction to _____. I now lay it down at the cross, where you shed Your blood and destroyed ALL addictions, so that I could live in complete freedom. I bind every stronghold off my life and sever all connections with the blood of Jesus. I loose the power of Your blood to completely deliver me and set me free. Precious Jesus, it is You that I want to be addicted to and nothing else. I ask You to forgive me for making _____ my personal god, which is idolatry instead of You. Deliver me now, from all powers of darkness that keeps me in bondage. I ask this, in Jesus's name. Amen.

*Jasmine Hartswick*

*For if we have been united together in the likeness of His death, certainly we also shall be in the likeness of His resurrection, knowing this, that our old man was crucified with Him, that the body of sin might be done away with, that we should no longer be slaves of sin.* (Romans 6:5-6)

*Stand fast therefore in the liberty by which Christ has made us free, and do not be entangled again with a yoke of bondage.* (Galatians 5:1)

*Therefore, if the Son makes you free, you shall be free indeed.* (John 8:36)

**3. Unrepented sin:** Sin that is not confessed or regretful.

Third, you must confess your sins to the Lord and ask for forgiveness. Repentance means that you are sorry for your sin, and you resolve in your heart and to God to turn away from it and try your best not to do it again. Repentance involves the way you think about God, yourself, and others. You do not want to bring unrepented sin into your marriage. Why? Because you will hinder your marriage from being able to grow and prosper.

*He who covers his sins will not prosper, but whoever confesses and forsakes them will have mercy.* (Proverbs 28:13)

*Those whom I love I rebuke and discipline. So be earnest and repent.* (Revelation 3:19 NIV)

464

*If we confess our sins, He is faithful and just to forgive us our sins and to cleanse us from all unrighteousness.* (1 John 1:9)

# Prayer

Dear Lord,

I come humbly before Your thrown of grace. I ask you to forgive me of all unconfessed sins. Search me and reveal anything to me that I need to confess. I bow before You now and surrender myself to Your will and righteousness. Give me clean hands and a pure hear. I am a sinner and fall short of Your glory. Help me to be diligent in my walk with You and convict me of sin through Your Holy Spirit, that I may instantly repent. Thank You Jesus for Your shed blood, that washes away all my sins and makes me white as snow. In Jesus's name, amen.

**4. Unforgiveness:** When you refuse or feel you are unable to forgive someone for hurting, betraying, or causing you emotional or physical pain. (This is the root to a plethora of physical, emotional, and spiritual suffering)

It brings and grows anger, bitterness, jealousy, tormenting thoughts, sickness, (cancer is a huge one) false accusations, unrest, suffering, pain, misery, etc. You give satan and his demons legal grounds over you when you do not forgive. Why would you want to bring this trail of destruction into your marriage? Believe me, you do not want to!

*"For if you forgive men their trespasses, your heavenly Father will also forgive you. But if you do not forgive men their trespasses, neither will your Father forgive your trespasses."* (Matthew 6:14-15)

*Then his master, after he had called him, said to him, 'You wicked servant! I forgave you all that debt because you begged me. Should you not also have had compassion on your fellow servant, just as I had pity on you?' And his master was angry and delivered him to the torturers until he should pay all that was due to him. "So, My heavenly Father also will do to you if each of you, from his heart, does not forgive his brother his trespasses." (Mathew 18:32-35) ,*

**Forgiveness was covered in my testimony, chapter nine. Go back to that chapter as many times as you need to.**

Forth, make sure you make your list of people you need to forgive and why. Pray the prayer in that chapter. This is one of the most important things you will need for your marriage to flourish. Forgiveness is one of the keys that will unlock the blessings God wants to give you as a married couple.

### 5. Generational Curses:

The sins of your ancestors can cause your spiritual bondage. The curse of sin that has been passed on from generation to generation.

*Then those of Israelite lineage separated themselves from all foreigners: and they stood and confessed their sins and the iniquities of their fathers. (Nehemiah 9:2)*

*You shall not bow down to them nor serve them. For I, the Lord your God, am a jealous God, visiting the iniquity of the fathers, upon the children, to the third and fourth generations of those who hate Me, but showing mercy to thousands to those who love Me and keep My commandments. (Exodus 20:5-6)*

*This day I call the heavens and the earth as witnesses against you that I have set before you, life and death, blessings, and curses. Now choose life, so that you and your children may live. (Deuteronomy 30:19 NIV)*

*The Lord is longsuffering and abundant in mercy, forgiving iniquity and transgression; but He by no means clears the guilty, visiting the iniquity of the fathers on the children to the third and fourth generation. (Numbers 14:18*

We inherit many behaviors and choices from our parents that aren't always a good influence on us. When we follow and live out a sinful belief or habit that opposes and resists the word of God and has negative effects on our lives or those around us, this is known as a generational curse. (Alcoholism, abuse, depression, infidelity, mental illness, and even poverty, to name a few)

Perhaps you've inherited a family curse. Maybe the curse has begun with you. Wherever the curse originated from, God already had a plan in place to break the cycle of ongoing bondage and destruction, in order to set you free. His Son's blood severs these curses off you, your children, and family forever.

## Repentance and salvation are the answer to live in freedom and abundance in Christ.

*Therefore, if anyone is in Christ, he is a new creation; OLD Things have passed and become new. (2 Corinthians 5:17)*

*Beloved friends, what should be our proper response to God's marvelous mercies? To surrender yourselves to God to be His sacred, living sacrifices. And live, in holiness, experiencing all that delights His heart. For this becomes your genuine expression of worship. Stop imitating the ideals and opinions of the culture (world) around you but be inwardly transformed by the Holy Spirit through a total reformation of how you think. This will empower you to discern God's will as you live a beautiful life, satisfying and perfect in His eyes.* (Emphasis mine) (Romans 12:1-2 TPT)

# Prayer

Precious Jesus,

I come before Your thrown room of mercy. I bring the sins of my forefathers and sins of my family lineage, including my own and ask for forgiveness for all our sins. Right now, in the name of Jesus and by the blood He shed on the cross, I ask that all generational curses be broken, severed, and rendered null and void off myself, my children, grandchildren, and future generations. Thank you for setting us free and delivering us from curses of the past. I now seal
that door with the blood of the Lamb. I reverse the curses and ask that all blessings, favor, supernatural provisions, healing, inheritance, and rightful justice be returned to my family. I declare and decree that everything that was stolen because of any generational curse be returned sevenfold. Thank You Lord Jesus, that I am a joint heir with You, because I accepted You as my Savior. Thank You that my family and I will now live a life in freedom and all the riches of Your glory according to Your will and purpose for our lives. Thank You Jesus, for Your precious and powerful blood that takes away ALL sin! Amen.

Jasmine Hartswick

## 6. Spoken Word Curses:

If you have ever spoken words over yourself, such as "I will never amount to anything," "I don't want to live anymore," "I'm sick and tired," I will never be able to do that," "I hate myself," or anything negative about yourself, you need to repent and renounce those words. If someone else spoke those types of words against you, or you spoke them against someone else, those words need to be broken. Remember there is power in our words.

*Reckless words are like the thrusts of a sword, cutting remarks meant to stab and to hurt. But the words of the wise soothe and heal.* (Proverbs 12:18 TPT)

*Your words are so powerful that they will kill or give life, and the talkative person will reap the consequences.* (Proverbs 18:21 TPT)

*"For by thy words thou shalt be justified, and by thy words thou shalt be condemned."* (Matthew 12:37)

# Here is a sample list of words:

## (These words may have been spoken against you or by you)

1. I/You will never amount to anything
2. I/You wish you were never born
3. I hate myself/you.
4. I/you am/are worthless
5. I/you am/are dumb and stupid

# Make your own list

1._____

2._____

3._____

4._____

5._____

6._____

7._____

8._____

9._____

10._____

# Prayer

Dear Jesus,

Thank you for shedding Your precious blood on the cross for me. I bring all word curses and negative words that I spoke about myself, someone else spoke over me, or I spoke against someone else. I ask You to break their power over me and the ones I spoke against with Your redeeming and healing blood. Set me free from all negative words, thoughts and feelings that have hindered, blocked, tormented my mind, or paralyzed me from moving forward or having any breakthrough in my life. I render powerless all word curses spoken against me or by me in each of these relationships. I break all word curses that have been spoken against me by people I know, or I didn't know. I renounce and rebuke all word curses and shut the mouth of the enemy right now, in Jesus's name. I believe I am who You say that I am. I can become who You called me to be. I can do what You have called me to do. I receive all that You have planned for my life with a heart of gratitude. Thank You Lord for setting me free by the blood of the Lamb and the words of my testimony. I speak Your living Word over my life. I ask, believing what I ask, and I receive it, in Jesus's name, Amen.

### 7. I had to break all soul ties from my past.

A soul tie is a link between two people in the soul realm. It links the two people's souls together. In marriage, God unites or links the two together and they become *one flesh.*

*Therefore, a man shall leave his father and mother and be joined to his wife, and they shall become one flesh.* (Genesis 2:2)

The purpose of this joining is to build a very strong, intimate, and healthy relationship that is unique to them and them alone. A soul tie can also, be formed between a strong friendship.

*Now when he had finished speaking to Saul, the soul of Jonathan was knit to the soul of David, and Jonathan loved him as his own soul.* (1 Samuel 18:1)

There can also be a negative result from a soul tie. The devil will absolutely take advantage of this and use it

475

against us, even years later from the relationship we had in the past.

Soul ties formed from having sex outside of marriage, defiles our body. The enemy of our soul knows this.

*And when Shechem the son of Hamor the Hivite, prince of the country, saw her, he took her and lay with her, and violated her. His soul was strongly attracted to Dinah the daughter of Jacob, and he loved the young woman and spoke kindly to the young woman.* (Genesis 34:2-3)

The devil can use our soul ties to make us *one flesh* with whomever we have sex with outside of marriage. We become one with whatever spirits they have. This could be very bad! satan mocks everything God does. Just as we become one with the Holy Spirit, we can become one with satan and his demonic spirits. Remember, I became one flesh with my ex-boyfriend and became one with his spirit of disobedience,
self-centeredness, and perverted, unclean spirits. We have no idea what we are getting ourselves into by sleeping with someone outside of marriage. This is why we get defiled in our bodies.

The devil brings back memories, even 30 years from our past, to make us remember the person or have dreams we have a soul tie with. We can even be locked into feelings for someone from our past because of a soul tie. These feelings seem to just pop out of nowhere. We can also, still be carrying those spirits in our lives. This is why they must be broken. If you don't break all the soul ties from your past, those are the type of people and spirits that you will attract. You will be ushering in the same type of people and demonic spirits that you became one with. These are also called *familiar spirits* because they know you. There are also familiar spirits through those who serve satan. These are his puppeteers and pawns, through being a palm, card, or crystal ball reader, psychic, fortune teller, medium, soothsayer, witch, and the like.

*Give no regard to mediums and familiar spirits; do not seek after them, to be defiled by them: I am the Lord your God.* (Leviticus 19:31)

*There shall not be found among you anyone who makes his son or his daughter pass through the fire, (be sacrificed) or one who practices witchcraft, or a soothsayer, (a person who seems to be able to tell the future; a false prophet) or one who interprets omens, (a sign or warning that something good or bad is about to happen) or a sorcerer, or one who conjures spells, or a medium, (the use of someone or something else as a way of communication) or a spiritist, or one who calls up the dead. For all who do these things are an abomination to the Lord and because of these abominations the Lord your God drives them out from before you. (Emphasis mine)* (Deuteronomy 18:10-12)

If you ever went to any of these types of people, for any reason, you need to repent and break off the familiar spirit that got attached to your soul. This too would be a soul tie. A very evil one. Because you opened yourself up spiritually to them.

Our words are powerful. There is power in our tongue. Our words can cause a soul tie to be formed. We must be careful what we speak! Have you ever told someone, "No matter what, I will love you forever?" Maybe you said to someone, "You will always be a part of my life." How about, "We will be friends for the rest of our lives." Have you ever made a vow, pact, or ungodly covenant with someone? Are there times you wish you had never known someone or that you were ever part of their lives, whom you spoke those words to? I know I have!

*Thou art snared with the words of thy mouth, thou art taken with the words of thy mouth.* (Proverbs 6:2)

# How to Break Soul Tie's

First of all, I had to repent for having ungodly relationships. I went before the Lord and asked Him to show me who I had to break off soul ties with. So, I took a piece of paper and wrote down the names of all the people He brought to my mind. I prayed out loud, so the enemy could hear my words. This is just a sample list with made up names, just to
give you an idea of what it might look like. This will include my old friends who I made a pact with or a friendship vow when we were younger. This covers many years of relationships, to include ex-boyfriends and ex-husbands.

Again, this is just a sample. Then say the prayer I prayed below but make it personal.

## Sample List

1. Lobo        6. Ronnie        11. Stacey

2. William     7. James         12. Mike

3. Brandon     8. Joseph        13. Alex

4. Carlos       9. Amanda       14. Rey

5. Mindy       10. Rhonda       15.Brenda

## Make Your Own List

1._____

2._____

3._____

4._____

5._____

6._____

7._____

8._____

9._____

10._____

11._____

12._____

13._____

14._____

15._____

16._____

17._____

18._____

# Prayer

Father,

I come before Your courts of heaven. I repent for having ungodly relationships and forming these ungodly soul ties. Right now, in the name of Jesus Christ, I break all soul ties with: (name each person on the list) and I render null and void any and all vows, pacts, promises, and covenants made with each of these people. I rebuke every demonic spirit that has attached itself to me through my past relationships and for any connections I made myself open to through witchcraft, palm or card readers, psychics, mediums, spells or seances and the like, and command them to leave, in Jesus's name. I thank You Lord, that I am covered and redeemed by the Blood of the Lamb, and the words of my testimony. Lord, your word says in Mathew 16:19: What is bound on earth, is bound in heaven, and what is loosed on earth is loosed in heaven. I bind all ungodly past soul ties and send them back to the person from which they came.

Especially ex-boyfriends or girlfriends and ex-spouses. I break all intimate relations I had with these people. I loose, the power they have had in my life with the blood of Jesus. I now bind myself to Jesus and loose the power of His Holy Spirit in my life. Thank You Lord, I am now free to live my life according to Your will and purpose for me, in Jesus most precious and powerful name. Amen!

## 8. Getting Rid of The Remnants

Do you still hold on to gifts that were given to you by another? Still have letters, cards, pictures or something that symbolized your relationship, and you just can't seem to get rid of it? This can become idolatry. Don't allow the enemy of your soul, to keep you in bondage. You need to get rid of them. You can't move forward if you still hold on to the past. I took another step of measure in making sure there was nothing left that would tie me to the past. With my ex-boyfriend, I returned all his photos and gifts. I tore up all his letters, cards, or anything I had that symbolized any affection towards me and threw them in the trash. With my ex-husband (Lobo), I literally had a bon fire and burned everything! Well, I did sell my ring, but I blessed it for the person who bought it for his wife. While the fire was burning, I broke all curses off myself. I began praying in tongues, as the Holy Spirit led me to. I did a walk through in my house and if I found anything at all, it was immediately destroyed. I would urge you to do the same.

**This is how I prayed against the remnants:**

Remember, you can always make the prayers more personal for yourself and change the words in these prayers.

# Prayer

Father God,

As I burn or trash, to get rid of these symbolic things, I ask You to remove any lingering residue or effect they may have had in my soul, (mind and emotions) body, or spirit. I repent for idolizing any of these objects. I cut off any ties with these symbols and objects, with the blood and name of Jesus. Amen.

Doing all of the above will certainly prepare you for the spouse that God has chosen for you.

Ask the Lord if there is anything else, He would have you do for yourself before you get married. You should, by now feel so much lighter in your spirit and have much more peace. If you need to go through the steps again, don't hesitate to do it. Remember, the enemy of your soul wants to keep you where you have been for so many years, but you have the victory! Amen!

*But thanks be to God, who gives us the victory through our Lord Jesus Christ.* (1 Corinthians 15:57)

*For sin shall not have dominion over you, for you are not under law but under grace.* (Romans 6:14)

Now that you have humbled yourself before the Lord and had a good cleansing, you are in a much better place to pray
for your spouse. As I shared with you in the Revelations chapter 21, go ahead and make a list of things you would like
in your spouse. Please go before the Lord before you do this, so that what you write down will align with what He has planned for you. Doing this is in no way placing a demand on our Lord for what you want. He will give us the desires of our hearts if they align with His will for us. So, go to a quiet place and allow the Holy Spirit to lead you in writing your requests. He will add what He wants for you or remove what He doesn't want for you. And when you surrender to His will, some of the things you asked for, won't even matter to you anymore. Sometimes, it will take longer for

our requests to manifest. You just need to be patient and wait on the Lord for His timing, but they will come to pass if you are in His will. You just have to trust Him.

## Make Your Request List for Your Spouse

1. _____
2. _____
3. _____
4. _____
5. _____
6. _____
7. _____
8. _____
9. _____
10. _____

# Prayer

Abba Father,

I pray for my brothers and sisters in Christ. I ask that You help them write down in their lists, the requests that You place in their hearts. Help them to be still in Your presence. May they not be so anxious in writing things down, so that You may speak to them, as to what You want for them in a spouse. I pray that they would surrender what their image is of their spouse, to the perfect image of what their spouse is in Your eyes. I pray they would focus on You, on Your ability, Your power, and Your promises for them. You are the God of the impossible! Help them to be faithful in reading, trusting, and believing Your word. Give them patience in waiting on You, until their hearts desires are fulfilled in marriage to the one You have chosen for them. I ask this in the precious name of Your Son, Jesus. Amen.

*You will keep him in perfect peace, whose mind is stayed on You, because he trusts in You.* (Isaiah 26:3)

*Commit your way to the Lord, trust also in Him, and He shall bring it to pass.* (Psalm 37:5)

*Now may the God of hope fill you with all joy and peace in believing, that you may abound in hope by the power of the Holy Spirit.* (Romans 15:13)

After you write down your requests for your spouse, place it inside your bible. This is a safe place, and you will be reminded to continue to pray for the spouse God has chosen for you.

# Chapter 28

# The Making Of A New Bride (Church)

It starts off with the king having an extravagant feast that lasted 180 days. Wow! That was some Celebration!

### The feast of Ahasuerus

Now it came to pass in the days of Ahasuerus (this was the Ahasuerus who reigned over one hundred and twenty-seven provinces, from India to Ethiopia), in those days when King

Ahasuerus sat on the throne of his kingdom, which was in the Shushan citadel, that in the third year of his reign he made a feast for all his officials and servants the powers of Persia and Media, the nobles, and the princes of the provinces being before him when he showed the riches of his glorious kingdom and the splendor of his excellent majesty for many days, one hundred and eighty days in all. (Esther 1:1-4)

## Refusal of Queen Vashti

*Queen Vashti also made a feast for the women in the royal palace which belonged to King Ahasuerus. On the seventh day, when the heart of the king was merry with wine, he commanded Mehuman, Biztha, Harbona, Bigtha, Abagtha, Zethar, and Carcas, seven eunuchs who served in the presence of King Ahasuerus, to bring Queen Vashti before the king, wearing her royal crown, in order to show her beauty to the people and the officials, for she was beautiful to behold. But Queen Vashti refused to come at the king's command brought by his eunuchs; therefore, the king was furious, and his anger burned within him. (Esther 1:9-12)*

In the next verses, we see that the king sought counsel on what to do with the disobedient queen.

*Then the king said to the wise men who understood the times, (for this was the king's manner toward all who knew law and justice, those closest to him being Carshena, Shethar, Admatha, Tarshish, Meres, Marsena, and Memucan, the seven princes of Persia and Media, who had access to the*

*king's presence, and who ranked highest in the kingdom)
"What shall we do to Queen Vashti, according to law,
because she did not obey the command of King Ahasuerus
brought to her by the eunuchs?" And Memucan answered
before the king and the princes: "Queen Vashti has not only
wronged the king, but also all the princes, and all the people
who are in all the provinces of King Ahasuerus. For the
queen's behavior will become known to all women, so that
they will despise their husbands in their eyes, when they
report, 'King Ahasuerus commanded Queen Vashti to be
brought in before him, but she did not come.' This very day
the noble ladies of Persia and Media will say to all the king's
officials that they have heard of the behavior of the queen.
Thus, there will be excessive contempt and wrath. If it
pleases the king, let a royal decree go out from him, and let
it be recorded in the laws of the Persians and the Medes, so
that it will not be altered, that Vashti shall come no more
before King Ahasuerus; and let the king give her royal
position to another who is better than she. When the king's
decree which he will make is proclaimed throughout all his
empire (for it is great), all wives will honor their husbands,
both great and small." (Esther 1:13-20)*

**Oh, my goodness! This beautiful queen is losing her
royal position and her crown!**

*And the reply pleased the king and the princes, and the king
did according to the word of Memucan. Then he sent letters
to all the king's provinces, to each province in its own script,
and to every people in their own language, that each man
should be master in his own house and speak in the
language of his own people. (Esther 1:21-22)*

493

## Decree to Search for Vashti's Replacement

*After these things, when the wrath of King Ahasuerus subsided, he remembered Vashti, what she had done, and what had been decreed against her. Then the king's servants who attended him said: "Let beautiful young virgins be sought for the king; and let the king appoint officers in all the provinces of his kingdom, that they may gather all the beautiful young virgins to Shushan the citadel, into the women's quarters, under the custody of Hegai the king's eunuch, custodian of the women. And let beauty preparations be given them. Then let the young woman who pleases the king be queen instead of Vashti." This thing pleased the king, and he did so. (Esther 2:1-4)*

## Preparation of Esther

*And Mordecai had brought up Hadassah, that is, Esther, his uncle's daughter, for she had neither father nor mother. The young woman was lovely and beautiful. When her father and mother died, Mordecai took her as his own daughter. So it was, when the king's command and decree were heard, and when many young women were gathered at Shushan the citadel, under the custody of Hegai, that Esther also was taken to the king's palace, into the care of Hegai the custodian of the women. Now the young woman pleased him, and she obtained his favor; so, he readily gave beauty preparations to her, besides her allowance. Then seven choice maidservants were provided for her from the king's palace, and he moved her and her maidservants to the best place in the house of the women. (Esther 2:7-9)*

Esther's (Hadassah) preparation takes a full year before she is brought before the king.

Not only was Esther beautiful in her figure and her face, but she obtained much favor with Hegai who was in charge of all
the virgins who were brought into the palace. She got an extra portion of beauty preparations, seven maidservants, special food, and she got the best place in the palace for the women!

## These were the days of her preparation:

Six months of oil and myrrh, and six months with perfumes, ointments, cosmetics, and preparations for beautifying women.

Now, you need to understand that all these women who were to be brought before the king, were gathered from all the provinces of his kingdom in Susa. This was a Persian Empire that went as far East to India and far West to Greece, which surrounded massive deserts, and sub-tropical areas along the Tigris and Euphrates Rivers. So, you can imagine that the kingdom weather broadcast would be hot, humid, and shortage of rain, which caused droughts everywhere and the provinces located far from the rivers were infernal hot! I'm sure that the winds from the Persian Gulf going south, stirred up some brutal sandstorms and some very dry winds that came in from the North. This doesn't make for a good skin care regimen. Their face, lips, and skin would be damaged from the heat. This would include very rough, cracked, and blistered skin. They also had to deal with all the insect bites which also, caused sores and sickness. Their hair too was damaged. Hence, the year-long preparation for Esther before she meets with the king.

*Each young woman's turn came to go in to King Ahasuerus after she had completed twelve months' preparation, according to the regulations for the women, for thus were the days of their preparation apportioned: six months with oil of myrrh, and six months with perfumes and preparations for beautifying women. (Spices and cosmetic treatments) (Esther 2:12)*

## Let the Preparations Begin!

First, let us begin with the oil of myrrh. My daughter-in-law, Sheila, gave me a book called "Healing Oils of the Bible" by David Stewart PhD. for Christmas. It was perfect timing as I used this book for reference for looking up the oils that were used to prepare the next Queen of Persia.

## A Quick Course in Chemistry

Because of the tiny molecular structure of the components of an essential oil, they are extremely concentrated. One drop contains approximately 40 million-trillion molecules. Numerically is a 4 with 19 zeros after it: 40,000,000,000,000,000,000. We have 100 trillion cells in our bodies, and that's a lot. But one drop of essential oil contains enough molecules to cover every cell in our bodies with 400,000 molecules. Considering that only takes one molecule of the right kind to open a receptor site and communicate with the DNA to alter cellular function, you can see why even one drop or inhaling a small amount of oil vapor can have profound effects on the body, brain, and emotions. *(pgs. 27,28 Healing Oils of The Bible*

Myrrh is like a servant to all other oils. It is a fixative that increases the longevity of the aroma any fragrance with which it is combined without dominating or overpowering that fragrance. Myrrh is one of those synergistic oils that

enhances the qualities of any oil with which it is mixed. But

myrrh is a wonderfully healing oil in its own right, one of the most versatile. It is antiseptic, supports the immune system,
enhances the body's natural defenses, helps you relax, help to manage stress and frustration, soothes the skin, is oxygenating to body tissues, is mood elevating, creates a sense of well-being, promotes overall health, vitality, and longevity. (*pg. 151 Healing Oils of The Bible*)

There are many uses for this precious oil, to include healing cracked and dried skin, facial wrinkles, and helps to clean out your bowls. So, imagine being pampered with myrrh oil for six whole months. What a transformation that would be! Surely this would be a process of cleansing, healing, purification, and renewal.

Now, let us look at the perfumes, spices, and beautifying cosmetics. Perfumes were generally applied as oil-based salves, and there are numerous recipes and representations of the preparation of perfume in temples all over Egypt. The most highly prized perfumes were Susinum (a perfume based on lily, myrrh, cinnamon), Cyprinum (based upon henna, cardamom, cinnamon, myrrh, and southernwood) and Mendesian (myrrh and cassia with assorted gums and resins, usually obtained by making an incision in a plant and allowing the juice which exudes to solidify). As you can see, spices were used to mix these very aromatic fragrances.

Beautifying cosmetics of the Persian empire were Kohl for the eyes, henna for hair color and also to decorate the body. The pomegranate juice was lavishly used for blush and lip stain. Honey was used as a natural moisturizer and cosmetic. It was used to clear acne and is a mild antiseptic. Coriander, fennel, juniper, cumin, and thyme were used as health promoting spices.

Six months of this treatment would ultimately hurl you into the finishing process to become the next Queen of Persia.

At last, we come to the conclusion of the preparations. Now we go to the beginning of a whole new love story!

## Crowning of a New Queen Bride

*So, Esther was taken to King Ahasuerus, into his royal palace, in the tenth month, which is the month of Tebeth, in the seventh year of his reign. The king loved Esther more than all the other women, and she obtained grace and favor in his sight more than all the virgins. So, he set the royal crown upon her head and made her queen instead of Vashti. Then the king made a great feast, the Feast of Esther, for all his officials and servants; and he proclaimed a holiday in the provinces and gave gifts according to the generosity of a king.* (Esther 2:16-18)

Queen Esther will be queen over the largest empire the world has ever seen! It was God who poured His favor on Esther. When we have His favor, we also have man's favor. Esther loved God with all her heart, she was dedicated, obedient, and fervent in prayer. She lived a life that pleased God and He knew He could trust her. Therefore, He divinely set her up to be the next queen, so that she could fulfill her destiny. To save her people from destruction!

*For if you remain completely silent at this time, relief and deliverance will arise for the Jews from another place, but you and your father's house will perish. Yet who knows whether you have come to the kingdom (your royal position) for such a time as this?"* (Emphasis mine) (Esther 4:14)

God has a plan and a purpose for each and every one of us. We were created with a special and unique destiny. All we have to do is ask God to reveal what His plan is for us.

What is it that you are supposed to be doing for God? Whatever it is, we must do it with the best of our ability. A teacher, a wife, a minister, working in the marketplace, a lawyer, a doctor, a preacher, an author, a CEO or a receptionist, it doesn't matter what it is, so long as we do all things in *excellence* as unto the Lord. Amen!

**When we accept Jesus as our Lord, we get our own feast day!**

*Let us be glad and rejoice and give Him glory, for the marriage of the Lamb has come, and His wife has made herself ready." And to her it was granted to be arrayed in fine linen, clean and bright, for the fine linen is the righteous acts of the saints. Then he said to me, "Write: 'Blessed are those who are called to the marriage supper of the Lamb!' And he said to me, "These are the true sayings of God."* (Revelation 19:7-9)

So, let me ask you this. Have you allowed the Lord to prepare you as the bride of Christ?

**Have you been called and are you prepared for the marriage supper of the Lamb?**

# Chapter 29

# The Preparation Chamber

**Preparation:** something done to get ready for an event, the action or process of making something ready for use or service or of getting ready for some occasion, test, or duty

**Chamber:** A natural or artificial space or cavity, a private room (Merriam-Webster)

I absolutely love the process of preparation, of my biblical role model, Queen Esther, before she was to be brought before the King Ahasuerus (Hebrew) or Xerxes (Greek).

We are going to look at the way God prepares us (male or female) to be His bride. In the days that we live in now, all

the beauty preparations in the marketplace are so easily at our disposal. You can go to just about any store or on-line website, to purchase what you want or need. Shampoos and conditioners, eye makeup, body lotions and perfumes, hair and nail accessories, cleansing and wellness products, even such products as to enhance what we lack. *That is the easy part.* This takes care of the outside of us. The outside appearance. It's the inside that we really need work on. *This is the hard part!* You can look at a beautiful woman or handsome man on the outside, but their attitude, actions, and personality make them really ugly. Yet, you can see a person who would be considered in the eyes of the world, an ugly person, but they can be kind, loving, giving and have an attitude of gratitude, which in turn makes them beautiful. It isn't the outside appearance that counts. It's what is in the heart and spirit of a person that matters. Beauty is in the eyes of the beholder. God is our beholder! What does He see when He looks at you?

I'm going to share how God prepared me as His bride and what He had to do with me while I was praying, believing, and waiting for my spouse.

I mentioned earlier that I was a single mom for eleven years. It then turned into thirteen years after my big mistake of marrying someone I knew I shouldn't have. You read that nightmare.

As I continued to wait on God, I remember one day I asked Him, "Lord, why is it taking so long for me to meet the husband You have chosen for me?" He said to me, "Because

I have you in a preparation chamber." He immediately gave me the understanding of what that meant. Just as His beloved Esther, went through her preparations, I now needed to go through my own personal cleansing and beautifying. My emotions, my memories, and my spirit had been mangled, beaten, and battered.

Even though I had forgiven everyone and everything that had been done to me and my family, I still needed healing and restoration. God had me in this chamber to prepare me for my future spouse, so that I wouldn't bring all this brokenness into our marriage.

If you have two broken vessels, you can't make a whole one. The cracked pieces won't fit together. You both need to be whole, or there will be a lot of heartache and strife in the marriage. If you are married already, God can still heal and make you whole. You just have to be willing to go through your own *chamber* and allow Him to do what He needs to do for you. You might need a chamber of healing, deliverance, forgiveness, salvation, or of revelation. Maybe all of these.

Since I was already saved, already had a heart of forgiveness, and had revelation of all that I had been through, I now needed to be prepared for my next chapter in life, which would include my true husband.

God had been taking me through a journey of healing, restoration, and teaching through this *preparation chamber* He had me in for so long; I didn't even know it. All I had to do was ask!

I now had to be fully surrendered to His will and plan for me. Even though the forgiveness was there, I still didn't have the time to heal because something else would come to pile on top of what I had just gone through. I had a lot of layers that needed to be peeled and torn away. I may have to go through some more spiritual pain, more cleansing and refining through the fire, humbled down low to extreme measures, but I knew it would all be worth it.

I saw a vision of my chamber. It was crystal clear and sparkled in the light. It was in the shape of an eight-sided cylinder. I knew this symbolized new beginnings, hope, and a new future for me. I was standing in the middle of this chamber. It had parallel strips of silver on the side, top, and bottom of it. Even though I had gone through my own hell on earth, I was being protected through it all. God kept me surrounded in His protection, so that the enemy would not prevail against me. I was being taken through a process.

## This is how He prepares His bride.

*Husbands, love your wives, just as Christ also loved the church and gave Himself for her, that He might sanctify and cleanse her with the washing of water by the word, that He might present her to Himself a glorious church, not having spot or wrinkle or any such thing, but that she should be holy and without blemish.* (Ephesians 5:25-26)

When we give our lives to the Lord, we become part of the body of Christ, His church. We first become His bride. How beautiful is that? We come to Him just as we are. Full of sin, full of failure's, fears, brokenness, guilt, and shame. Just plain dirty. The great thing is that He accepts us just the way we are with open arms. He knows all the details of our life. We can't hide anything from Him.

*And there is no creature hidden from His sight, but all things are naked and open to the eyes of Him to whom we must give account.* (Hebrews 4:13)

I am now going through seasonal changes in my preparation chamber, where God is sanctifying, healing, restoring, and cleansing me from my past. You see, our transformation, and being changed and conformed to His image and as the bride of Christ, is a daily and lifelong process. It doesn't just happen overnight. Although, I have experienced past issues in my life that He immediately took away. And I know of innumerable testimonies on the miraculous in people being delivered and set free instantly. However, some are not.

# Living Waters

In this season of life, He really wanted to wash away all the turmoil, trauma, pain, and spiritual paralysis it all had on my life. There were times when I would feel His *living waters* being poured upon me all around. In the chamber, it was like this gushing flow of water would come pouring out of all sides of the chamber. It was so refreshing, so cleansing, and so pure. Almost, like standing in a heavenly car wash. I was getting the ultimate, spiritual *deluxe* package.

God's living waters brings refreshment, cleansing, healing and purification to our hearts and minds.

*And He said to me, "It is done! I am the Alpha and the Omega, the Beginning and the End. I will give of the fountain of the water of life freely to him who thirsts.* (Revelation 21:6)

*But let justice run down like water, And righteousness like a mighty stream.* (Amos 5:2)

*The Lord will guide you continually, and satisfy your soul in drought, and strengthen your bones; You shall be like a watered garden, and like a spring of water, whose waters do not fail. (Isaiah 58:11)*

*He who believes in Me, as the Scripture has said, out of his heart will flow rivers of living water."* (John 7:38)

# Consuming Fire

The same thing would happen at different times, but then instead of water, *fire* would be pouring out. When the fire came, I could feel the heat of the flames, but not in the sense of burning me. I knew the consuming fire of God at this time, was burning out old roots of sin, strongholds, the effects of trauma, and all the junky filth that was left behind from my past. All the dross was being removed permanently. At the end of this washing with fire, I felt His freedom, strength, and connection to His perfecting power over me.

*Behold, I have refined you, but not as silver; I have tested you in the furnace of affliction.* (Isaiah 48:10)

*I will turn My hand against you, and thoroughly purge away your dross, and take away all your alloy.* (Isaiah 1:25)

**Definition of dross**: *Metallurgy*: the scum or unwanted material that forms on the surface of molten metal; waste or foreign matter: impurity, chaff, junk, garbage, debris, and effluvium (an invisible emanation *especially* an offensive exhalation or smell)

**Definition of alloy:** An admixture that lessens value; an impairing alien element a compound, mixture, or union of different things (Merriam Webster)

No wonder we must be refined in the fire! All that junk mixed together. Until we are truly purified, I don't even want to know what I smelled like in the presence of the Lord. I'm sure I didn't smell like the Jasmine flower!

*But He knows the way that I take; when He has tried me, I shall come out as gold.* (Job 23:10)

# Anointing Oil

Just like the living waters and consuming fire came and filled my chamber, there was a third outpouring. I would get bathed in the luxurious oils and perfumes from heaven. It was, as a heavy mist coming forth from a waterfall, where I would get soaked in the sweet-smelling aroma of His presence. Just as Queen Esther was bathed and massaged in the most expensive oils and perfumes in her time, I too was lathered and massaged with the priceless treasure of the Holy Spirit and drenched in the incense of His love, peace, and joy.

*Let him smother me with kisses, his Spirit-kiss divine. So kind are your caresses, I drink them in like the sweetest wine! Your presence releases a fragrance so pleasing over and over poured out. For your lovely name is Flowing Oil. No wonder the brides-to-be adore you. Draw me into your heart. We will run away together into the king's cloud-filled chamber.* (Song of Solomon 1:2-4 TPT)

*Jesus of Nazareth was anointed by God with the Holy Spirit and with great power.* (Acts 10:38 TPT)

514

**The Holy Spirit is symbolic of oil, which brings His presence and power in our life.**

*Moreover, the Lord spoke to Moses, saying: "Also take for yourself quality spices, five hundred shekels of liquid myrrh, half as much sweet-smelling cinnamon, (two hundred and fifty shekels) of sweet-smelling cane, five hundred shekels of cassia, according to the shekel of the sanctuary, and a hin of olive oil. And you shall make from these a holy anointing oil, an ointment compounded according to the art of the perfumer. It shall be a holy anointing oil.* (Exodus 30:22-25)

*You are passionate for righteousness, and you hate lawlessness. This is why God, your God, crowns you with bliss above your fellow kings. He has anointed you, more than any other, with His oil of fervent joy, the very fragrance of heaven's gladness.* (Psalm 45:7 TPT)

Jesus, as the Master perfumer, took the ingredients from His heavenly garden to formulate a fusion of fragrances, essential oils, and spices; uniquely for me. This beautiful mixture of holy elements and liquid was poured into me like an alabaster jar, filling me with His holy anointing oil. How glorious it is, to be called and prepared as the bride of Christ. Each one of you has a very intimate and distinct formulation that is prepared exclusively for you from the Lord.

I thank God for His continued mercy and grace in my life. I thank Him for loving me so much that He wouldn't let me stay the way I was.

# Prayer

Dear Lord,

I pray for your beloved ones. May they have a surrendered heart towards your plans for them. Give them the hope of Your glory to transform them into the bride of Christ. I pray that they freely enter into their own personal *preparation chamber*. Give them the desire to experience the washing, burning, and saturation they need in Your divine presence. May they call upon You, our Savior, Healer, Redeemer, Deliverer, Forgiver of our sins, and Lover of our souls. I pray they would allow You to reveal to them, anything in their lives that needs to be dealt with before they are joined to their chosen spouse. Prepare them and their spouse for a marriage with You, then with each other. Draw them into the bridal chamber to experience Your pure and perfect love for them. I ask this in the name of our Betrothed, Jesus. Amen!

*Jasmine Hartswick*

# Chapter 30

# Ushering in Your Spouse The One God Has Chosen For You

Now, let us get down to God's business of how to usher in your spouse using His spiritual kingdom realm.

**Ushering in**: Cause or mark the start of something new. herald, mark the start of, signal, ring in, show in, set the scene for, pave the way for, start, begin, introduce, open the door to, get going, set in motion, get underway, kick off, launch pave the way for, open the door, set in motion, initiate, launch. To celebrate the beginning of something. (Britannica Dictionary)

I wanted to put the definition of what *Ushering In* means, so you can get a general idea of what this chapter is going to teach you. I'm going to share with you what I personally did to *usher in* my spouse with the help and the leading of the Holy Spirit. God is faithful to help us in all things; all we have to do is ask Him.

*The woman came and knelt before him. "Lord, help me!" she said.* (Matthew 15:25)

*I can do all things through Christ who strengthens me.* (Philippians 4:13)

*Surely God is my help; the Lord is the one who sustains me.* (Psalm 54:4 NIV)

*Let us therefore come boldly to the throne of grace, that we may obtain mercy and find grace to help in time of need.* (Hebrews4:16)

After my second divorce and AFTER I got saved, I knew what type of husband I deserved. The Bible is very clear on how God wants the husband to treat his wife and how the wife should treat her husband. Let's look at some scriptures to align ourselves with the type of spouse and marriage God wants for us.

# What a Marriage Should Be

*Wives, submit to your own husbands, as to the Lord. For the husband is head of the wife, as also Christ is head of the church; and He is the Savior of the body. Therefore, just as the church is subject to Christ, so let the wives be to their own husbands in everything.* (Ephesians 5:22-24)

Gentlemen, I would like to kindly remind you not to try to abuse this scripture. This is not by any means allowing you to twist these words to accommodate yourself, in forcing your wife to do something that is against the Word of God. This will not please God. So long as you are being obedient in the ways that you are to treat your wife and ask her to do something that aligns with His word, then the wife should not have a problem doing what you ask. Wives, just as you submit to God, it should be easy for you to submit to your husband. (If he is living a life according to the scriptures and being a Godly husband). Since Jesus is our spouse, and He gave you the husband as your earthly spouse, then you should submit to him as you would Jesus. Both of you should be *Jesus* to each other.

*Husbands, love your wives, just as Christ also loved the church and gave Himself for her, that He might sanctify and cleanse her with the washing of water by the word, ^that He might present her to Himself a glorious church, not having spot or wrinkle or any such thing, but that she should be holy and without blemish. So, husbands, ought to love their own wives as their own bodies; he who loves his wife loves himself. For no one ever hated his own flesh, but nourishes and cherishes it, just as the Lord does the church. For we are members of His body, of His flesh and of His bones. "For this reason, a man shall leave his father and mother and be joined to his wife, and the two shall become one flesh." This is a great mystery, but I speak concerning Christ and the church. Nevertheless, let each one of you in particular, so love his own wife as himself, and let the wife see that she respects her husband.* (Ephesians 5:25-33)

A healthy marriage must have mutual respect. There is the stereotype that says men need respect and women need love, but both spouses need love and respect. In a marriage, we must be tenacious in showing respect and love to one another. They come hand in hand. This is a joint premium benefit to the marriage.

**Respect:** a feeling of deep admiration for someone or something elicited by their abilities, qualities, or achievements. Due regard for the feelings, wishes, rights, or traditions of others. (Oxford English Dictionary)

## How can the wife respect her husband?

### 1. By helping and assisting him

The way she interacts with her husband, allows him to know that she is there to be helpful and willing to assist in what he is trying to accomplish. She can serve him in giving advice and letting him know he is not alone in the marriage. She can serve him in different ways to help him become the best he can be and the best at what he does.

## 2. She can honor parameters that are established for him

There are certain responsibilities that are meant to be for the husband alone. The wife shouldn't feel it necessary to get involved in every situation. The husband feels respected when the wife supports him in doing his job, without trying to do the job for him. She shouldn't try to take control of everything.

## 3. By loving and encouraging him.

She always looks out for his best interest. She tells him the truth, even if it hurts. She encourages him when he's down and prays with him to lift him up. She reminds him who he is in Christ. She gives him words of affirmation. She speaks to him in love.

## 4. By showing him that she trusts him

By trusting him, you give him the confidence that he is not going to fail. You allow him to accomplish hard tasks by believing in him. This makes him feel adequate in himself and in his work.

## 5. By listening to him.

If you do not listen to what your husband has to say, he feels very disrespected. He feels that what he has to say isn't important enough for you to listen. Sometimes, we may interfere when our husband is in the middle of a conversation with us. We don't let him finish talking. We disrupt his conversation with us by assuming we already know the answer or the end of what he is saying. This can cause a lot of frustration. We need to keep silent and listen to him with love and understanding until he is finished talking. This gives him a deep feeling of respect from us. Listening gives him, his desire to be heard.

## 6. By nurturing a loving intimate relationship

Let's face it. Men need sex. If a wife will make a joint effort to identify and understand her husband's sexual needs, he will feel a great level of relevant respect. For most couples, sex is a very important way of showing their love for each other. If a man doesn't feel his wife wants to connect with him sexually, he feels disrespected because he can't separate sex and respect in a marriage. God created sex for the marriage. We become one flesh during intimacy with our spouse. It is supposed to be a holy union between a husband and wife. It is the most intimate way we show each other love. So, husbands to be...know that if you hurt your wife or get her angry, she is not going to want to have sex with you because she will be reacting according to her emotions. Women think with logic of emotion, men think with logic of reason. It will do the husband good to be respectful and loving to his wife, if he expects her to be intimate with him. Believe me, this is golden advice!

There are so many other ways to show respect to your husband. I just wanted to give a few examples that will shed some light on the matter. The husband can also use these examples for the wife. Marriage is a partnership that deserves equal love and respect. These two go hand in hand and are vital in a marriage.

*Husbands, in the same way be considerate as you live with your wives and treat them with respect as the weaker partner and as heirs with you of the gracious gift of life, so that nothing will hinder your prayers.* (1 Peter 3:7 NIV)

This scripture is very important for every man who hopes to become a husband, or already are one. Read the last part of that scripture. It is warning you that if you do not respect your wife, your prayers will be hindered! If you belittle your wife, are disrespectful to her, abusive, or you dishonor her in any way, you are disobeying God. By disobeying God, you dishonor Him and disrespect Him. By the same saving grace in faith through Christ, the wife is co-heir with you. She is your equal and should be treated as so. The husband is to treat his wife with love, honor, care, and protection, just as he would to someone that is more fragile than himself. He should love his wife as God loves her.

Unless the husband repents of any wrongdoing against his wife and changes that behavior, his connection in communicating with God, will not be fully opened. His prayers will be hindered.

And the wife should love and respect her husband as she does the Lord. Abuse and disrespect are not part of the marriage God wants for a husband or wife. And yes, ladies that includes you not being abusive to your husband. This issue doesn't only pertain to men. Women can be just as abusive as any man. That is why it is relevant for both men and women to go through the steps taken in chapter twenty-seven, BEFORE you get married.

*He who finds a wife finds a good thing and obtains favor from the Lord.* (Proverbs 18:22)

## How can the husband express love to his wife?

**1.** He can buy her gifts of appreciation: Flowers, perfume, massages, a week-end vacation, special jewelry, a new outfit, etc.

**2.** By helping her with the house chores.

**3.** Help taking care of the kids and homework.

**4.** Taking her out on dates.

**5.** Running a bubble bath for her and making a cup of tea.

**6.** Showing her love and affection with hugs and kisses.

**7.** Taking your time by emotionally connecting with her during intimacy.

**8.** Tell her how much you love her and why.

**9.** Let her know with words of affirmation how important she
is to you.

**10.** Just be there for her when she needs you the most.

There are many ways to express our love and affection to one another. Find ways of doing so that would utterly surprise your spouse. We have a very creative God. Ask Him for ideas.

# The Virtuous Wife

*Who can find a virtuous wife? For her worth is far above rubies. The heart of her husband safely trusts her; So, he will have no lack of gain. She does him good and not evil All the days of her life. She seeks wool and flax, and willingly works with her hands. She is like the merchant ships; she brings her food from afar. She also rises while it is yet night, and provides food for her household, and a portion for her maidservants. She considers a field and buys it; from her profits she plants a vineyard. She girds herself with strength and strengthens her arms. She perceives that her merchandise is good, and her lamp does not go out by night. She stretches out her hands to the distaff, and her hand holds the spindle. She extends her hand to the poor,*
*yes, she reaches out her hands to the needy.* She is not afraid of snow for her household, *for all her household is clothed with scarlet. She makes tapestry for herself; her clothing is fine linen and purple. Her husband is known in the gates when he sits among the elders of the land. She makes linen garments and sells them and supplies sashes for the merchants. Strength and honor are her clothing; she shall rejoice in time to come. She opens her mouth with wisdom, and on her tongue is the law of kindness.She watches over the ways of her household and does not eat the bread of idleness. Her children rise up and call her blessed; Her husband also, and he praises her: "Many daughters have*

*done well, but you excel them all." Charm is deceitful and beauty is passing, but a woman who fears the Lord, she shall be praised. Give her of the fruit of her hands, and let her own works praise her in the gates. (Proverbs 31:10-31)*

*Love is patient, love is kind. It does not envy, it does not boast, it is not proud. It does not dishonor others, it is not self-seeking, it is not easily angered, it keeps no record of wrongs. Love does not delight in evil but rejoices with the truth. It always protects, always trusts, always hopes, always perseveres. Love never fails. (1 Corinthians 13:4-7 NIV)*

**Why does love never fail? It is because God is love and He can never fail!**

The above scripture describes the attributes and essence of what a spouse and marriage should be. Whether the wife or the husband, they should always put their spouse before themselves.

*Greater love has no one than this, than to lay down one's life for his friends. (spouse) (emphasis mine) (John 15:13)*

This scripture isn't just talking about a life and death situation. We can literally take this scripture and apply it to our marriage.

**These are some examples of how we can lay down our own lives for our spouse.**

♥ Sometimes we need to go to the hospital for different reasons and times. The situation could seem to be

serious, or it could be just a checkup. We accompany each other, no matter what we had planned for our day, to let the other, know that we care about them and want to know they are getting the care they need to get better. We need to let our spouse know that they matter to us, and we will be by their side in good times and bad, as well.

♥ Whenever something needs to get done for one or the other, we lay down our own agenda and inconvenience, to put the needs of the other before our own.

♥ I will always wash his clothes before I wash mine.

♥ If either of us gets sick, we will make runs to the store to get medicine, certain drinks or foods that will help the other get better. My husband goes beyond and above in this. He brings home fresh soup from the restaurant instead of serving me canned soup.

♥ There are times we need to put everything aside, just to be there for moral support or to just listen.

♥ If for some reason, one can't perform their regular chores, the other steps in to give a helping hand.

♥ If my husband needed one of my body parts to keep him alive, I wouldn't hesitate to give it to him. He too, would do this for me.

♥ Sometimes we just have make sacrifices for one another, to show them that they matter, are worthy, and significant to our life.

You get the picture. No matter how small or big the sacrifice we make, we are to put each other first. We lay down our life to make our spouse's life come first. I know without a shadow of doubt, my husband would literally lay down his life for mine. I would do the same for him because that is what love does. That is what Jesus did for us!

*Therefore, as the elect of God, holy and beloved, put-on tender mercies, kindness, humility, meekness, longsuffering; bearing with one another, and forgiving one another, if anyone has a complaint against another; even as Christ forgave you, so you also, must do. But above all these things put on love, which is the bond of perfection.* (Colossians 3:12-14)

The **bond of perfection** is our marriage to Christ when we get saved. His love is perfect. It is Pure, holy, and unconditional. His love for us is the perfect example of what our earthly marriage should be.

In all the above scriptures, as the elect (chosen ones) of God, pertaining to marriage, we should put it all into practice in our everyday life. This makes for a beautiful, happy, and fulfilled marriage! It will be difficult at times. You will have the marriage according to the time and effort you put into it. If you apply all the scriptures mentioned above into your marriage, it should prepare you for the hard times, the battles you will face, and any difficulties the enemy may throw your way. Just do everything in love, as Jesus loves us.

*Two are better than one, because they have a good reward for their labor. For if they fall, one will lift up his companion. (spouse) But woe to him who is alone when he falls, for he has no one to help him up. (Emphasis mine) (Ecclesiastes 4:9-10)*

## (1 Corinthians 13:4-7 NIV)
## Sums it all up for us.

*Love is patient, love is kind. It does not envy, it does not boast, it is not proud. It does not dishonor others, it is not self-seeking, it is not easily angered, it keeps no record of wrongs. Love does not delight in evil but rejoices with the truth. It always protects, always trusts, always hopes, always perseveres. Love never fails.*

**Everything we say and do, good or bad, "ushers" (summons) something or someone into our lives.**

There is a spiritual response or reaction in the spirit realm (heaven or hell) to what we speak and do. The devil knows the Word of God and he can quote it better than most any of us. But he absolutely cannot operate in the power of it, and he is powerless against it. We as Christians believers have all power and authority to operate in the living Word of God when we speak it. His spirit lives in us!

541

Now, if you want to *usher* in that spouse, then what type of spouse do you want brought into your life? Remember that satan, the father of lies, will come in and mock everything God does. He will send the fakes, the wolves, and the imposters to try and trap you into believing that someone or something was sent from God. By this point in the book, I am guessing that you want the one God has for you.

## It's Time To Do It God's Way

We need to use God's way of *ushering in* (pave the way, introduce, open the door) the things and especially the spouse God has for us.

We know how to attract in the physical realm. Men and women dress nice, we style our hair nicely, ladies put on makeup, women use perfume and men use cologne. When we are out and about or on a date, we put on our best behavior. We want to attract the opposite sex, in hopes of gaining that special someone. But satan knows this by getting information from his monitoring spirits and will begin a subtle plan to lure in the wrong person to cause havoc and destruction. This happened to me!

Now, you may meet someone who is nice and seems to have it all together, but if they are not the one God wants for you, you will be cheating yourself out of the blessings God wants for both of you.

Even if you do marry or already have married someone who was not God's choice for you, He can still bless you. And it will only come from a mutual agreement between the both of you to follow all the scriptures, take all the steps, and advice to begin a journey of working towards the love and marriage God wants for you. It's not too late to fall in love with your spouse. God can place that love in your heart.

# Ushering in Your Spouse

### The first thing you need to do is pray.

I looked back at my past relationships and compared them to what type of relationship I should have with my spouse, according to God's standards. When you pray, ask God to help you make a list of the type of spouse God wants for you. I remember telling God that I didn't want my husband to be of certain ethnic backgrounds. Not because I was prejudice, but because I had labeled them as bad men due to the behavior and abuse, I saw them display in mine and some of my friend's marriages. After a while, God convicted my heart to let me know that not all men of those ethnicities were bad or evil. I repented for allowing that wrong thought pattern into my heart and then asked Him to remove any unforgiveness in my heart towards these men. As I did this, I set myself free from any hinderance that would stop me from meeting the man God had chosen for me. I even told Him that it didn't matter anymore to me, where my husband came from. Whether he was Black, White, Hispanic, or Chinese, I knew I would love him because he was the one for me from God.

**The spouse God has for you will be a reflection of Jesus our Bridegroom in the flesh, whom God our Father sent just for you.**

Oh, how this knowledge excited me and filled me with a joyous expectation!

As I sat down to write my own list, it was by the leading of the Holy Spirit that I would ask God for the specific things I wanted in my spouse. (See chapter 21) He allowed me to write down that I didn't want a man with a pot belly, but in the end, even that didn't matter to me anymore. Yes, the Lord will give us the desires of our heart, but they must align with the things He wants for us. He will put those desires in us. He will also remove any desires that are not from Him if we allow Him to. And if you really want that perfect match for you from the Lord, then you will surrender your own wants and desires for His. You can cry, beg, whine, and tantrum to get what you want from God, but don't blame Him if He gives it to you and it turns into a nightmare. He will just look down and say, "Are you ready to surrender your will, your plans, and your thoughts over to Me and receive the blessings that I have planned for you?" Please, brothers and sisters, save yourself a lot of heartache!

*"For My thoughts are not your thoughts, nor are your ways My ways," says the Lord.* (Isaiah 55:8)

*Now to Him who is able to do exceedingly abundantly above all that we ask or think, according to the power that works in us, to Him be glory in the church by Christ Jesus to all generations, forever and ever. Amen. (Ephesians 3:20-21)*

**I began to pray for my husband and ask God to prepare our hearts for each other.**

I spiritually laid hands on him and prophesied over him. I thanked God that he was indeed a man after God's own heart. I declared that he was so in love with Jesus and that he would serve Him with a servant's heart. I spoke a lot of scriptures over him and asked God to protect him wherever he was. I proclaimed that he would be filled with humility and be totally surrendered to His Creator. I asked Jesus, to make him into His image, as a husband. I covered him with the blood of Jesus and asked God to send His angels to encamp around him, to minister to him, and help protect his identity and destiny.

*For He shall give His angels charge over you, to keep you in all your ways. In their hands they shall bear you up, lest you dash your foot against a stone.* (Psalm 91:11-12)

I asked God to keep his heart pure and for the Holy Spirit to convict his heart of sin with a holy conviction. I prayed for Abba Father to bless the work of his hands and for him to be a good steward of everything he was blessed with, especially his finances. I also asked the Lord for my husband to be praying for me. If the Holy Spirit put something in my heart to pray for, I would pray it for my husband. I asked for the Holy Spirit to cleanse us, wash us, purify us, and prepare our hearts for the day that we would be divinely connected. This went on for years. Yes, sometimes I would get discouraged, but I knew that the word of God was infallible, so I redirected my focus on His promises and not let the waiting time overtake me. I was not going to let the enemy steal my faith or hope.

*Now faith is the substance of things hoped for, the evidence of things not seen.* (Hebrews 11:1)

*He is our father in the sight of God, in whom he believed, the God who gives life to the dead and calls things that are not as though they were.* (Romans 4:17)

*Therefore, I tell you, whatever you ask for in prayer, believe that you have received it, and it will be yours.* (Mark 11:24)

## I would always quote scripture out loud.

All the scriptures that I have been using in the chapters is what I would pray out loud and proclaim over myself, my husband, and marriage. I would encourage you to do the same. Angels are attracted to God's living Word. God has His army of angels of every rank and division to help us in all things.

Bless the Lord, you His angels, who excel in strength, who do His word, Heeding the voice of His word. (Psalm 103:20)

## What you speak out of your mouth either causes life or death.

*Death and life are in the power of the tongue, and those who love it will eat its fruit.* (Proverbs 18:21)

*Whoever guards his mouth and tongue Keeps his soul from troubles.* (Proverbs 21:23)

*For by your words, you will be justified, and by your words you will be condemned."* (Matthew 12:37)

*But those things which proceed out of the mouth come from the heart, and they defile a man.* (Matthew 15:18)

*Pleasant words are like a honeycomb, sweetness to the soul and health to the bones.* (Proverbs 16:24)

*She opens her mouth with wisdom, and on her tongue is the law of kindness.* (Proverbs 31:26)

These scriptures tell us that you either bless with your words or curse with it. You either speak life, or death. If you speak blessings with your mouth, you will reap blessings, but if you curse with your mouth, that is what you will reap.

**Speaking God's Word is a very important key to *ushering in* your spouse.**

Proclaiming what God says about you and your spouse through His word, plays an essential part in vesting into your future together. I have given enough truth through God's written word, what a marriage should be in the eyes of God, and how we should treat and speak to each other. Putting all these scriptures into practice, speaking God's word over yourself and your spouse will benefit you and prepare you for your spouse.

*"Assuredly, I say to you, whatever you bind on earth will be bound in heaven, and whatever you loose on earth will be loosed in heaven.* (Matthew 18:18)

In this scripture, you can bind (impose a legal or contractual obligation on) anything that the devil would try to attempt against you. You have the power to do this by the blood of the Lamb and in His name, Jesus. Let me be clear. Unless you are saved, you have no power over the devil. Why? Because it is the power of Jesus that lives in us that gives us the authority over our enemies.

*When the seventy missionaries returned to Jesus, they were ecstatic with joy, telling him, "Lord, even the demons obeyed us when we commanded them in your name!" Jesus replied, "While you were ministering, I watched satan topple until he fell suddenly from heaven like lightning to the ground. Now you understand that **I have imparted to you** my authority to trample over his kingdom. You will trample upon every demon before you and **overcome every power satan possesses**. Absolutely nothing will harm you as you walk in this authority. (Luke 10:19 TPT)*

*You are of God, little children, and have overcome them, because He who is in you (Jesus) is greater than he (satan) who is in the world. (Emphasis mine) (1 John 4:4)*

## You bind the enemy first.

**Bind:** To confine, restrain, or restrict as if with bonds; (Blood of Jesus)
**To constrain** what is unlawful with legal authority (power and authority of Jesus)

We have authority to arrest the demonic hosts of hell that come against us, our loved ones, our marriage, and any area of our life. So, when you bind something that comes from

hell, you are forbidding and prohibiting it from happening. You are putting it in God's spiritual chains.

**You then loose the works of the enemy.**

**Loose:** to set free; release; remit or discharge (Blood of Jesus)

We have authority to command the hosts of hell to loosen their works, curses, assignments, and hinderances on us or our loved ones, in Jesus's name and by the power of His blood.

*He raised us up with Christ the exalted One, and we ascended with Him into the glorious perfection and **authority** of the heavenly realm, for we are now co-seated as one with Christ!* (Ephesians 2:6 TPT)

## This was my decree:

(An official order issued by a legal authority)

Lord Jesus,

I thank You for giving me power and authority over all the powers of darkness. I thank You that no weapon formed against me, my spouse, or our marriage shall prosper. We are redeemed from the hands of the enemy and delivered from every power of darkness. Right now, in the name of Jesus Christ of Nazareth, I bind you satan and all your demons. And in the name and by the blood of Jesus, I declare and decree you to loosen any and all weapons of darkness you have placed on us. I bind and rebuke all your works, plans, plots, and schemes. I loose your assignments, curses, hinderances, and agendas off myself, my family, and my spouse. I render null and void everything that you have caused to come against us, by the blood of and in Jesus's name. Amen.

**Your future marriage is something that you should pray for before it comes to pass.**

After you bind and loose the enemy off yourself, spouse, and marriage, you can then loose the power of the Holy Spirit into your lives. Bind the word of God in your hearts and lives and ask the Holy Spirit to fill you and your spouse with all the fruits of His Spirit. Everything in the scripture below should be what your marriage portrays.

*But the fruit of the Spirit is love, joy, peace, longsuffering, kindness, goodness, faithfulness, gentleness, self-control. Against such there is no law.* (Galatians 5:22-23)

## Prayer for your spouse

Abba Father,

I ask You to finish what You started in myself and my spouse. I ask for protection over us and our future relationship together. I pray that You fill us both with Your love, understanding, a forgiving heart, Your wisdom and discernment. I pray that You would reveal to us our purpose, calling, and gifts as an individual. Teach us how to nourish and grow what you have called us to do. When the day comes that You bless us with our divine connection to each other, I pray that our calling in life would just flow together in unity as husband and wife. Help us to know how to help each other fulfill our destinies, according to the will and purpose for us as individuals and as a couple. I ask You to remove anyone who is a hindrance or a bad influence in our walk with You. Surround my spouse with Christian's who will help them develop a true and strong relationship with You. Kindle a fire within them to search the things of Your kingdom, to hunger and thirst after You, and to read Your word daily. Holy Spirit lead them towards the right paths and keep them from stumbling along the way. Keep them under the shadow of Your wings. I pray that you fill us with a love for each other that only comes from You. I ask all this in Your precious name, Jesus. Amen!

## Remember that there is no perfect marriage.

The only one that is perfect is the one we have with Jesus. A three-fold cord can't be broken. In marriage, that cord is the husband, wife, and the Holy Spirit. There is solidity and longevity when God is in it.

I pray that this book has been a blessing to you and that you will use all the information, scriptures, steps, and my own personal experiences, to help you **usher in the spouse**, God has chosen for you.

As the bride of Christ, may we all yearn to have that holy and intimate relationship with our Bridegroom, Jesus!

Until the next book, much love, and blessings to you all!

# Conclusion

I want to encourage each one of you to believe that no matter what you are going through right now, there is hope and a Helper. Each difficulty, every hardship, all suffering, and heartache can and will be used for the good of others. Including yourself. God has a plan for your life. He allows us to go through certain things and times in our lives to prepare us for what He has in store for us. To prepare us for our destinies. Yes, sometimes it is the enemy of our souls who hates us so much that he causes havoc and destruction. But 1 John:4 says this: *You are of God, little children, and have overcome them, because He who is in you is greater than he that is of this world.*

You read my story. And looking back, I can honestly say that satan tried very early in my young adulthood to try to take my life, in order to stop what God wanted to do in my life. The eighteen-wheeler that slammed into us, the shotgun that was pointed at me by the neighbor, the car accidents I was in throughout the years, but didn't mention, the man who tried to abduct me, Lobo the fake, and of course the times I should have been dead. God preserves our lives so that we can fulfill our callings and gifts. Whatever that may be for you. We are all intertwined in His great plan.

The void in my life all those years was Jesus. It was He that filled the hole in my heart, it was He that filled me with a love I could have never fathomed, and it was He who filled me with the fruits of His Spirit and made me whole.

559

He was the only One who could make me truly happy. The void in my heart was my bridal relationship with my Bridegroom, Jesus.

Trust God because He knows what He is doing. If you allow Him to, He will take you through a journey of healing, growth, transformation, and purpose. And when you have reached that season in your life, when you have been in your *Preparation Chamber,* God will release you to meet your spouse. The one whom He has chosen for you. If you truly want that *One*, then surrender yourself to the Lord and allow Him to move on your behalf. Go through all the steps and prayers in this book as many times as needed to get the head knowledge of His love for you into your heart. You are His and He is yours. He is your first and eternal Bridegroom. Ask the Holy Spirit to help you Love Jesus the way He deserves to be loved.

I want to thank you the reader, for supporting my ministry by purchasing and reading this book. I would greatly appreciate, any of you who would kindly leave a review of this book.

If you were one who gave your life to the Lord by praying the prayer of salvation, we would love to hear from you so that we can celebrate with you and send more information. Contact us at jasminehartswick@queensofvalorministry.org If any of you would like to know when the next book of this series is coming out, or future events, we'd love to hear from you as well.

Again, thank you for your support.

**I close with this, my dear brothers and sisters:**

*The Lord bless you and keep you; the Lord make His face shine on you and be gracious to you; the Lord turn His face towards you and give you peace.* (Numbers 6:24-27)

## I rejoice with you, as you usher in and encounter your spouse!

*A person may have many ideas concerning God's plan for his life, but only the designs of His purpose will succeed in the end.*

(Proverbs 19:21 TPT)

_ _._ _ _ ꭗ

*Jasmine Hartswick*

# About Jasmine Hartswick

Jasmine was called into ministry after experiencing a life of extreme dreadful and horrendous encounters. One of those was a devastating fall, but after two years of suffering, she received a miraculous healing. God had been preparing her to be used to bring healing and deliverance to the sick and those who are broken and hurting. She is the Founder of Queens of Valor Ministry. Her passion is to empower women to become brave, steadfast, and powerful warrior brides for the kingdom of God. She has been teaching and ministering for over twenty-five years. Jasmine is a loving wife, mother, grandmother, writer, author, guest speaker, and designer. She creates one-of-a kind wedding bouquets as part of her ministry and uses part of the proceeds to help support the homeless and various shelters and charities around the world. You can go to queensofvalorministry.org to purchase a bouquet that was uniquely made, anointed with oil, and prayed over for the future bride, or if you are led to support this ministry through your generous donation. We are very grateful for any amount.